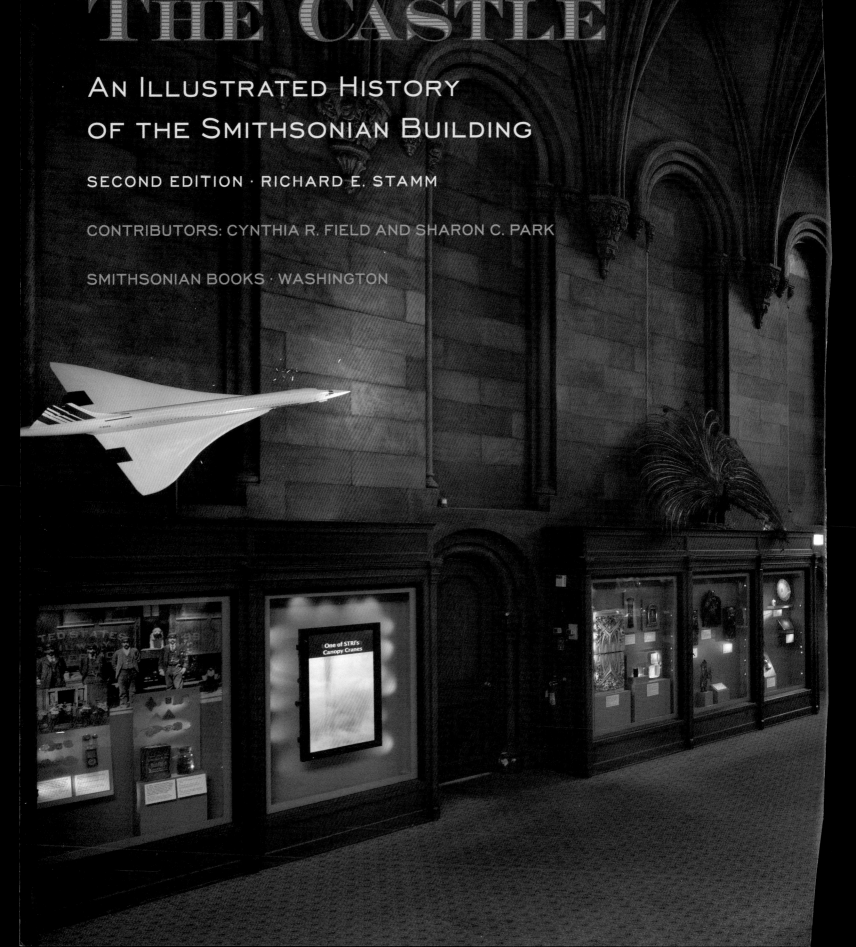

THE CASTLE

AN ILLUSTRATED HISTORY
OF THE SMITHSONIAN BUILDING

SECOND EDITION · RICHARD E. STAMM

CONTRIBUTORS: CYNTHIA R. FIELD AND SHARON C. PARK

SMITHSONIAN BOOKS · WASHINGTON

One of STRI's
Canopy Cranes

Funding for this book was provided in part by the
Smithsonian Institution Scholarly Press and the
Smithsonian Institution's Office of Architectural History
and Historic Preservation.

Produced by Smithsonian Books
Carolyn Gleason, Director
Christina Wiginton, Project Editor

Edited by Diane Maddex, Archetype Press, Inc.

Designed by Robert L. Wiser

LIBRARY OF CONGRESS CATALOGING-IN-PUBLICATION DATA

Stamm, Richard E.
   The Castle / Richard Stamm ; contributors, Cynthia R.
Field and Sharon Park. — Second edition.
   p.   cm.
   Summary: "The more than 150-year history of the
Smithsonian's striking Castle, featuring the stories of
workers and residents"— Provided by publisher.
   Includes bibliographical references and index.
   ISBN 978-1-58834-351-2 (pbk.)
   1. Smithsonian Institution Building (Washington, D.C.)
2. Public buildings—Washington (D.C.) 3. Museum
buildings—Washington (D.C.) 4. Washington (D.C.)—
Buildings, structures, etc. I. Field, Cynthia R. II. Park,
Sharon C. III. Title.
   NA4227.W2F53 2012
   727'.60009753—dc23
                                              2011047608

17   16   15   14   13 | 5   4   3   2

Printed in China

Smithsonian Books titles may be purchased for educational, business, or sales promotional use. For information, please write:

Special Markets Department
Smithsonian Books
P.O. Box 37012, MRC 513
Washington, D.C. 20013-7012

ILLUSTRATION CREDITS

Unless otherwise indicated, all illustrations are part of the
Smithsonian collections. We extend our gratitude to the
Smithsonian photographers who contributed images to this
publication, particularly Eric Long.

12. National Archives, RG 77, neg. 90-4.
13 (top). Indiana Historical Society.
13 (bottom). Picture Collection, Indiana State Library.
15. Avery Architectural and Fine Arts Library, Columbia
University.
18. Courtesy the New-York Historical Society, New York City.
27 (right, top and bottom). Courtesy SmithGroup,
Washington, D.C.
42. National Portrait Gallery, NPG.77.261.
70 (right). Washington Gas Light Company, 1948.
71 (top). Private collection.
85. Courtesy Ellen Dorn, 2009.
106. Courtesy Library of Congress.
122. U.S. Treasury Department.
129. Courtesy The Kiplinger Washington Collection.
159. Athenaeum of Philadelphia.

SUPPLEMENTARY CAPTIONS

1. The Castle's south side in winter. Photograph by Eric
Long, 2010.
2–3. The Commons in the West Wing. Photograph by Eric
Long, 2011.
5. The North Towers, by James Renwick Jr. Engraving
by W. Roberts, from Robert Dale Owen, *Hints on Public
Architecture*, 1849.
8–9. The south facade of the Castle. Drawing by
Richard E. Stamm, 1996.
36–37. The north facade of the Castle. Drawing by
Richard E. Stamm, 1993.
192. A transverse section of the hall of the West Range,
portraying the proposed decoration scheme. Drawing by
Cluss & Schulze, May 1888.

Contents

Foreword

G. WAYNE CLOUGH

Opposite: The Enid A. Haupt Garden in the South Yard of the Smithsonian Castle. Photograph by Eric Long, 2010. Top: The first Smithsonian seal, by Edward Stabler, ca. 1847. Above: The mosaic of the second Smithsonian seal, located at the entrance of the Regents' Room, by Augustus Saint-Gaudens, ca. 1900. The Smithsonian seal was updated to the now widely recognized starburst in 1965, which was again modified in 1998.

If you want to explore the history of the Smithsonian Institution, the Castle is the perfect place to start. It is a local Washington, D.C., story with all the nineteenth-century political intrigue and maneuvering surrounding what the new Institution should be. It is also a national story, because the Smithsonian has always belonged to the American people. And it is an international story, because from day one the Institution has sought to show the world a picture of America and America a picture of the world.

The building, made of red sandstone, red brick, and black iron beams, with walls up to three feet thick and a mélange of towers ranging from seven to twelve stories high, has endured many changes and challenges, including a brutal fire in 1865 and, more recently, an earthquake in 2011 followed within days by a hurricane. So far, it has passed all the tests.

The Castle has embraced a national museum filled with curiosities, science laboratories, lecture halls, libraries, an art gallery, a children's room, dormitories, and more. Now it holds the Institution's administrative headquarters as well as a visitors center showcasing a sampling of the Smithsonian's many treasures. Bison once roamed outside, and owls took refuge inside. At one time the Star-Spangled Banner was repaired here. The Castle was also once a home: the first Secretary of the Smithsonian, Joseph Henry, and his family actually lived upstairs in the East Wing. My desk now sits where Henry slept. Located directly beneath the Henry living quarters at one time was the Laboratory of Natural History, which produced what Henry described—and loudly derided—as "a very pungent stench." That problem, thankfully, is long gone.

Presidents and politicians, kings and queens, judges, actors, authors, everyday Americans, and international visitors have all strolled the halls of the Castle and admired its beauty. But perhaps the most famous dignitary in the Castle is one who never set foot on U.S soil when he was alive—our founder, the English scientist James Smithson. His crypt is in the north entrance. It is a powerful symbol that reminds us that an act of private philanthropy started the Smithsonian, which thrives today thanks to the support of the American people.

Rick Stamm came to the Smithsonian in 1975. He knows every nook, cranny, and secret of the Castle, as he so deftly demonstrates in the pages that follow. We thank him, again, for his work on this revised edition.

In a sense, the Castle stands out more today than it did a century and a half ago, when it stood alone on the National Mall. Our nation does not have many castles, but the doors of the Smithsonian's Castle are tall and open daily—free of charge. Please come and visit America's Castle.

GIVING FORM TO THE

PART ONE

SMITHSONIAN MANDATE

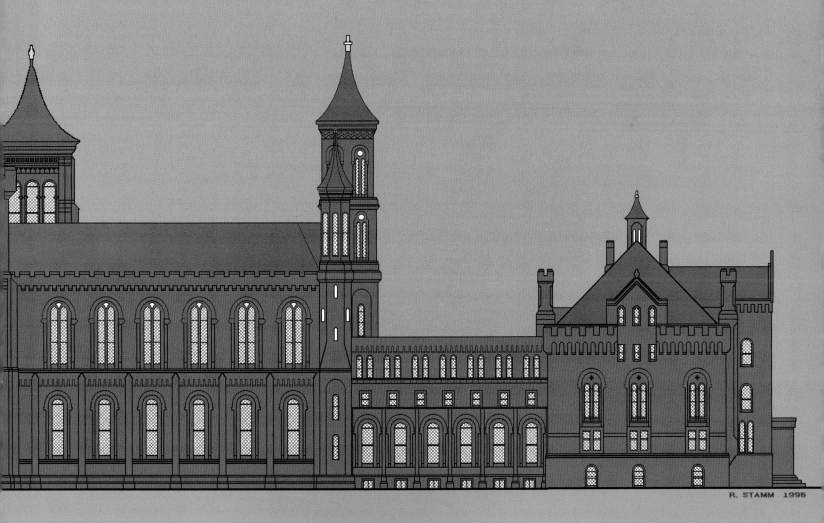

R. STAMM 1996

A Symbol for the Institution

CYNTHIA R. FIELD

Years before the Smithsonian's establishment by Congress in 1846, programmatic ideas for a building to house the new Institution began to take shape. Projected uses ranged from a museum and an art gallery to an astronomical observatory and a national library as well as an agricultural college and a teacher training institution. Each of these programs would have necessitated a distinctive space: a tall and unobstructed room for a museum, skylighted art galleries, a domed space for the observatory, a well-lit, lofty space for the library, and lecture halls for teaching courses suitable to a college.

Giving physical form to the Smithsonian's broad mandate for "the increase and diffusion of knowledge among men," as expressed in the bequest of James Smithson (ca. 1765–1829), presented the Institution's governing board with a formidable task. The numerous functions imposed by Congress after lengthy debate—eleven bills were introduced and tabled between 1838 and 1845—required a building unlike any in mid-nineteenth-century America. Eager to put forth his own vision for the Smithsonian Building, Regent Robert Dale Owen transformed the vague directions into a specific program. His brother, David Dale Owen, helped him translate the program into a proto-plan, which laid out a series of spaces to accommodate the needs of a museum, a gallery of art, a library, and a teaching and research facility.

Commensurate in importance with this effort was the expression of the plan in a medieval revival architectural form. A conceptual design, annotated by the architect of public buildings, Robert Mills, was presented to numerous architects in the United States for further development. Of the designs submitted, that of James Renwick Jr. most sensitively responded to all the requirements.

During a period in American architecture when a building's style was meant to evoke an underlying message, the choice of a medieval revival style was a deliberate identification with collegiate buildings. This decision was confirmed repeatedly throughout the design's evolution. In contrast to classical public buildings, which evoked ancient democracies, the Smithsonian took on a form related to the late-medieval English university, denoting the combination of private funds and public function.

THE DESIGN GAINS FORM

As early as 1841, Robert Mills (1781–1855) had submitted a plan for a building to house the Smithsonian Institution, which some supporters of the privately funded National Institute for the Promotion of Science and the Useful Arts had hoped would be integrated with it. The National Institute, created by an act of Congress in 1841, was a private organization for the collection of natural history specimens that required ample exhibition space along with

Opposite: The south facade of the Smithsonian Castle, fronting the parterre of the Enid A. Haupt Garden in the South Yard, 2010. Above: James Smithson, miniature by Henri Joseph Johns, 1816.

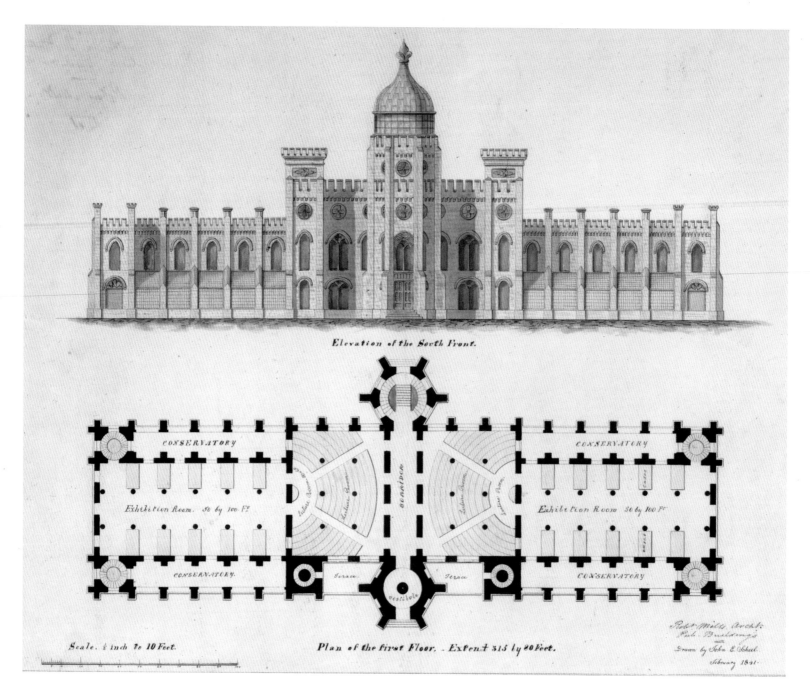

Elevation of the South Front.

Scale. ¼ inch to 10 Feet.

Plan of the first Floor. – Extent 315 by 20 Feet.

National Institute for the Promotion of Science, with the Smithsonian Building. Rendering by Robert Mills, February 1841.

lecture halls and an observatory. In his *Discourse on the Objects and Importance of the National Institution for the Promotion of Science,* its president, Joel Poinsett, explained:

The lovers of science, literature, and the fine arts, residing in the District, felt sensibly the absence of those resources which are found elsewhere, and are necessary for the attainment of knowledge. They . . . formed an association, and applied themselves to collect specimens of geology and mineralogy, and other objects of natural history. . . . The Institution for the Promotion of Science and the Useful Arts, will, as its name indicates, embrace every branch of knowledge.[1]

Rather than the classical style of the numerous public buildings he had designed for the U.S. government, Mills used a romantic medieval style to establish a distinction between

Below: Photograph of Smithsonian Regent Robert Dale Owen, a congressman from Indiana and author of *Hints on Public Architecture*. Bottom: Portrait drawing of David Dale Owen, who assisted his brother with plans for the Smithsonian Building, 1852.

the Smithsonian Institution and government buildings. He based his Smithsonian proposal on his 1839 plan for a library with an observatory at West Point; that building's most arresting feature was a double-curved (ogee) dome housing the observatory, which Mills modeled on the Tom Tower of Christ Church (College) at Oxford University.[2] The association of this feature with a university was surely intended, because Mills envisioned the Smithsonian Building as part of a complex for an agricultural college.[3] By placing all the stairs in the towers, he created a large, uninterrupted museum space on the top floor to house the National Institute's collections. The choice of a medieval revival style and the effective use of towers for circulation remained central to the later design development of what became known, despite its lack of military or defensive function, as the Castle.

Because he was especially concerned that the Smithsonian Building be a fit expression of its functions, Robert Dale Owen was in correspondence with his brother as early as August 1845 to develop a preliminary plan. Robert Dale Owen (1801–77) was a cofounder of the Utopian community of New Harmony, Indiana, with his father and later an Indiana congressman who brokered the legislative agreements founding the Institution, while David Dale Owen (1807–60) was one of the nation's leading field geologists and a gentleman architect who had designed an admired laboratory for New Harmony. Intending the Institution to function as a center of free public education and to include a training center for teachers, Robert Dale Owen identified features that would remain in the planning process: four or five lecture rooms, including one for chemistry with a student laboratory and another for geology with provision for using large-scale visual aids, and a meeting room for the governing board. This all-encompassing plan also included sizable spaces for a museum, a library, conservatories, and an astronomical observatory. A medieval college was conjured up through Owen's evocative request for a "piazza, or cloister, for the use of students in wet weather . . . in keeping with the style of architecture suggested."[4]

Robert Dale Owen proposed that the brothers adopt from Robert Mills's plan the uninterrupted museum room running the length of the building's central block. He also accepted Mills's suggestion of an "Anglo Saxon" style, redefining the term by saying, "I believe, that, by going back to the pure Norman, with its Saxon arches & simple forms, you may provide something well suited for the purposes in view."[5] Although David Dale Owen's plans have been lost, the detailed description he wrote to accompany his design of October 10, 1845, remains. His building consisted of a central block three stories high with wings on each side connected to the main body by low stretches called ranges.[6] On the third floor were two mixed-use rooms for demonstration lectures, specimen exhibitions, and the gallery of art; on the second floor was a large museum space for the natural history objects; on the first story were the library stacks, a reading room, and a lecture hall seating seven to eight hundred people.

After having reviewed David Dale Owen's plans and drawings, Mills, at Robert Dale Owen's request, completed another design for the Smithsonian in September 1846. In his revised design, Mills adopted the wings and ranges of Owen's layout. The medieval revival style and the staircase towers were retained. Battlements and buttresses suggested the early English medieval, while the mix of window treatments—round headed, pointed, square headed—spanned four centuries. Mills acknowledged that "our associations with great literary institutions are assimilated with the Saxon style of architecture in these buildings."[7]

With the exception of locating a lecture hall in the central block, Mills arranged the space as Owen had: a library on the first floor, a museum on the second, and galleries for art and demonstration lecture rooms on the third. Mills planned to accommodate four lecture halls, along with attached offices, in the wings. The "piazzas" remained on the north side and the conservatories on the south. Mills introduced a niche over the entrance for a statue of James Smithson. The observatory, which had occasioned the distinctive dome of the 1841 proposal, was now situated in the octagonal stair tower on the north side, which was also to have a great clock.

Under Robert Dale Owen's leadership, the Smithsonian's Board of Regents, on which Owen served as head of the Building Committee, rapidly selected both site and building. On September 9, 1846, only two days after the Board's first meeting, Owen presented his

"Perspective of the Smithsonian Institution, agreeably to the Design. . . ." Rendering by Robert Mills, 1846.

brother's plan, with drawings and specifications, as well as Mills's refinement. News of the proposed architectural commission was published in Washington newspapers, although word of the project had already spread among architects and builders.[8]

To obtain plans for a Smithsonian Building from a wide range of established architects as quickly as possible, Owen and other members of the Building Committee embarked on a tour of the northeastern states. The Owen drawings were shown, along with descriptive specifications in the form of the Owen brothers' edited correspondence. From the evidence of some of the competition drawings, it seems likely that the Mills scheme of 1846 was also shown. Certain elements—such as the porte cochère (carriage porch), skylights for the lecture halls, an exhibition space for Smithson memorabilia, and an office for the Secretary—appeared in neither design but were mentioned in these discussions. A special plea was made to have the whole structure designed to be reasonably fireproof.[9]

RENWICK ENTERS THE COMPETITION

Among the architects visited on this trip was twenty-eight-year-old James Renwick Jr. (1818–95), highly regarded for his Gothic-style Grace Church in New York City. Even before the Building Committee's September trip, Renwick—already sympathetic with the organization of spaces and the decidedly romantic articulation of the facades—may have executed his earliest scheme as a building in the Gothic style. Several elements suggest the influence of Robert Mills's 1841 design.[10] Like the Mills plan, Renwick's sketch (a north elevation and a plan) featured a tower modeled on the Oxford example of Christ Church and depicted a building only two stories high, although the Owen plan called for three stories. Had he already met with the Building Committee, Renwick would have understood that the members preferred a clearly Romanesque style over the early Gothic style favored by Mills. As might be expected of someone who had not yet learned of the Owens' program for the building, Renwick set forth largely undifferentiated spaces, with the exception of two lecture halls to the south of each wing.

The lecture halls had been important to the development of the Owen brothers' plan, representing a means of providing free public education to all. With this "auditorium" sketch, Renwick appeared to have been working out aspects of the Mills-Owen plan discussed on the Building Committee's trip. The amphitheater configuration of the lecture hall existed in Mills's 1841 project. David Dale Owen's specifications also included a semicircular theater for lectures in anatomy on the third story of his central building. Whatever source he used, Renwick was now paying close attention to the requirements of the competition models.

Renwick's winning entry was likely quite close to his south elevation drawing from 1846.[11] The Romanesque scheme provided three stories to accommodate the library on the first floor, the museum on the second, and the gallery of art on the third. Renwick's use of buttresses, which deflect the thrust of interior masonry vaults, suggests that he had employed vaulting to provide the fireproof construction requested by the Building Committee on its visit. The south tower in the center of the building featured a protruding

Portrait of James Renwick Jr., holding his plans for St. Patrick's Cathedral, New York City. Painting by John Whetten Ehninger, 1853.

bay known as an oriel window for the Regents' Room in the shape selected by Robert Dale Owen from the antiquarian John Henry Parker's *Glossary of Terms Used in Grecian, Roman, Italian and Gothic Architecture*.[12] Renwick's placement of the "piazzas" (open cloistered walkways) on the south side, rather than on the north as in the Owen-Mills plan, may have stemmed from an effort to avoid the shadier side of the building.

Robert Dale Owen considered the east end an example of the whole design approach he advocated, letting the architecture's style be adapted to the plan to enhance the building's fitness to function:[13]

The entire rectangle of that wing was laid out as a Chemical Lecture room, with a gallery on three sides. . . . It was decided, that the seats in the main body of the Lecture room should be placed on an inclined surface, rising to the gallery floor and connecting with it; and that the usual entrance for the audience should be, not below, where delicate and fragile apparatus was exposed, but by a staircase to the gallery floor, whence the audience should descend, on either side of the inclined plane, to its seats. To carry into effect this arrangement, a stairway outside the Lecture room was required. It was obtained within a porch projecting from the eastern front; and as, in a porch of suitable proportions, the requisite height could not be gained without making the stairs too steep, a small outer porch was added, with a few steps therein.

Above: Smithsonian Building, north elevation in the Gothic style, with a floor plan. Drawing by James Renwick Jr., 1846. Opposite, top: Smithsonian Building, south elevation in the Romanesque style. Drawing by James Renwick Jr., 1846. Opposite, bottom left: Smithsonian Building, auditorium. Drawing by James Renwick Jr., 1846. Opposite, bottom right: Smithsonian Building, east elevation. Drawing by James Renwick Jr., 1846.

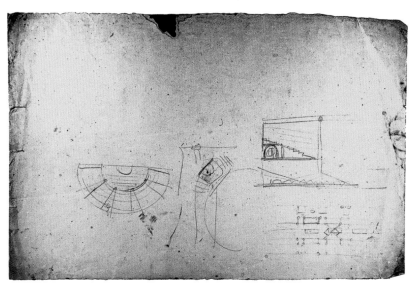

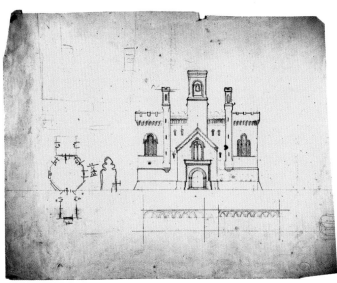

Thus the peculiarities of internal adaptation in this wing stamped upon its eastern elevation the exterior it now presents; the general effect being, I think, pleasing and harmonious.[14]

The chimneys in Renwick's drawing of the east elevation contained flues for the smelting operations that were to be part of the chemical laboratories located in this area. His design for the chimneys mimicked the form of the bell tower in the center, which was described as "Norman."[15] Renwick similarly described the interlaced arches between the chimneys as "Norman" in his specifications to the stonecutters.[16]

Although the architects had been told to submit their plans to the Board of Regents by December 25, the Building Committee had already settled on Renwick's design by November 30.[17] This premature selection caused what Secretary Joseph Henry (1797–1878) called "a tempest among the architects,"[18] but the reason for Renwick's victory was clear. Designs that failed to adhere to the Owen-Mills "Norman" model were all losers; only Renwick's design included, as the Building Committee explained, "all the accommodations demanded by the charter."[19]

INTERPRETING THE BEQUEST

With the selection of Henry, a distinguished professor of physics at Princeton University, as the Smithsonian's first Secretary, cost became a dominant design factor.[20] Henry's interpretation of "the increase and diffusion of knowledge among men" differed radically from that of Robert Dale Owen. The Secretary believed that "increase" meant the "discovery of new truths" by original research and that "diffusion" would properly be handled through scholarly publication. Soon he concluded that the building would drain the slender resources that should be dedicated to the creation of the Institution itself.

On his arrival in December 1846 to take up his new position, Henry attempted to halt the building plans. His goal was to prevent the deflection of Smithsonian funds from research into the building.[21] As a result of his efforts to persuade the Board to erect a much less costly building, the plans were altered to cut the central building from three stories to two.[22]

Renwick's model, submitted with his entry in 1846, presented the scheme that the Building Committee had selected.[23] By the time the presentation renderings were made in 1848, however, Renwick had reduced the building to two stories by removing the windowed ground level. Also eliminated were one tower on the West Wing and two entrances on either side of the porte cochère. An interesting addition was the false gable between the towers, a form Renwick also used on his Romanesque-style Church of the Puritans in New York City.

Because of this reduction of the design, Renwick was faced with the challenge of fitting all the program's requirements into two-thirds of the space. As a result, the interior plan was much altered. The second-level museum floor remained undisturbed, but the third-floor gallery of art was moved to the West Wing, where it could retain the

Church of the Puritans, New York City. Rendering by James Renwick Jr., 1846.

Top: Smithsonian Building, north facade. Rendering painted by Louis Townsend and drawn by H. C. Moore, June 1848. Above: Smithsonian Building, south facade. Rendering painted by Louis Townsend and drawn by H. C. Moore, June 1848.

skylights that the Building Committee had specified. The library space in the lower half of the Main Building was reduced to accommodate the large lecture hall formerly in the West Wing.

James Renwick had become an architect by observation and education. Through his father, an architectural amateur who had proposed a collegiate Gothic building as early as 1813, and through other members of his family, he had generous exposure to architecture and the other arts. As a student at Columbia College between 1831 and 1836, he received an education in science and engineering. Although he had little firsthand experience with the craft, his early buildings—such as Grace Church and Calvary Church in New York City and the Smithsonian Building—were unusually sure

in the employment of materials and bold in the mixture of design elements. His use of Gothic Revival at both Grace Church and Calvary Church was sophisticated in successfully combining continental and British forms.[24] For the Smithsonian, he integrated German Romanesque sources for the design of the east entrance doors, the west cloister, and several towers with the English collegiate model for massing, and he used Norman moldings for decorative detail. Examining Renwick's specifications for the building, Regent William Jervis Hough stated that he found "them elaborately and minutely drawn, both in reference to detail of the work and permanence and durability of the structure."[25]

In mid-nineteenth-century Washington, the Smithsonian Building was distinctive in its physical elements: a horizontal linear mass punctuated by numerous vertical accents, the whole in a deep red-colored stone. Although its motifs and details were technically Romanesque, it owed little to the massive walls and heavy, roughly articulated forms of traditional Norman architecture. The building's rhythmic linear massing flowed on each side from a dominant central block through low connectors to wings. Although the east and west wings balanced each other, they were far from identical: one a rectangular block with battlements and chimneys, descending to an entrance porch on the east end, the other resembling a chapel with a projecting apse. Carrying the contrast to a finer level, the two cloistered walkways on the north facade were strongly dissimilar.

Heightening the building's picturesque quality was the impression of asymmetry created by the nine architecturally diverse towers. The central motif was twin towered: one tower short and finished with a pointed roof, the other taller, changing almost imperceptibly from square at the base to octagonal. Marking the point at which this flag tower became octagonal were four pepper-pot pinnacles. The Campanile and two additional towers, including one at the northwest corner, brought the facade on the National Mall to a total of five towers. All of them housed necessary functional spaces and enhanced the building's silhouette by accenting its horizontal mass.[26]

In striking contrast to the north facade, the building's south side was dominated by a massive, square, battlemented central tower with an attached octagonal stair tower rising well above it. The tower was divided into three sections, punctuated by a grand round-arched door on the first floor, a projecting oriel window on the second, and an elongated version of the windows in the East Wing on the third. Two other towers—one octagonal staircase tower and one square elevator tower for freight—contributed to the south facade's asymmetry.

Constructed of red sandstone quarried in Seneca, Maryland, this dramatic building was unique not only in style but also in material. As several building materials were under consideration in early 1847, the building might have been constructed of light-colored marble, gray granite, or tawny sandstone. Its richly tinted stone was chosen by weighing studies conducted by David Dale Owen, in his role as geologist, and Charles Page, a physical scientist who reported on durability, with such aesthetic considerations as the visibility of shadows and detail and suitability for the medieval style.[27]

Opposite, top: North facade of the Smithsonian Building, three years after its completion, 1858. Opposite, bottom: South facade of the Smithsonian Building, ca. 1858–64.

A PHILOSOPHICAL FOUNDATION

The building was grounded in its own philosophical theory, explicated in a book of considerable intellectual power. Authorized by the Board of Regents in 1846 as a description of the plan and the architectural style, this book was entitled *Hints on Public Architecture*. In the hands of its author, Robert Dale Owen, *Hints* became a treatise on the appropriate architectural expression of purpose in public buildings.[28] Owen's cogent argument for the Smithsonian's medieval revival style made a strong appeal to the intellect. His language, concept, and examples were drawn from the work of the widely influential John Claudius Loudon (1783–1843), who based his architectural principles on the theory of Scottish Common Sense philosophers of the eighteenth century.

Having established Loudon's architectural principles for the use of forms expressive of function, Owen argued that, beginning with a well-grounded, functional plan, a good designer could find in the numerous medieval styles an architectural expression suitable to the character and fitness of the structure.[29] As further evidence, Owen added cost-related statistics. His impressively detailed comparison of the costs per cubic foot of the Smithsonian Building with other major public buildings, such as the Treasury Building and the Patent Office, sought to show how cost effective the medieval revival style was.[30]

This form was chosen for its expression of the American character and its association with collegiate institutions. Owen defined the nation's character in terms such as vigor, flexibility, independence, and practical economy. These characteristics he translated into flexible space use, picturesque silhouette, and practical use of native materials,

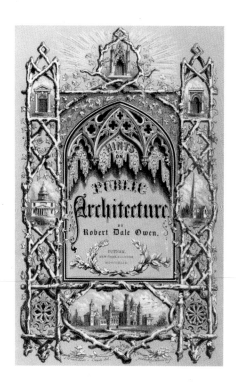

Above: Frontispiece from Robert Dale Owen, *Hints on Public Architecture,* 1849, with wood engravings of the Smithsonian Building, including the West Wing (bottom left); the South Tower (bottom right); the Campanile (opposite, top); the Octagonal Tower on the south side (opposite, bottom left); and the southern gateway (opposite, bottom right).

all of which he contended could be ascribed only to medieval architecture.[31] He concluded that the Smithsonian Building design had the qualities deserving "to be named as a National Style of Architecture for America."[32] Also inherent in the medieval style and the building's linear massing was an association with the traditional English college. That Owen intended the Smithsonian Building to be read as a collegiate building was apparent in his own statement: "nor do I believe that anyone, of moderately cultivated taste, in looking upon that building, would mistake its character, or connect it, in his mind, with other than a scientific or collegiate foundation."[33]

The potency of *Hints on Public Architecture* lay in its combination of the visual images, the persuasive argument, and Owen's frequently poetic language. These elements were expressions of the aesthetic that characterized both Renwick and Owen. When it was published in 1849, *Hints on Public Architecture* was adorned with a series of eight engravings of Renwick drawings illustrating aspects of the building, nine additional views by other artists, and renderings of several other Renwick buildings. A close collaboration between Robert Dale Owen and James Renwick was apparent, based on a shared belief in an architecture that was historically informed but not doctrinaire.

Hints on Public Architecture set the Smithsonian Building apart as the embodiment of an aesthetic philosophy. In the correspondence of the Owen brothers, the emphasis had already been on evolving a plan that suited the multiple functions that the building would serve. Robert Mills and both Owens had selected the medieval revival style and certain architectural forms for their expressive power. As a result of this predetermined design approach, the choice of architect and the evolution of the design led to a building that symbolized an idea while it housed an institution.

CHANGES WITH THE TIMES

SHARON C. PARK

The 1846 design of the Smithsonian Building by James Renwick Jr. and the Board of Regents retains much of its original integrity—changes over time have, for the most part, been well integrated. Now fondly called the Castle, this iconic building is still the embodiment of the architectural ideals outlined in Robert Dale Owen's *Hints on Public Architecture* (1849). The building that was intended for "the increase and diffusion of knowledge" would find ways to accommodate a balance of research and exhibition needs while serving as the Institution's administrative headquarters. Today the Castle remains the symbol of what has evolved into the largest museum system in the world.

This picturesque red sandstone building on the National Mall has been through numerous changes: partially rebuilt after a devastating fire, altered to respond to the changing focus of various Secretaries and as the Institution grew to accommodate expanding collections, upgraded with new building systems, and redefined for both the public's use and the Smithsonian's administrative functions. Three major periods of alterations were carried out by noted architects, typically with deference to Renwick's initial design. The most visible changes were made by a series of Washington architects, including Adolf Cluss and his partner, Paul Schulze, in the late nineteenth century; Hornblower & Marshall in the first part of the twentieth century; and Chatelain, Gauger

Opposite: The West Range, looking west, with the gray-green color scheme suggested by Adolf Cluss. Photograph by Eric Long, 2011. Below: A contemporary Mall view of the Castle, whose East Wing was modified and whose North Tower roof was restored after a damaging fire in 1865.

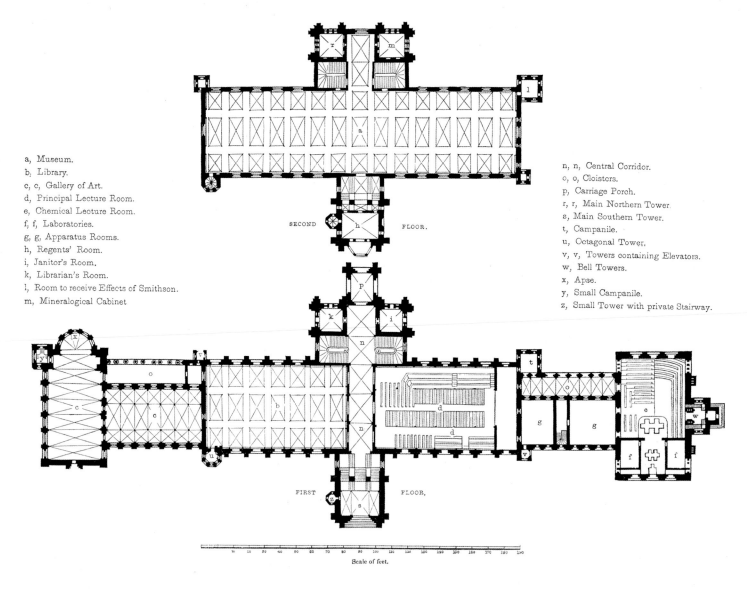

a, Museum.
b, Library.
c, c, Gallery of Art.
d, Principal Lecture Room.
e, Chemical Lecture Room.
f, f, Laboratories.
g, g, Apparatus Rooms.
h, Regents' Room.
i, Janitor's Room.
k, Librarian's Room.
l, Room to receive Effects of Smithson.
m, Mineralogical Cabinet

n, n, Central Corridor.
o, o, Cloisters.
p, Carriage Porch.
r, r, Main Northern Tower.
s, Main Southern Tower.
t, Campanile.
u, Octagonal Tower.
v, v, Towers containing Elevators.
w, Bell Towers.
x, Apse.
y, Small Campanile.
z, Small Tower with private Stairway.

SECOND FLOOR.

FIRST FLOOR.

Scale of feet.

Floor plan of the Smithsonian Castle, by James Renwick Jr. Engraving by J. H. Hall, from *Hints on Public Architecture*, 1849.

& Nolan in the mid-twentieth century. In one early renovation, a residence for the family of Joseph Henry, who served as the first Secretary from 1846 to 1878, was added to the East Wing in 1855. Some roof modifications were made in the late nineteenth century, but the exterior seen today is much as Renwick envisioned it. As with all historic buildings, infrastructure improvements have occurred periodically; renovations of aging systems, other alterations, and new programmatic uses will no doubt take place in the future.[1]

THE FIRST STAGE

Built over a period of eight years, from 1847 to 1855, the building's various sections opened as they were completed and paid for from the accrued interest generated from James Smithson's bequest. When finished, the 453-foot-long building included the East and West Wings, the East and West Ranges, the Main Building in between, and nine towers. One of most interesting architectural features was the Castle's system of galleries (mezzanines), which encircled the Lower Main Hall and the West Wing's library; these defining features provided additional, higher-level spaces for displaying objects and allowed visitors a more intimate experience with the exhibits. The flexible

Below: The West Range, with galleries (mezzanines) providing second-level access to collections, ca. 1857. Bottom: Museum visitors near the display cases in the West Wing, ca. 1857. Right, top: Cutaway model based on the Castle's appearance about 1860, showing in yellow the sections lost in the 1865 fire, including the center lecture hall. Right, bottom: A bird's-eye view of the Castle exterior. Model based on its ca. 2010 appearance.

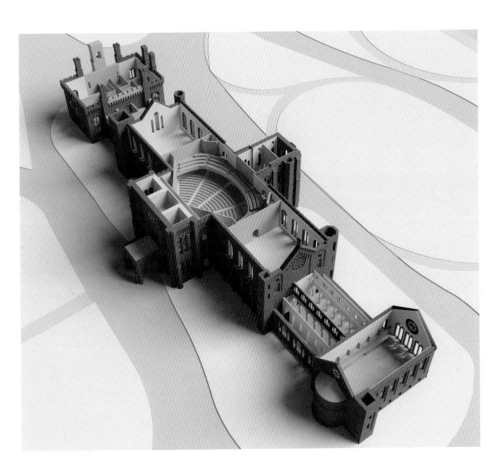

floor plan kept vertical circulation primarily in the towers, leaving large spaces that could be reconfigured as priorities changed.

Although the architect's original plans called for fireproof construction, cost-saving measures were implemented. As a result, much of the building's interior was constructed of lighter-weight, combustible wooden framing members. In 1865 a devastating fire on the upper floors of the Main Building destroyed a magnificent public lecture hall with excellent acoustics and seating for more than 1,500 attendees, as well as an apparatus hall and a major art collection of Native American portraits. The building's top floor was rebuilt and reconfigured by Cluss & Schulze, a local firm noted for its fireproof institutional buildings, including city markets and award-winning schools. Cluss (1825–1905) would continue to work on the building for two decades and was responsible for increasing the building's efficiency by raising the roof over the East Wing and the East Range to gain additional floors, rebuilding the West Range interior in fireproof materials, and inserting floors into the North and South Towers during the reconstruction after the fire. With little impact on the Castle's exterior, much of the early work, still in place today, became a blend of the work of James Renwick and Adolf Cluss.

Cluss, who had been born and trained in Germany, worked closely under Spencer Fullerton Baird (1823–87), the second Secretary of the Smithsonian. Baird's interests were supporting collections research and exhibitions, rather than the scientific research that had been Secretary Henry's primary focus. Consequently more space was dedicated to museum and public visitor services. Secretary Baird, who served from 1878 to 1887, substantially increased the Institution's collections, particularly by accepting the displays from the 1876 Philadelphia Centennial Exhibition, which the Castle could not accommodate. Baird then hired Cluss to design and supervise the construction of a new National Museum adjacent to the Castle for the expanded collection. Completed in 1881, this is the polychrome Victorian building known today as the Arts and Industries Building.

TWENTIETH-CENTURY MODIFICATIONS

At the turn of the twentieth century, Secretary Samuel Pierpont Langley (1834–1906) hired the local architecture firm Hornblower & Marshall to undertake some renovation work within the Castle. Known for its classical residences and public buildings, including the Army and Navy Club in Washington and the U.S. Custom House in Baltimore, the firm of Joseph Hornblower (1848–1908) and James Marshall (1851–1927) created a room in the East Wing dedicated to art and graphic arts. A plaster frieze copying the art of the Parthenon was added to this room. The firm even designed the art tables and the flat files for the print collection.

Two of the most notable public changes to the building carried out by Hornblower & Marshall were the dedication of the South Tower's first floor to the Children's Room in 1901 and the opening of a crypt for Smithson's remains in the North Tower in 1905. The charming Children's Room, with its low display cases, encouraged families to visit the museum and to engage a younger audience. The motto over the door was

Top: The East Wing, with its original roof configuration, and the missing roofs on the Main Building and the lower North Tower, lost in the 1865 fire, ca. 1866. Above: The Arts and Industries Building, built in 1881 adjacent to the Castle, ca. 1900.

"Knowledge Begins in Wonder," a new approach to "the increase and diffusion of knowledge." The space was converted into offices in 1942, but its original colors and decorative ceiling have since been restored. Alexander Graham Bell, the noted inventor of the telephone who was a Smithsonian Regent, went to Italy in 1903 and secured the remains of James Smithson, who died in Genoa in 1829. Bell's trip was designed to bring the Smithsonian's benefactor to a country to which he had been so generous but had never visited. As a suitable crypt for Smithson, Hornblower & Marshall reconfigured a small room off the north entrance that remains his final resting place.

Although the collections continued to grow, the Castle was not able to accommodate all of them. Hornblower & Marshall was commissioned again by the Smithsonian to design the second National Museum, now known as the National Museum of Natural History. It opened in 1910 and took most of the exhibits from the Lower Main Hall, leaving the Castle's primary public space in need of a new function. Secretary Charles Doolittle Walcott (1850–1927), a paleontologist who had a special interest in art, used this opportunity to exhibit graphic arts and John James Audubon prints in the galleried spaces of the Lower Main Hall. Shortly thereafter, in 1914, Walcott engaged Hornblower & Marshall to convert a portion of the Lower Main Hall into a library. All the exhibit cases and the gallery balconies were removed to make room for library stacks at the east and west ends of what became known as the Great Hall. Some of the balcony railings were reused, but the hall's configuration was radically changed and its two-hundred-foot length was shortened. The hall remains today in this reduced configuration, without the mezzanines, serving as a visitor orientation space.

In the years surrounding World War I and the subsequent depression in the 1930s, the Smithsonian, like other public institutions, had few resources for expansion or modernization. It was not until the mid-twentieth century that significant funds were again spent to upgrade and modify the Castle. Under the leadership of Secretary Leonard Carmichael (1898–1973) and Secretary S. Dillon Ripley (1913–2001), the Smithsonian underwent phenomenal growth, with the creation of new museums and research centers. The Institution hired the Washington architecture firm Chatelain, Gauger & Nolan to undertake a full renovation of the systems in the Castle and to construct offices for the Woodrow Wilson International Center for Scholars, for which the building served as host until it was relocated elsewhere in Washington. The architects, led by Leon Chatelain Jr. (1902–79), were known for their Westmoreland Congregational Church, Washington Gas Light Company, and Kiplinger Building; Chatelain was a leader in barrier-free design and served two terms, from 1956 to 1958, as president of the American Institute of Architects.

Mirroring earlier efforts to make more efficient use of space, the Upper Main Hall was subdivided with a new floor to create two levels of offices for the Wilson Center. The Smithsonian's need for expanded administrative spaces grew along with its expanded museums and research centers; since the Wilson Center moved out in 1998, these spaces have been adapted to house other offices and support functions. A small portion of the original high-ceilinged space is still evident in the current library.

Below: The southwest corner of the Children's Room in the South Tower, ca. 1900.
Bottom: The Great Hall, with its galleries (mezzanines) removed, ca. 1920.

During Secretary Ripley's tenure (1964–84), a furniture collection for the Castle was established to provide Victorian furnishings and decorative arts appropriate to the offices and the meeting rooms. By using period pieces from the collection, the interior's picturesque quality has been enhanced. The Victorian furnishings in the current Regents' Room, for example, help connect it to the nineteenth-century era when the Castle was first designed.

THE HEART OF THE INSTITUTION

Although few changes have been made to the Castle in the last fifty years, the construction of the Quadrangle beneath the Enid A. Haupt Garden in the South Yard in the 1980s has provided needed support services. Jean-Paul Carlhian, of Shepley, Bulfinch, Richardson and Abbott, converted the yard's 4½ acres into underground spaces for the Arthur M. Sackler Gallery, the National Museum of African Art, and the S. Dillon Ripley International Center. The garden not only adds a lovely Victorian setting for the Castle's south entrance, it also provides underground truck access and a loading dock off Independence Avenue to service the Castle. Without expanding its footprint aboveground, the Castle is now more integrated into needed behind-the-scenes service functions, all of which reduce the wear and tear on the public spaces above.

The only Renwick-designed interior space that retains its original spirit is the West Wing, now known as the Commons. Although its roof structure and decorative ceiling plasterwork were replicated in 1891 as part of the fireproofing project by Edward Clark (1822–1902), then serving as architect of the Capitol, it still conveys the effect that Renwick envisioned—a strong sense of design, magnificent vaulted spaces, and an abundance of natural light. Historic cases now house examples of the significant work being undertaken by museum curators, scientists at the Smithsonian's research centers, and ongoing programs throughout the Institution. The exhibits change to feature new initiatives under the twelfth Secretary of the Smithsonian, G. Wayne Clough, particularly educational outreach and the use of Internet communication that together bring more information to a worldwide audience.

The Castle's most significant period of architectural expression was its first sixty years, when the building functioned as an all-purpose institution. From 1847, when construction started, until about 1910, the building exhibited its full capacity as anticipated by Renwick. Beginning around 1910, as collections continued to move out of the Castle to other Smithsonian museums, the building ceased to serve as a self-contained museum and became more of an administrative space for the Institution. Designated a National Historic Landmark in 1965, the Castle's primary period of architectural significance rests within its early decades.[2]

More detailed information and stories about life in the Castle are provided in the following chapters of this book. In looking at the building's various sections, it is clear that the elegance of the interior spaces and their details all speak to the Renwick era, even when put to use in more modern forms. They continue to serve as embodiments of the Smithsonian's prominence as an American institution.

Above: The kiosk entrance to the S. Dillon Ripley International Center in the Quadrangle, 1996. Opposite, top: First-floor plan today, identifying building components and towers. Opposite, bottom: Section through the Castle, showing the Lower and Upper Main Halls, floors, and towers.

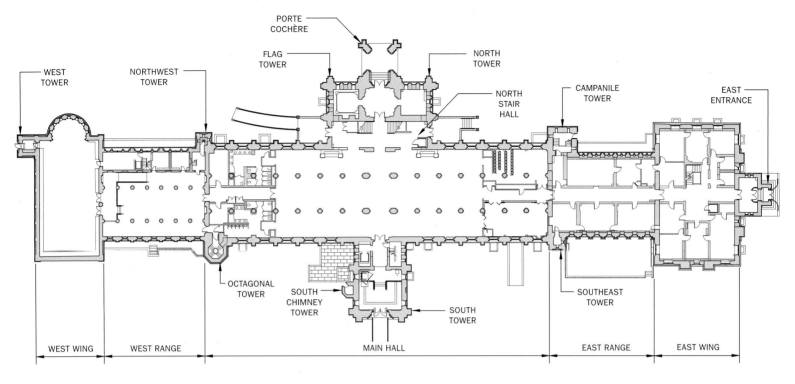

WEST TOWER

NORTHWEST TOWER

PORTE COCHÈRE

FLAG TOWER

NORTH TOWER

NORTH STAIR HALL

CAMPANILE TOWER

EAST ENTRANCE

OCTAGONAL TOWER

SOUTH CHIMNEY TOWER

SOUTH TOWER

SOUTHEAST TOWER

WEST WING

WEST RANGE

MAIN HALL

EAST RANGE

EAST WING

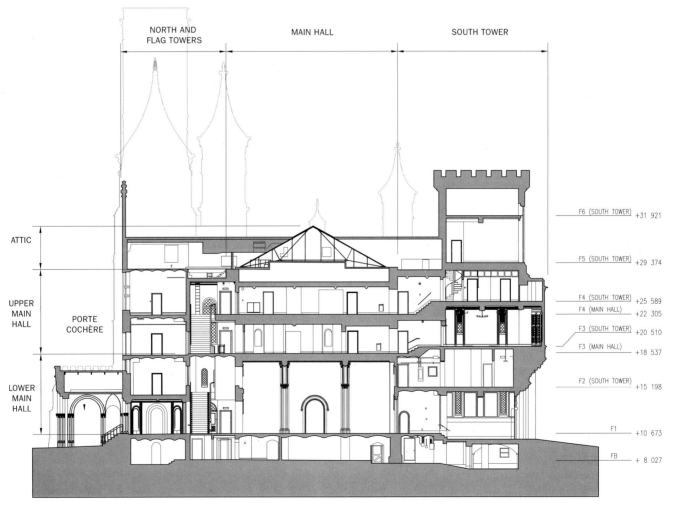

NORTH AND FLAG TOWERS

MAIN HALL

SOUTH TOWER

ATTIC

UPPER MAIN HALL

PORTE COCHÈRE

LOWER MAIN HALL

F6 (SOUTH TOWER) +31 921

F5 (SOUTH TOWER) +29 374

F4 (SOUTH TOWER) +25 589
F4 (MAIN HALL) +22 305

F3 (SOUTH TOWER) +20 510
F3 (MAIN HALL) +18 537

F2 (SOUTH TOWER) +15 198

F1 +10 673

FB + 8 027

1829. *James Smithson dies in Genoa, Italy, on June 27.*

1835. *The United States is notified of the Smithson bequest.*

1838. *The bequest, amounting to half a million dollars, is brought to the United States. Congress begins debate over how to carry out Smithson's intent.*

1845. *Robert Dale Owen and David Dale Owen collaborate to develop a plan for the Smithsonian Building.*

1846. *An act organizing the Smithsonian Institution is passed by Congress. The Building Committee of the Board of Regents selects the plan of James Renwick Jr. for the Smithsonian Building. Joseph Henry, a professor of physics at Princeton University, is elected the Institution's first Secretary.*

1847. *The cornerstone of the building is laid on May 1. Work on the exterior of the East Wing and the East Range is completed by December 31.*

1848. *The West Wing and the West Range are under construction in August, which also marks the beginning of the foundation work for the Main Building.*

1849. *The East Wing and the East Range are completed and occupied.*

1850. *The West Wing and the West Range are occupied, while the Main Building is roofed and the towers are partially completed. Part of the Lower Main Hall collapses during construction; an investigation recommends a fireproof reconstruction.*

1851. *The exterior of the building is completed on December 31.*

1852. *Joseph Henry sends a letter to Renwick, stating that his services are no longer wanted. Barton S. Alexander of the U.S. Army Corps of Engineers oversees the building's fireproof interior reconstruction.*

1855. *The Lower Main Hall opens to the public with the annual fair of the Metropolitan Mechanics' Institute. An apartment for the Henry family is created in the East Wing.*

1857. *The first guidebook to the Smithsonian, illustrating many of the Castle's interior spaces, is published.*

1858. *Cloisters on the building's north facade are enclosed. The galleries and cases in the Lower Main Hall are completed and arranged to house the museum collections, following the transfer of items from the National Institute for the Promotion of Science and the Useful Arts.*

Right, top: Joseph Henry. Photograph by Mathew Brady, ca. 1865. Right, center: Spencer F. Baird, ca. 1880. Right, bottom: Samuel P. Langley, ca. 1900. Opposite, top: Charles Doolittle Walcott, ca. 1910. Opposite, center: Charles Greeley Abbot, ca. 1950. Opposite, bottom: Alexander Wetmore, 1944.

1865. *A massive fire on January 24 destroys the Upper Main Hall and the primary towers, as well as their contents.*

1866. *Adolf Cluss, a Washington architect, is appointed the architect of the Castle's renovation. He reconstructs the South Tower, adding three floors and inserting iron columns for support, doubling the amount of office space.*

1871. *The floor of the West Wing is made fireproof and raised to provide a Laboratory of Natural History in the basement.*

1872. *Reconstruction of the Upper Main Hall is completed. The East Wing and the East Range are cleared of all museum-related functions and repurposed for the Smithsonian's administrative uses.*

1874. *Paintings, statuary, and engravings belonging to the Institution are deposited with the Corcoran Gallery of Art.*

1878. *Secretary Henry dies, and Spencer Fullerton Baird, a professor of natural history at Dickinson College, is elected the second Secretary of the Smithsonian.*

1881. *A new National Museum building, including many specimens transferred from the Castle, is opened in what is now known as the Arts and Industries Building. Telephones are installed in the East Wing offices of the Castle.*

1882. *The galleries of the Lower Main Hall are given over to curators' space.*

1883. *A statue of Joseph Henry is dedicated in front of the Castle.*

1884. *The East Wing and the East Range are fireproofed and enlarged by Adolf Cluss and his partner, Paul Schulze.*

1887. *The West Range is also fireproofed by the Cluss & Schulze firm. Samuel Pierpont Langley, an astronomer and aviation pioneer, is elected the third Secretary of the Smithsonian.*

1891. *The roof of the West Wing is rebuilt with fireproof materials.*

1895. *Electricity is supplied to the building by a new dynamo installed in the basement of the South Tower.*

1900. *The Art Room is created in the East Wing.*

1901. *A Children's Room opens in the South Tower.*

1904. *The remains of James Smithson arrive in the United States, brought from Italy by Alexander Graham Bell.*

1905. *A crypt containing Smithson's remains is created inside the Castle's north entrance.*

1907. *Charles Doolittle Walcott, an invertebrate paleontologist, is elected the Smithsonian's fourth Secretary. A proposal is made to house a National Gallery of Art in the Upper Main Hall and a Sculpture Hall in the West Wing.*

1911. *The opening of another new National Museum building (now the National Museum of Natural History) allows the transfer of natural history specimens from the Smithsonian Building.*

1914. *Renovation of the Lower Main Hall includes removal of galleries and the addition of new lighting.*

1916. *The Lower Main Hall is reopened with graphic arts exhibits, and a library is established with new steel book stacks, located at either end of the hall.*

1928. *Charles Greeley Abbot, an astrophysicist and astronomer, is elected the fifth Secretary of the Institution.*

1940. *The Lower Main Hall is renovated for the Index Exhibit, showcasing the breadth of the Smithsonian collections. With the hall receiving a new decor, thirty feet at each end are lost to office space; steel book stacks are enclosed behind these walls.*

1945. *Alexander Wetmore, an ornithologist and avian paleontologist, is elected the Smithsonian's sixth Secretary.*

1953. *Leonard Carmichael, a psychologist who was president of Tufts University, succeeds Wetmore as the seventh Secretary of the Institution.*

1959. *The Lower Main Hall in the Main Building gains a new name, the Great Hall, which has been used since then for this communal gathering place.*

1964. *The Smithsonian's National Museum of History and Technology opens, permitting the transfer of all remaining exhibits (graphic arts) still located in the Castle. S. Dillon Ripley, an ornithologist who became director of the Peabody Museum of Natural History, is elected the eighth Secretary of the Institution.*

1965. *The Department of Botany is transferred from the Upper Main Hall to the Natural History Museum.*

1970. *Renovation of the Castle is completed; the roof of the lower North Tower is reconstructed from old photographs. The Woodrow Wilson International Center for Scholars is installed in newly created floors occupying the former Upper Main Hall.*

1971. *The West Wing is opened as the Commons dining room.*

1975. *The South Shed, the Astrophysical Observatory, and the Air and Space Building are demolished, and the Victorian Garden is created in the Castle's South Yard to observe the nation's Bicentennial.*

1980. *A statue of Saint Dunstan, restored after its arrival from Westminster Abbey, is installed in the niche of the South Tower.*

1981. *The Victorian Garden is removed for construction of the Quadrangle underground museum complex.*

1984. *Robert McCormick Adams, an anthropologist and archeologist who served as provost of the University of Chicago, succeeds S. Dillon Ripley as the Smithsonian's ninth Secretary.*

1987. *Major renovations in the Great Hall are begun, and the Enid A. Haupt Garden is completed.*

1988. *The restored Children's Room is opened in the South Tower.*

1989. *A visitor information center and a reception center for Smithsonian Associates are opened in the Great Hall.*

1994. *I. Michael Heyman, who had served as chancellor of the University of California, Berkeley, is elected the Institution's tenth Secretary.*

1996. *The Smithsonian celebrates its 150th anniversary with programs, concerts, and a spectacular fireworks display. A bell is also finally dedicated and installed on the roof of the tall North Tower.*

1998. *The Woodrow Wilson Center moves out of the building, freeing space for administrative offices.*

2000. *Lawrence M. Small, president and chief executive officer of the Federal National Mortgage Association, is elected the eleventh Secretary of the Smithsonian.*

2003. *The Commons dining room is closed and replaced with exhibits.*

2004. *New exhibits are installed in the West Wing and opened to the public.*

2008. *G. Wayne Clough, a civil engineer and president of the Georgia Institute of Technology, is elected the Institution's twelfth Secretary.*

2009. *Night at the Museum: Battle of the Smithsonian recreates the Castle and inspires a temporary exhibit of one of the film's central props—the "Pile of Loot."*

2010. *The West Range hosts an exhibit of jewelry worn by Madeleine Albright, America's first woman secretary of state.*

2011. *An earthquake measuring 5.8 on the Richter scale damages five of the East Wing's chimneys on August 23.*

Opposite, top: Leonard Carmichael, ca. 1953. Opposite, center: S. Dillon Ripley, ca. 1980. Opposite, bottom: Robert McCormick Adams, 1989. Left, top: I. Michael Heyman. Photograph by Jeff Tinsley, 1999. Left, center: Lawrence M. Small. Photograph by Jeff Tinsley, 1999. Left, bottom: G. Wayne Clough. Photograph by Amanda Lucidon, 2011.

PART TWO

THE CASTLE FROM EAST

TO WEST

Richard E. Stamm 1993

THE EAST WING
AND THE EAST RANGE

The East Wing and the East Range were the first portions of the Castle to be completed and occupied. For more than a year, all the functions of the fledgling Smithsonian were carried on within these walls: in offices for the Secretary and the librarian, a lecture hall, two laboratories, and an Apparatus Room. Joseph Henry, the Institution's first Secretary, made significant changes to the East Wing to support his view of the Smithsonian as a research institution, rather than a public teaching college. The early functions were relocated as the other sections of the building were gradually completed and the spaces of the East Wing and the East Range were repurposed.

The most significant change to the East Wing was the construction of living quarters for Joseph Henry and his family in 1855. From the workrooms directly beneath the

Opposite: The Art Room on the second floor of the East Range, now used as a meeting space for the Under Secretary for History, Art, and Culture. Photograph by Eric Long, 2011. Right: Joseph Henry, his wife, Harriet (standing), and his daughters Helen, Caroline, and Mary (from left) on the Smithsonian grounds near their home. Photograph by Titian Ramsay Peale, 1862.

living quarters, the International Exchange Service concurrently disseminated scientific publications to scholarly institutions, both domestic and abroad. Laboratories occupied the first floor of the East Range.

Spencer Fullerton Baird, who was the Institution's second Secretary from 1878 to 1887, devoted more space in the East Wing and the East Range to the Smithsonian's expanding administrative requirements. Since the early 1870s, the offices of the Secretary and the support staff have been located in the building's east end, which serves as the Institution's administrative headquarters. Special-use rooms were also created here by the various Secretaries, including the Art Room, the Smithsonian Archives, and the Secretary's parlor and meeting room.

ALL UNDER ONE ROOF

Planning for the Smithsonian Building had begun before Joseph Henry was appointed Secretary in December 1846.[1] Once in Washington, he expressed his opposition to the construction of such a large and ornate building, stating: "The great danger is that they will think themselves obliged by law to go on with the construction of a magnificent building which will absorb all the funds."[2] Although the Castle's exterior was James Renwick's design, Regent Robert Dale Owen had begun laying out every detail of the interior even before the Institution's plan of organization was adopted.[3] By 1849, however, Henry was making changes to Owen's plans, if hesitantly at first.[4]

Construction of the building proceeded in stages, with the East Wing and the East Range completed and occupied early in 1849.[5] The first lecture delivered in the wing's new lecture hall occurred on April 30 of that year. Henry was so displeased with the acoustics, the seating, the lighting, and the ventilation of the Owen-designed hall that he immediately set to work with the architect, reconfiguring it to his own specifications.[6] By June 1849, Henry stated that a "much more convenient lecture room will be provided than that given in the plan as shown in Owen's book."[7]

A rough drawing of Henry's plan sketches seats curving around the speaker's table, which was placed at the door from the range. A gallery opposite the table would span nearly the room's entire width.[8] Henry set his plan into action, and by January 1850, less than a year after the East Wing had been completed, the entire interior was gutted and his new lecture hall constructed. Rising to the full two-story height of the wing and terminating in a vaulted ceiling, it measured 75 feet long, 45 feet wide, and about 30 feet high.[9] As shown in a rough drawing labeled "Plan adopted," Henry had eliminated the gallery facing the speaker's table, but even without it, the room held "990 persons at 16 inches to each."[10] By the end of 1850, with twenty-five lecture series completed, Henry noted that the hall was already too small to accommodate the large crowds wishing to attend: "Should large audiences continue it may be well to provide a larger lecture room in the main building."[11]

In addition to the lecture hall, the East Wing and the East Range by then housed the offices of the Secretary and the librarian, an Apparatus Room, and two laboratories. The

Below: Detail of the first East Wing lecture hall, from *Hints on Public Architecture*, 1849. Bottom: The Secretary's revised plan for the lecture hall. Drawing by Joseph Henry, 1849.

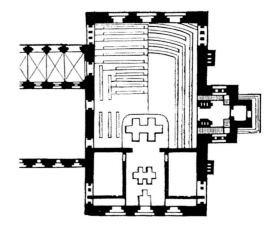

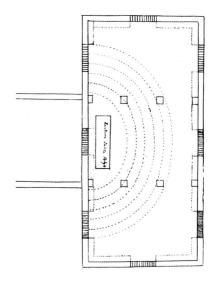

Top: The Chemical Laboratory. Woodcut from William J. Rhees, *An Account of the Smithsonian Institution*, 1857. Above: The Laboratory of Natural History. Woodcut from Rhees, *An Account of the Smithsonian Institution*, 1857.

latter were located directly behind the speaker's table in the East Range, providing easy access to specimens and equipment for lecturers conducting scientific demonstrations. The Chemical Laboratory adjoined the lecture hall, separated by a thick masonry wall and a large arched iron door for fire safety. The Laboratory of Natural History, the smaller of the two rooms, was separated from the Chemical Laboratory by a narrow hallway and a staircase that led to the offices above. The laboratories occupied these spaces from 1849 to 1872.[12]

The Laboratory of Natural History was used for studying, examining, and cataloguing the Institution's natural history specimens, while the Chemical Laboratory was used by qualified professionals for chemical experiments. Research resulting from the use of both laboratories was published in the Smithsonian's *Contributions to Knowledge*, which was distributed worldwide, reaching scientists and scholars with a passion for new information.[13] That passion was best expressed in 1853 by Alexander Winchell, at the time a twenty-nine-year-old student of natural history who would later become one of the most renowned geologists in the country. In a long letter to Assistant Secretary Spencer Baird arranging the donation of his collections to the Smithsonian in exchange for copies of *Contributions to Knowledge*, he wrote: "[T]o be once in the atmosphere of the Smithsonian Institution. . . . If I could once step within its threshold, it seems to me my eager eyes and ears and understanding would drink in a world of wonders and knowledge."[14]

HIS HOME, HIS CASTLE

With the completion of the Main Building early in 1855, several changes occurred. The East Wing's lecture hall was moved to the Upper Main Hall in the new section, and the East Wing was divided into two stories. The lower floor consisted of a large room used for the Institution's International Exchange Service and storage of extra copies of Smithsonian publications.

In the upper story of the East Wing, living quarters for Secretary Henry and his family were constructed. When he was appointed secretary in 1846, he had been promised that in addition to his yearly salary of $3,500 he was to be allotted $500 a year for rented housing "until a residence shall be prepared for you."[15] Nine years passed, and Henry and his family were still living in rented accommodations close by the Smithsonian Building.[16]

The laboratories that remained on the first floor of the adjoining range proved to be a constant source of annoyance for Henry and his family because of foul odors seeping up into the living quarters.[17] Despite the fumes and other annoyances, Henry was generally pleased with his living situation. "[W]e have very pleasant and commodious apartments in the Smithsonian building," he stated.[18]

A cutaway drawing created when the apartment was built shows that a long, steep staircase descended from the Henry household to the east door, the family's private entrance. The stairs were treacherous, as Henry recorded: "Sad accident happened at about half past eleven to Mrs. Henry. . . . I heard a loud crash and called to Mrs. H. to know what it was but receiving no answer the idea occurred to me that she had fallen down the stairs.[19] Plans were then drawn to reconfigure the staircase to rise at a less steep angle.[20]

A floor plan of the Henry living quarters in the East Wing shows a series of eight main rooms as well as several smaller service rooms. The bedrooms and Henry's private study, placed in between two of them, were located along the suite's south side, while the dining room and two parlors occupied the north side.[21] The suite was connected by a doorway to the rooms in the range, which had earlier served as offices for the Institution. By 1872, after collections were removed from the East Wing and with more office space created during the post-fire reconstruction, these rooms were incorporated into the Henrys' living quarters. Bedrooms then occupied the three rooms formerly used as offices by Spencer Baird and the paleontologist Fielding B. Meek and one that had been a study for young scientists.[22] An artist's studio for the Henrys' eldest daughter, Mary (1834–1903), was created in the long room across the hallway.[23]

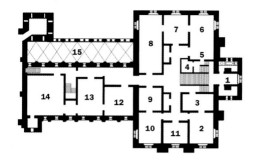

Floor plan of the Henry family living quarters: 1. Water closet and bathroom (north) and pantry (south). 2. Joseph Henry's bedroom. 3. Middle bedroom (east). 4. Pantry. 5. Stairs from the first floor and to the attic. 6. Dining room. 7. Small parlor. 8. Parlor/Music Room. 9. Middle bedroom (west). 10. Southwest bedroom. 11. Joseph Henry's private study. 12–14. Former offices later converted into bedrooms. 15. Mary Henry's studio.

DOROTHEA DIX VISITS

One of the Secretary's visitors, a family friend since about 1848, was Dorothea Dix (1802–87), the noted social reformer and activist for the indigent insane. She often dined with the Henrys in the Castle.[24] The Secretary's opinion of the building was one she shared. In a letter to President Millard Fillmore written after seeing the partially completed building, she was scathing in her assessment: "And then in near proximity stands the Smithsonian edifice (or mass of deficient edifices), a monstrous pile of misshapen towers, arches, columns, etc., a reproduction of the defects of by-gone semi-barbarous periods, a strange blot on the brow of advancing science and a strange commentary on the aims of those who were rather boastful in their announcement of the high purpose of 'cultivating the arts' and diffusing 'useful knowledge.'"[25]

During the Civil War, Dix served as superintendent of Union Army nurses. Within days after the fall of Fort Sumter, she traveled to Washington to offer her services to the president in establishing a hospital for wounded soldiers in the city. Although the government had not taken over the Castle for its use during the war, Dix was given a room in the basement of the East Wing in which to store medical supplies.[26] When, after several months of tireless work, a "feeble and exhausted" Dix walked across town to the building to inspect her supplies in the storeroom, Henry asked her why she did not ride. She explained that her expenses were so great that she could not afford to hire a carriage. Without her knowledge, Henry wrote to Secretary of War Simon Cameron on his friend's behalf, requesting that a wagon and a driver be put at her disposal by the War Department. Cameron referred the matter to President Lincoln, who immediately approved the request.[27] On learning of the offer, Dix refused. "I give cheerfully my whole time, mind, strength and income, to the service of my country," she responded.[28]

Dorothea Lynde Dix, the noted social reformer. Daguerreotype, ca. 1849.

The dining room of the Henry family apartment on the second floor. Photograph by Titian Ramsay Peale, 1862.

A series of photographs of the Henry apartment's three main rooms was taken by the artist Titian Ramsay Peale, a personal friend of Henry.[29] The dining room, the parlor, and the Music Room were often used for the reception and entertainment of visitors. Henry's daughter Mary reported one such occurrence in 1864: "A meeting of the Board of Regents last evening. We were in the Parlor when they came in for supper." Vice President Hannibal Hamlin, General George Totten, Senator W. P. Fessenden, and William W. Seaton, a former mayor of Washington, formed the party.[30] A bust of George Washington, visible in the Music Room, was the topic of one of Henry's letters: "We are all well

except Mary, who met with an accident, in the falling on her head of a bust of Washington from the top of a clothes press. She was shutting the door of the press, when the bust came down,—cut her temple and broke in one of the side bones of her nose."[31]

Directly below the apartment and connected by a separate stairway was the kitchen, a pantry, and a dormitory room for the Henrys' servants and cook, Margaret DeBeust.[32]

LIFE ABOVE THE MUSEUM

Although the Henrys maintained a relatively comfortable upper-middle-class lifestyle, living above the museum always had peculiar drawbacks. Less than a year after moving into their second-floor apartment, the family was plagued both by foul smells emanating from the laboratories and by the assorted vermin that were attracted to the specimens stored in rooms below. A long-time employee, Solomon G. Brown, wrote to Spencer Baird in 1856, reporting that Secretary Henry awoke one day with a terrible headache, which he attributed to the smells emanating from fish specimens. In a state of bad

Above and opposite: The Music Room of the Henry family apartment. Photographs by Titian Ramsay Peale, 1862.

humor, Henry decided to rid the building of all museum specimens that day, but after his excitement abated he changed his mind.[33]

Henry probably rued that decision, however, for less than a year later he instructed Brown to "take all the skins about the building to the cock loft above the lecture room and arrest and kill every flea, for I am tormented."[34] The large animal hides were hoisted up by block and tackle and lowered through the skylight in the roof, where, as Chief Clerk William Jones Rhees put it, "I expect the fleas will have fine times."[35] But that was not the end of the flea infestation, as Brown related afterwards: "I do not perceive that the scratching has fallen off any for on my way out this afternoon I met Mr. McPeak with one hand down his back and the other in his bosom. He looked at me and said 'Solomon do you know anything that keeps away the confounded animals—if I do not get something soon they will eat me and my old woman up.' I told him as I passed him in haste with a smile to wrap himself in a buffalo hide."[36]

Many references were made to exterminating fleas and other insects on museum specimens. A special room was set aside for the task, designated with the ominous title "poisoning workroom."[37] But the plague persisted for years. In 1867 Henry wrote:

I have been for the last two weeks the solitary occupant of the Eastern portion of the Norman Castle. I say solitary rather unadvisedly since I have had more company than desired in the way of visits from fleas and mosquitoes. The house is swarming with the former, which have been disturbed in their occupancy of the packing rooms below. They have given me little or no rest.[38]

In a letter to his wife, he wrote more on the topic:

I have [now] been free from annoyance from mosquitoes, and last night gained a complete victory over the fleas. When the war commenced I was driven from my bed in the middle parlor to the one in the corner room and back again. As the enemy did not scruple to attack me when least prepared for defense, and in the midst of darkness, I felt justified in adopting a similar kind of warfare, and had recourse to a poisonous atmosphere of the vapor of camphor. I strewed this substance in a pulverized condition over the field of conflict, and by this means put the enemy to flight.[39]

Baird's collections not only gave off offensive odors and attracted fleas, they also proved appealing to a more sinister pest. As Rhees reported to Baird in 1871: "The dwelling is almost uninhabitable on account of the dead rats. The Professor [Henry] advertised for a rat killer and a man came who killed 38 in one night, but many more have probably died in their holes."[40]

In an attempt to completely separate the Smithsonian's museum and administrative functions, Henry had all the specimens removed from the East Wing to a room in the West Wing basement in 1872.[41] The problem was moved but not solved, however, as Henry noted shortly afterward: "A very pungent stench pervaded the building yesterday from the fish collected by Professor Baird. The stench is too offensive to the visitors of the Institution to be allowed."[42]

Finally, in 1875, odors from the specimens being prepared for display at the Centennial Exhibition in Philadelphia became so noxious in the lower parts of the building, and the "diffusion of the effluvia" through the other parts proved so intolerable, that Henry

took decisive action. Southwest of the Castle, he ordered construction of a small brick building (named the Laboratory of Natural History) to accommodate the photographer, the taxidermists, and those engaged in the study of the "offensive specimens."[43] After twenty years of annoyance, Henry had at last triumphed over the vexing problem.

It can be said that not only was Henry's home his castle, but in fact the entire Castle was his home. On finding themselves temporarily displaced while the living quarters were being painted, the Henrys simply relocated to the museum. As Mary recalled: "[W]e eat in the kitchen and use the laboratory as a parlor. . . . We are very cozy among the chemicals tonight."[44] Once, to entertain the young daughter of a visiting friend, the usually reserved Joseph Henry and his wife, Harriet, played hide-and-seek with her among the exhibit cases in the cavernous museum hall.[45] What a sight it must have been to see the eminent professor frolicking among the minerals, shells, stuffed birds, and mummies![46]

During the heat and humidity of summer, which Mary described as "the malarious [sic] atmosphere of Washington," the Henrys, like many other families of their stature, would leave the city for the cooler north, sometimes returning as late as early autumn. In October 1862, while the rest of the family was still away, Henry's eldest son, William, became gravely ill. The family rushed back to Washington, but within a day or two, Will had passed away. Mary later recorded the sad event in her diary:

I went upstairs into the dining room. The house looked chill and desolate. After a little while Mother said I might see him but I was not prepared for the change in him. It was a terrible shock, but the smile he gave me was inexpressibly sweet and I can never forget it. His hand was so thin, so damp and cold that I had to kneel down and lean my forehead on it to hide my tears. He was very restless, requiring to be moved from one bed to another every 10 or 15 minutes, Hannah, and Henry the watchman carrying him like a child. Towards morning he was very much worse [and] his breathing frightened me after a while, it was so very peculiar and his eyes were only half closed. Will lay quietly for a short time and then started suddenly upright with a wild look in his eyes crying out "Oh they are chaining him, they are chaining Father." He was himself again in a few moments and asked to be moved into the next room, then to a couch in the same room. After that he was moved from bed to bed continually answering all our entreaties that he would remain quiet with his plaintive "move me . . . please move me." Hannah [the maid] then made some change in his dress and laid him upon the large bed in the corner room. I bathed his head with cologne and putting my lips near his ear sang to him in a low tone. He grew quiet as soon as I commenced to sing, but his breathing soon frightened me as it had in the morning. I went into the next room to call Father and Professor Baird. He breathed two or three times more softly. I could hear nothing then and asked Professor Baird with my eyes if he were dead. Professor Baird bowed his assent. Mother and I closed his eyes, the expression of his face was exquisitely peaceful.[47]

The Henrys, especially Joseph, were devastated, and Mary later observed that he had grown touchingly gentle since Will's death. "He speaks of him quietly and cheerfully," she said, "but we can see that it is telling upon him."[48] Christmas 1862 was particularly melancholy; the family spent the day quietly, not receiving any of their many callers. After exchanging modest gifts of drawing instruments and books, Mary summed up their holiday by saying, "The happiest part of the day has been sitting at Father's feet and hearing him read 'The Lady of the Lake.' I enjoyed not only the beautiful poem itself, but Father's intense

Opposite: The small parlor of the Henry family apartment. Photograph by Titian Ramsay Peale, 1862. Above: The bedroom in the southwest corner of the apartment where William Henry, the Secretary's son, died in 1862. Photograph by Thomas W. Smillie, ca. 1878.

enjoyment of it. It has been a day of pain in spite of all our efforts."[49] Mary's pain had not yet subsided by New Year's Eve, when she wrote: "We watched the old year out and the new year in. Nell and I sat in Father's study until the heavy boom of a cannon told us the old year was dead. I shall not soon forget that sound; it was the last of the year that knew our Will."[50]

Mary Henry was known to be an amateur artist, sometimes spending afternoons sketching with friends in Georgetown Cemetery.[51] For more than five years during the mid-1860s, she could be found in the laboratory on the first floor, patiently sculpting a portrait bust of her father.[52] Perhaps realizing, as she put it, that she "had no talent," Mary finally gave up on the bust and switched to painting, which may have prompted the creation of her studio.[53] Light to the long, narrow atelier came from two skylights and a row of portal windows.[54] As seen in a photograph taken about 1878 by the Smithsonian's

Below: Mary Henry's studio in the East Range, with an 1849 Renwick chair (near the far wall) designed for the Regents' Room. Photograph by Thomas W. Smillie, ca. 1878. Opposite, top: Joseph Henry's study, in between the bedrooms, in the family's second-floor apartment. Photograph by Thomas W. Smillie, ca. 1878. Opposite, center: Joseph Henry's bedroom at the time of his death. Photograph by Thomas W. Smillie, ca. 1878. Opposite, bottom: John H. Richard's studio in Mary Henry's former studio space, displaying the scientific illustrator's hand-painted plaster fish casts and earlier paintings of reptiles, amphibians, and fish, ca. 1880.

first full-time photographer, Thomas W. Smillie (1843–1917), six easels were set up amid a variety of props, suggesting a class or a group working together.[55] Among the props was a large plaster bust of Apollo that originally came to the Smithsonian in 1858 as part of the collections of the defunct National Institute. Both the bust and a Renwick chair, also shown, remain in the building to this day, catalogued as part of the Smithsonian Institution Castle Collection.

Mary's studio was recorded as part of a second set of photographs taken of the private rooms in the Henrys' living quarters. Thomas Smillie also documented the Secretary's study, which was between Henry's own bedroom and one in the southwest corner.[56] The view of the first Secretary's bedroom, notable for its chairs facing the bed, reveals the event that had just occurred: his death on May 13, 1878. Soon afterward, the first Secretary's family moved from the building that had been their home since 1855.

FROM FAMILY LIFE TO OFFICIAL USE

After Joseph Henry's death in 1878, the family's second-floor rooms in the East Wing were converted into offices and the artist's studio on the range's second floor was given over to the scientific illustrator John H. Richard (1807–81).[57] He first worked in the Smithsonian's Laboratory of Natural History from 1852 to 1855, drawing fish, reptiles, and amphibians for several reports of the government's exploratory expeditions.[58] After moving to Philadelphia in 1855, Richard continued to illustrate Smithsonian publications for the next twenty years, often coloring the drawings of the ornithologist Robert Ridgway.[59] In 1875 Richard returned to Washington to prepare the Smithsonian's natural history exhibits for the 1876 Centennial Exhibition in Philadelphia. He was engaged primarily in painting plaster casts of fishes modeled by the Smithsonian's taxidermist, Joseph Palmer, although several of his handcolored fish drawings were also displayed in the exhibition. Richard's final project before his death in 1881 was the preparation of the Smithsonian's fish casts for the 1880 Fishery Exhibition in Berlin, for which the Smithsonian was awarded the grand prize.[60] A photograph of him in his studio, posing with examples of his life's work spread out about him, was taken approximately a year preceding his death.

Before the Henry family's second-floor apartment was repurposed as administrative offices for the Institution in 1879, Assistant Secretary Spencer Baird and his assistants had offices in two rooms on the first floor of the East Range.[61] Seven years earlier Joseph Henry had removed the laboratories from the range's first floor, renovated the rooms, and converted them for his office. When Baird became Secretary on Henry's death in 1878 and moved into that office, he brought with him an innovative desk that he had purchased in 1876 from the Wooten Desk Company of Indianapolis.[62] First patented in 1874 by William S. Wooten, this desk when opened provided a drop-down writing surface, as well as scores of pigeonholes and letter boxes that exemplified the old adage, "A place for everything and everything in its place." The London dealer for Wooten desks declared that "with this desk, one has absolutely no excuse for slovenly habits."[63] Wooten's "Patent Cabinet Office Secretary" came in three sizes in each of four

Top left: Spencer Baird's office in the East Range, showing his Wooten desk (left foreground). Photograph by Thomas W. Smillie, ca. 1878. Bottom left: Chief Clerk William J. Rhees's office in the East Range, formerly the Chemistry Laboratory, with the balustrade dividing the office. Photograph by Thomas W. Smillie, ca. 1878.

grades—ordinary, standard, extra, and superior—and when closed and locked secured its contents from dust and intrusion.[64] Baird's standard Wooten desk today is located in the political history collection of the National Museum of American History.

In describing his new office in the East Range in 1872, Henry had revealed that the old Chemical Laboratory was also reconfigured to accommodate the Smithsonian's chief clerk, William J. Rhees, as well as other staff: "The partitions have been removed from the adjoining room occupied by Solomon [Brown]; and the large room thus produced has been carpeted and otherwise fitted up for Mr. Young, Luck and the other assistants connected with my office."[65] Separating Rhees's work area from the rest of the staff was a low railing formed from newel posts and balustrades with a decorative wire grill attached.

A FIREPROOF ENLARGEMENT

Although the former Henry family living quarters were used as offices for the Secretary and his staff from 1879 until early 1883, the wooden frame interior was considered highly flammable. Secretary Baird appealed to Congress, and an appropriation of $50,000 was granted for the complete fireproofing of the wing and the connecting range. The architecture firm Cluss & Schulze submitted plans to the Regents to add two floors to the East Wing and one to the range, increasing to 12,500 square feet the amount of usable office space.[66]

The rather daunting task of coordinating the relocation of the staff and offices to temporary quarters during the renovation fell to William J. Rhees, who was put in charge of "all matters relative to the removal of property, furniture, fixtures, stores etc." Many of the employees were moved to rooms in the North and South Towers and to portions of the Main Hall in the Castle, while Rhees moved to the Regents' Room and Secretary Baird took an office in the new museum building next door (now the Arts and Industries Building). Rhees was thorough, detailing not only the relocation of staff but also providing estimates of the number of various workers needed for the move, as well as the amount each was to be paid.[67]

The reconstruction took about a year to complete, allowing some of the new offices to be occupied early in May 1884. However, the funding proved insufficient to finish the interiors of the rooms on the top two floors.[68] When completed, the East Wing and the East Range housed the offices of the Secretary and his assistants, the International Exchange Service, the registrar's office, the chief clerk's office, the librarian, a post office, a reference library and reading room, the Archives, laboratories, several rooms for

Chief Clerk William J. Rhees, who was also an inventor.

RENAISSANCE MAN RHEES

William Jones Rhees (1830–1907) was the Smithsonian's chief clerk from 1852 until 1890, after which he continued as the Institution's archivist until his death. In addition to being a founder of the Washington, D.C., chapter of the YMCA and a member of many civic and professional organizations, Rhees was for eight years a trustee of the Washington public schools, a position that provides insight into an interesting sideline of his. In 1867, with his patented design for a slate frame for use in schools, Rhees added inventor to his impressive list of accomplishments.[69] Endorsed by Joseph Henry and the secretary of education, among others, and advertised in the Smithsonian's 1869 guidebook, Rhees's innovation was adopted by the school board for use in all of the District's public schools.[70] The slate frame featured a built-in foot ruler that moved in a groove covering a shallow compartment for storing a pencil, an eraser, and a sharpener. Touting its many advantages over regular slates, the Smithsonian advertisement declared that "it promotes a habit of neatness and order—a place being provided for the pencil, the pencil can always be put in its place."[71]

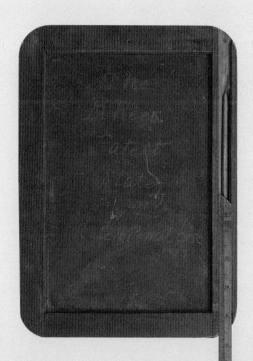

Rhees's patented ruler and pencil case slate, used in District of Columbia schools.

artists and researchers working on the collections, and a large office for the National Academy of Sciences.[72]

The architects managed to add the two floors while maintaining the building's architectural character. By adjusting the height of the floors within the original structure, three floors then occupied the same vertical space as the previous two; one floor was added under a new, more steeply pitched roof. In Cluss's words: "The exterior architecture was simply modified by resetting all the architraves and cornices at such levels as to enable valuable space within the building to be made useful [and] by enlarging some of the windows as necessary."[73] Cluss reused most of the Seneca sandstone removed during reconstruction, replacing all of the original decorative detail and adding a small quantity of new stone for the range's new third floor, the dormers, and the extended east facade.[74]

In designing the second-floor layout, Cluss had closely followed the room arrangement from Henry's time. However, he relocated and reconfigured the staircase around an open stairwell, eliminating the long, steep staircase that rose from the east entrance. The layout of the rooms in the basement and on the first and third floors also followed the configuration of those on the second floor, but the rooms of the fourth floor were necessarily smaller because of their position under the roof's gables.

THE INTERNATIONAL EXCHANGE SERVICE

When the renovation of the East Wing and the East Range was completed, the offices of the Smithsonian Institution International Exchange Service returned to the first floor, while the service's shipping and packing rooms occupied rooms in the basement below. Established in 1848, the service distributed scientific publications to American and foreign institutions, government departments, societies, and individuals around the world.[75] Joseph Henry eloquently summed up the value of this Smithsonian function: "The worth and importance of the Institution are not to be estimated by what it accumulates within the walls of its building, but by what it sends forth to the world."[76]

Two photographs taken in 1892 by Coates Walton Shoemaker, a clerk in the service who later became chief clerk, show the first-floor offices of George H. Boehmer, chief clerk, and Ferdinand V. Berry, assistant in charge of foreign exchanges. The two department heads posed in spacious, well-lighted offices appointed with up-to-date office furniture and equipment. Their desks, chairs, revolving bookcases, and letter file cabinets were all in the contemporary Eastlake style, while the tall bookcases in both offices were repurposed from the former balcony laboratories of the Lower Main Hall.[77] Although ample light poured in from the north- and south-facing windows, gas chandeliers provided additional light on dark days and both offices were warmed by steam radiators.

The International Exchange Service offices remained on the first floor until 1893, when a suite of dark and damp rooms in the basement was renovated into well-lighted, comfortable offices and the entire operation was consolidated downstairs.[78] A remarkable set of photographs documents the basement office of the chief clerk over a period

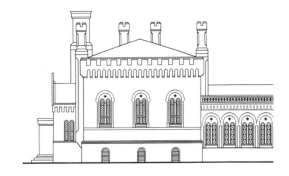

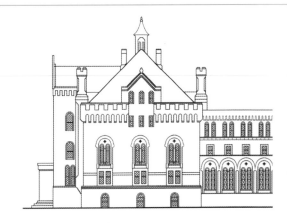

Top: North facade of the East Wing before the 1883–84 renovation. Drawing by Richard E. Stamm, 2005. Above: North facade of the East Wing after the 1883–84 renovation. Drawing by Richard E. Stamm, 2005. Opposite, top: George H. Boehmer, chief clerk of the Smithsonian International Exchange Service, in his first-floor office. Photograph by Coates Walton Shoemaker, 1892. Opposite, bottom: Ferdinand V. Berry, assistant in charge of the Smithsonian International Exchange Service's Foreign Exchange Division, in his first-floor office, whose world maps were reminders of the service's scope and reach. Photograph by Coates Walton Shoemaker, 1892.

of twenty-four years. In the first photograph, dating from 1908, a young Frank E. Gass takes notes from the chief clerk, Washington Irving Adams. By 1912 the office had been modernized and rearranged with contemporary office furniture. A clean-shaven Gass, seated at the corner desk, shares the office with Chief Clerk Shoemaker; a young man is seated at a Gammeter Multigraph, a machine for duplicating letters or forms. Two years later, in 1914, little in the office had changed, except that Miss J. Stark had replaced the young man at the duplicating machine and Mrs. L. C. Boehmer assisted in the office. Eighteen years later, in 1932, the aging Shoemaker and Gass still occupied their assigned desks, while Gass's daughter-in-law Mary operates a Burroughs adding machine by the door. Shoemaker retired at the age of eighty-one in 1941 after more than fifty-nine years of service to the Institution. Gass, who started as a messenger in 1886 at the age of fifteen, also retired that year; however, because of the severe manpower shortage during the war, he returned to work within a year as acting chief

Top, left: Office of the chief clerk, International Exchange Service, showing Frank E. Gass taking notes from Chief Clerk Washington Irving Adams, 1908. Top, right: Chief Clerk Coates Walton Shoemaker (left) and Frank Gass (center) in the modernized office, with a young assistant seated at a duplicating machine, April 1912. Above, left: Shoemaker and Gass, with Miss J. Stark now at the duplicating machine, November 1914. Above, right: Shoemaker and Gass, assisted by Mary Gass at a Burroughs adding machine, November 1932.

clerk in the International Exchange Service office, finally retiring in 1946 after almost sixty years at the Smithsonian.

The shipping rooms were located immediately adjacent to the offices of the International Exchange Service in the basement below the Main Hall. Hundreds of thousands of packages annually moved in and out of these cramped quarters; at its peak during the postwar decades of the 1950s and 1960s, well over a million packages were processed each year.[79] Although steam pipes, electrical conduits, and water pipes were beginning to encroach on the basement ceiling, the rathskeller-like groin vaulting is clearly visible in a photograph from about 1930.

The International Exchange Service offices were moved out of the Castle to new quarters in the Arts and Industries Building during fiscal year 1966.[80] The old basement offices were then converted into laboratories for the Division of Radiation and Organisms, which studied photomechanisms in plants.[81] After the laboratories were moved to Rockville, Maryland, in 1970, the offices were reassigned to the Smithsonian's Protection Division. Finally, in 2001, the employee food-service unit, which for many years had occupied several rooms on the other side of the hallway, was newly renovated, expanded, and renamed the Castle Staff Deli. A new seating area for the deli created in the old exchange offices was decorated with historic photographs of the International Exchange Service, which had been terminated in 1983–84.[82]

The basement shipping room of the International Exchange Service, with its original groin vaulting, ca. 1930.

THE INSTITUTION'S HEADQUARTERS

When the renovated East Wing was reoccupied in 1884 following the fireproof additions, Secretary Baird located his office in the Henrys' former dining room in the northeast corner of the second floor. However, when Samuel Pierpont Langley (1834–1906) became Secretary in 1887, he took as his office the room at the opposite side of the wing that had been Joseph Henry's bedroom. It has remained the Secretary's office ever since. Charles Doolittle Walcott (1850–1927) served as Secretary from 1907 until his death twenty years later. A photograph by Thomas Smillie shows him seated at his cluttered desk about nine months after the death of his second wife, Helena. A small portrait of her printed on a transparent material appears ghostlike in the window.

What had been the second bedroom of the Henry suite was by 1912 an office for the Secretary's support staff. In the hallway adjacent to the Secretary's office, visitors would wait to be received in the sitting area behind a screened alcove. Tables and chairs were provided for messengers; electric call bells, mounted on the door frames, alerted them when they were needed. Although electric service had been installed in the East Wing

Below: Secretary Charles D. Walcott at his desk in the Secretary's office. Photograph by Thomas W. Smillie, 1912. Opposite: The second-floor hallway adjacent to the Secretary's office. Photograph by Thomas W. Smillie, ca. 1900.

HELENA WALCOTT, SMITHSONIAN NOBILITY

The Smithsonian's fourth Secretary, Charles D. Walcott, was first married at age twenty-two in 1872 to Lura Ann Rust. She was a frail young woman who died after only four years of marriage. For the next twelve years, Walcott devoted himself to the science of geology. He married Helena Breese Stevens, daughter of the former mayor of Madison, Wisconsin, in 1888, and the couple had four children between 1889 and 1896. Helena Walcott often accompanied her husband on his geological expeditions, in addition to serving as official hostess at Smithsonian functions after he became Secretary.[83] Her portrait was painted by Karl Bror Kronstrand (1875–1950), a Swedish artist who specialized in creating portraits of European nobility, especially women. Beginning in 1910, he embarked on a four-year quest to paint the most notable (and beautiful) women of the United States.[84] Helena Walcott sat for her portrait on April 17, 1911, in the presence of her husband and four children. Less than three months later, she was killed in a tragic train accident.[85]

Portrait of Helena Walcott, the wife of Secretary Charles D. Walcott. Oil wash on canvas by Karl Bror Albert Kronstrand, 1911.

offices in 1895, it was still not completely reliable for lighting in 1900.[86] The use of chandeliers equipped with both electric lights and gas burners provided a backup against power interruptions.[87] As an amenity offered to visitors and staff alike, a brass cuspidor (spittoon) on the floor atop a small decorative mat was readily available for use. Cuspidors were common sights in public places during the second half of the nineteenth century and the early decades of the twentieth century. Most often made of brass (polished, embossed, painted, or plated), they were also available in cast iron, enameled tin, and porcelain.[88] Appearing to guard the hallway from intruders, two mannequins dressed in Japanese armor flanked the archway leading to offices in the East Range. The framed portrait hanging at the base of the staircase was that of Robert Hare (1781–1858), among the Smithsonian's earliest donors and one of its first honorary members.[89]

The publications staff and the appointment clerk occupied adjoining offices on the East Range's second floor, directly adjacent to the chief clerk's office. In the absence of electrical sockets in the walls, additional desk lamps in the publications office were plugged directly into the chandelier. The chief clerk's office, on the other hand, had been updated with a modern electric fixture that replaced the outdated combination gas-electric chandeliers.[90] Telephones, thirty of which had been installed in Smithsonian offices in 1881, were quite commonplace by 1914.[91] The development of the telephone had a profound effect on the conduct of business and society in general during the late nineteenth and early twentieth centuries—much as the personal computer and the Internet have done in recent years.

Located above on the third floor, Smithsonian publications continued to be the primary means of diffusing knowledge well into the twentieth century. After the publications editor,

The chief clerk's office, picturing (left to right) James G. Traylor, Henry W. Dorsey, and John Ure Perkins. Photograph by Thomas W. Smillie, 1914.

Presentation of the Langley Medal to Charles Lindbergh (third from right) by William Howard Taft (far right) in the Regents' Room on the second floor. Also pictured are future Secretary Alexander Wetmore and then-Secretary Charles G. Abbot (standing at left), 1927.

Alonzo Howard Clark, died in 1919, Webster Prentiss True was appointed his successor. The publications office was reorganized and renamed the Editorial Division in 1939. After several subsequent administrative changes, it ultimately became the Smithsonian Institution Press in 1966.[92]

A large room adjoining the Secretary's office had been converted for use as the meeting room of the Board of Regents in 1904, when the old Regents' Room in the South Tower was used as a temporary resting place for James Smithson's remains. The Regents met in this space for the following sixty-four years, until their former South Tower chamber was restored for their use. Smithsonian Secretary Charles Greeley Abbot (1872–1973), who served from 1928 to 1944, joined members of the Board of Regents gathered around a specially designed oak meeting table at the December 8, 1927, meeting of the Regents for presentation of the Langley Medal to Charles Lindbergh for outstanding achievement in aviation for his nonstop flight across the Atlantic. William Howard Taft, chief justice of the United States and former president, presented the award to Lindbergh.[93]

MODERNIZATION OF THE EAST WING

Two world wars and an economic depression took their toll on the Castle's infrastructure and systems. The antiquated heating, electrical, and plumbing systems were all desperately in need of replacement by the time S. Dillon Ripley (1913–2001) was appointed Secretary in 1964.[94] By then the decor of the offices in the East Wing and the East Range can only be described as bleak: green asbestos tiles covered the wooden floors, egg-crate fluorescent lighting fixtures had replaced the gas chandeliers, and the furnishings consisted of drab metal desks and filing cabinets. Ripley soon initiated plans for a complete renovation of the building with the two-fold goal of updating the mechanical systems and restoring the interior spaces with period furniture and fixtures to complement the building's nineteenth-century architecture. To that end, the Smithsonian Furnishings Collection (now the Smithsonian Institution Castle Collection) was established in 1964 under the special assistant to the Secretary, Richard H. Howland, and later the Castle curator, James M. Goode.

Photographs from the mid-1970s show the Secretary's staff working at antique desks in offices furnished with nineteenth-century tables and chairs, beneath restored and electrified gas chandeliers. Paintings and sculpture on loan from the Smithsonian's art museums graced the walls, and period decorative objects sat on the mantels of working fireplaces. Ripley's renovation had restored a Victorian elegance to the rooms not seen since the Henry family made this their home. Almost thirty years later, the rooms were again redecorated for a new Secretary to include exhibit cases filled with objects from the various Smithsonian museums—serving as a tour in microcosm of the Institution's vast holdings.

Above, left: The Secretary's office in the 1970s. Photograph by Richard Hofmeister, 1976.
Above, right: The Secretary's parlor. Photograph by Alfred F. Harrell Jr., 1980.

Right: The Secretary's office today.
Photograph by Eric Long, 2011.
Below: The Secretary's reception suite.
Photograph by Eric Long, 2011.

Opposite: The Secretary's parlor. Photograph by Eric Long, 2011. Above: Andy Warhol during his visit to view the Smithsonian Institution Castle Collection, 1977.

The Smithsonian's Furnishings Collection received a surprise visit in 1977 from the artist and cultural icon Andy Warhol (1928–87). Warhol, who was just beginning to collect nineteenth-century American Empire furniture, requested a tour of the Castle's collection of antique furniture and decorative arts. He met with Goode and the Assistant Secretary for History and Art, Charles Blitzer, who occupied the former publications office space on the third floor. Warhol's own collection eventually grew to include many fine examples of American Empire furniture, as well as pieces representing the full range of nineteenth-century styles.[95]

FROM ART ROOM TO MEETING SPACE

After the fire of 1865, the Smithsonian's nascent art collections were loaned to the Library of Congress and the Corcoran Gallery of Art for safekeeping.[96] It was not until 1896 that the Regents authorized their return. A special room was later prepared primarily to house the Marsh collection of prints and engravings, the Smithsonian's first art purchase. George Perkins Marsh (1801–82), a statesman and an early member of the Board of Regents, had amassed a large and valuable collection—including such artists as Dürer, Rembrandt, and Da Vinci, as well as folios of old Italian and German masters—which he sold to the Smithsonian in 1849.[97]

The large room opposite the Secretary's reception suite, which had been the book-keeper's office since 1884, was converted into the Art Room for the study and display of the engravings.[98] The room and its furnishings, designed between 1899 and 1900 by the architecture firm Hornblower & Marshall, measured 32 feet long, 14 feet wide, and 11 feet, 10 inches high. Surrounding the room was a frieze of plaster copies in reduced size of a part of the Elgin marbles from the Parthenon. Below the frieze hung a series of photographs, copies of famous master portraits published by Adolphe Braun (1811–77).[99] The two large cases flanking the doorway were designed with an elaborate system of hardware that enabled the drawers to be raised almost vertically for viewing the prints.[100] Several bookcases constructed of quarter-sawn oak delicately carved with floral motifs were placed around the room for holding important artworks, small bronzes and other art objects decorated the room.

The Art Room continued to house the collection of prints and engravings as late as about 1963, when the graphics arts collections were moved to the newly completed Museum of History and Technology (now the National Museum of American History). By 1972, when the space served as the office of Under Secretary James Bradley (1910–84), only the replica Parthenon frieze remained as a reminder of the room's previous function. With a few exceptions, such as the nineteenth-century chandeliers and an antique partners' desk, the office had modern furniture.

By the time that the astronaut Michael Collins was appointed Under Secretary in 1978, many more period pieces of furniture from the Smithsonian Furnishings Collection were being used in the office, most notably a walnut library table–desk with four fancifully carved griffin supports dating from about 1890. Before becoming the Under Secretary, Collins had been the director of the National Air and Space Museum (1971–78), overseeing construction of the museum's new building on the Mall.[101] Collins, an Air Force colonel, had earlier participated in NASA's Gemini 10 (1966) and Apollo 11 (1969) flights.

The Under Secretary retained the former Art Room space until 2000, when it became the office of the newly created position of Under Secretary for American Museums and National Programs.[102] Now used as a meeting room for the Under Secretary for History, Art, and Culture, it is furnished with a large oak table, one of three designed by Hornblower & Marshall in 1900 for use in the building. At the far end of the room is a Wooten desk similar to the one used by Spencer Baird in his first-floor office (*see page 38*).

THE FOURTH FLOOR

In 1894 a room on the fourth floor of the East Wing was converted for the "valuable and somewhat voluminous archives of the Institution." This space contained twenty-nine specially built walnut cases with shelves and drawers that were quickly filled with letters, drawings, diagrams, photographs, plans of the buildings and grounds, and copies of original papers of the Institution's Secretaries.[103] Beneath a portrait bust of Joseph Henry, possibly an 1879 plaster cast of an original by the prominent American sculptor Clark Mills (1810–83),[104] sat a Harvard coal-burning stove made by the Fuller, Warren Company of Troy, New York.[105]A photograph taken about 1897 shows a bronze commemorative plaque commissioned as a gift to James Smithson's alma mater,

Top: The Art Room on the second floor of the East Range, ca. 1903. Above: Michael Collins in same space, then the Under Secretary's office, 1979.

Pembroke College, Oxford.[106] Above the plaque, mounted into the wall, was the mouthpiece of the so-called oral annunciator, one of the speaking tubes installed throughout the East Wing in 1884 to serve as an intercom system.[107] When the Archives Room was remodeled in 1913, the wooden door panels in the cases were replaced with glass to allow the contents to be seen without opening the doors.[108]

By the mid-1960s the doors of the 1894 cabinets were completely removed for better access to document boxes; to provide improved lighting for researchers, modern eggcrate fluorescent light fixtures were hung from the pressed-metal ceiling. Although the importance of maintaining the Institution's archival documents was always recognized, it was only during this period that the unit acquired its own permanent staff and the collections were fully described and catalogued with quality finding aids. The Smithsonian Archives was temporarily relocated during the complete renovation of the East Wing and the East Range from 1968 until March 1970, when it was moved into larger, newly renovated quarters in the former west library stacks on the first floor.[109] In fiscal year 1976, the Archives was again moved, this time to new quarters in the Arts and Industries Building.[110]

With the Archives no longer occupying the fourth-floor spaces, its former reading room and adjoining offices were reassigned to the Institution's general counsel. The old Archives Room was then furnished with an extension table, a rolltop desk, and lighting fixtures from the Castle Collection. Two matching late-nineteenth-century Renaissance Revival gas chandeliers were electrified, replacing the fluorescent fixture. A handsome hall mirror of the same style occupied the space where Henry's bust and the Harvard heater had been.[111] The glass doors were then restored to the 1894 wall cabinets. With an increased demand for work space by the general counsel's staff and less reliance on the traditional library, the room since the late 1990s has served as an office for Smithsonian lawyers.

Below, left: The Smithsonian Archives on the fourth floor, ca. 1897. Below, right: Samuel T. Surratt, who was appointed the Smithsonian's first archivist in 1965, assisting a researcher in the Archives Room; he left in 1969 to become the first archivist for CBS News.

THE MAIN BUILDING

With its distinctive pair of tall towers marking the Mall facade, the Castle's massive central section is its focal point. Both levels of this two-story portion, called the Main Building, were designed to hold the Institution's public functions: library, lecture halls, and museum. Joseph Henry opposed the construction of such a large building and considered the public uses to be parochial—capable of attracting only a local audience. Reasoning that Smithson's bequest would be better spent on scientific research and publication ("increase and diffusion"), he endeavored to delay or dispense entirely with the building's center portion. As early as October 1847, Henry contemplated connecting the East and West Wings with a screen or a covered walkway. However, he was overruled, and by 1850 the Main Building was under roof and work was progressing to complete the interior as planned.

THE LOWER MAIN HALL

Opposite: The Great Hall of the Main Building, originally known as the Lower Main Hall. Photograph by Richard Strauss, 1992.
Above: The Great Hall, with visitors at the 1976 exhibit The Federal City: Plans and Realities.

From the beginning, the Smithsonian Building's Lower Main Hall was intended as a public area. During the planning phase, this hall was to be divided between a public library and a lecture hall. However, after the space was finished, it was filled with exhibits of natural history specimens, many of which were transferred from the defunct National Institute for the Promotion of Science and the Useful Arts.[1] Although no legislation governing it had been passed by Congress, the term "National Museum" was unofficially adopted for the collections exhibited in the Lower Main Hall beginning about 1859. Springing from this one great hall, the original collections eventually grew to fill three additional Smithsonian museums opened in 1881, 1911, and 1964. With the launching of each new museum and the removal of collections from the original building, the use of the space was reconsidered. After the first National Museum building (now called the Arts and Industries Building) was opened in 1881, the exhibit space in the Castle's Main Hall was divided between curatorial and public functions. The completion of the National Museum of Natural History in 1911 prompted the hall's conversion into a library, with related graphic arts exhibits sharing the space. The hall was again cleared in the 1960s, when the graphic arts displays were transferred to the newly erected National Museum of History and Technology. A public information center was then created in the space and a new name, the Great Hall, was adopted.

The information center was refined and updated over the next twenty years, with exhibits emphasizing the origins and development of both the Smithsonian and Washington, D.C. Foreign dignitaries, heads of state, and cultural figures were ceremoniously received here throughout the 1960s and the 1970s. In the 1980s the renovated Great Hall became the official home of the reception center for visitors and the Smithsonian Associates, serving as the gateway to the entire Smithsonian Institution.

A SINGLE GRAND SPACE

The 1849 plan of the building's first floor shows a large lecture hall in one half of the hall, with a library occupying the rest of the space. A long corridor connected the two main entrances to the building on the north and the south (*see page 26*). This plan was abandoned even before the Main Building was completed in 1855. A lecture hall had been constructed in the already completed East Wing, and the library occupied the entire West Wing. In place of the lecture hall, Joseph Henry envisioned a room to house a collection of scientific instruments, a "museum of apparatus."[2]

When the interior structure of this area collapsed during construction, Henry recorded in his desk diary that "four men were working in the Apparatus Room when they sensed the south east part of the floor to begin to sink. They sprung to the door leading

Sheet-music cover for the "Institute Polka and Schottisch." Lithograph by A. Hoen & Company, Baltimore, published by Hilbus & Hitz Music Depot, Washington, D.C., 1855.

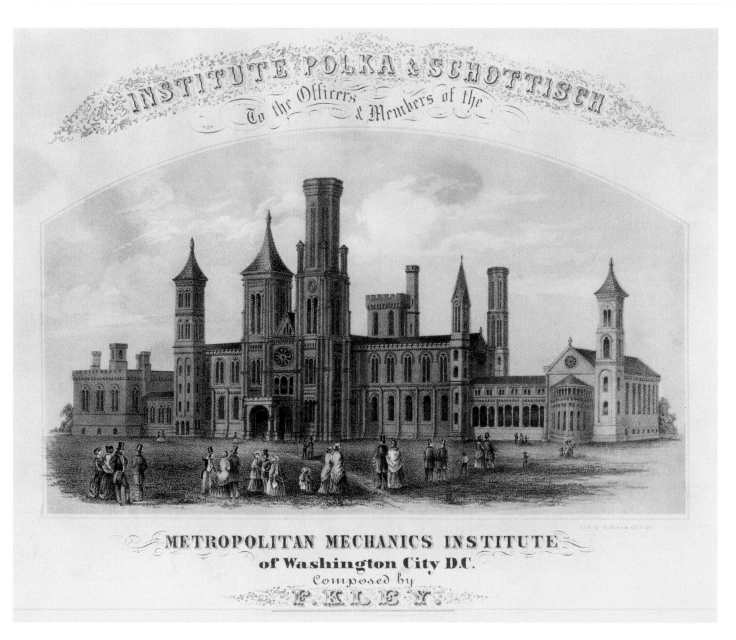

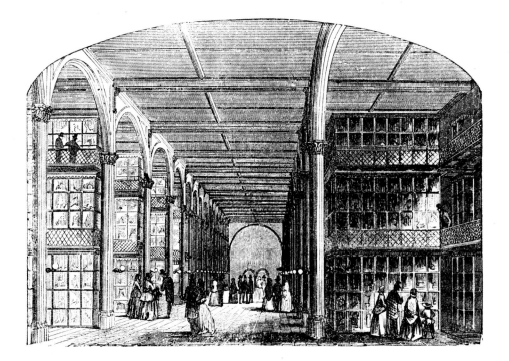

The Lower Main Hall, showing the proposed triple-teared galleries behind the arches. Woodcut from Rhees, *An Account of the Smithsonian Institution*, 1857.

into the Library part and miraculously escaped injury."[3] An independent panel was convened to investigate the cause of the accident, as well as the building methods used.[4] The report persuaded the Regents to adopt James Renwick's original plan to fireproof the building to make it safe for the collections. By the time the reconstruction began, Renwick had been replaced by Barton S. Alexander (1819–78), an engineer on active duty with the U.S. Army Corps of Engineers. The hall was rebuilt with fireproof materials, using brick vaults and iron beams, as a grand single space measuring 200 by 50 feet.

Although finished in 1854, the large first-floor hall remained empty until 1855. The Metropolitan Mechanics' Institute requested permission to use the hall for its 1855 fair, which Henry supported as a way of "favorably exhibiting the Smithsonian building to the public."[5] The exhibition, held on February 8, 1855, provided manufacturers, tradesmen, artisans, and inventors an opportunity to display their products.[6] In honor of this occasion, Frederic Kley composed a polka and schottisch dedicated to the officers and members of the Mechanics' Institute; the sheet music was published that year by Hilbus & Hitz Music Depot of Washington.[7] A second polka, called the "Smithsonian Polka," was composed during the same year by W. Bergman, a music teacher, and also published by Hilbus & Hitz.[8] These dances, likely written to commemorate the building's opening, each featured the image of the Castle on the cover.[9]

After the closing of the Mechanics' Institute exhibition, Joseph Henry intended to have three tiers of exhibit cases constructed in the bays along the hall's north and south sides, which were formed by the two rows of columns that ran its length.[10] Although that arrangement was never constructed, an engraving shows the room with the triple-tiered proposal as if it had actually existed.[11] The gas sconces attached to the columns, as depicted in the engraving, were also never installed.

FILLING THE LOWER MAIN HALL

In the foreground of a stereograph made in 1858 of the museum's hall can be seen a large deformed ball mounted atop an exhibit case. The twelve-inch diameter limestone ball was part of an experiment by James Crutchett in 1847 to illuminate the city from the old dome of the U.S. Capitol. The scheme employed a "Drummond Light," which produced an intense beam of light by spraying ignited gas onto a ball or disc of lime (giving rise to the term *limelight).* The apparatus consisted of the ball positioned inside a glass-enclosed lantern mounted on a ninety-foot pole atop the Capitol dome; gas was pumped from a generating apparatus on the ground through pipes attached to the dome's roof.[12] The experiment was a moderate success, but the ball was subsequently struck by lightning, removed from the dome, and given to the Smithsonian in 1848.[13] In preparation for the transfer of the government collections from the defunct National Institute to the Smithsonian in 1857, exhibit cases designed by Thomas Ustick Walter, the architect of the Capitol, were constructed in the bays and on the galleries of the Main Hall.[14] Joining them were large whitewashed slant-top exhibit cases transferred from the Patent Office to the Smithsonian in August 1858 and placed in the center of the room.[15] Labeled the "Ball struck by lightning" in the Smithsonian guidebook, Crutchett's sphere was installed the following October.[16]

By 1860 the cases in the Main Hall were filled with natural history specimens, many of them collected by officers of exploratory and surveying expeditions, such as the Wilkes Expedition of 1838–42. In addition to preserved specimens of birds, fishes, mollusks, reptiles, and other wildlife, the museum also displayed such exotic items as Egyptian and Peruvian mummies and the so-called cannibal-cooking pots from the "Feegee Islands." Collections were not limited to dead, preserved specimens, however— live snakes from New Jersey were in good company with other living animals.[17] John Varden, the caretaker, revealed that one room in the museum was a veritable menagerie. As he wrote in 1862: "I have instructed James to get young birds, bull frogs or live

Henry M. Bannister and Henry W. Elliott, with Henry Horan, the watchman, near the Washington Monument model in the Lower Main Hall, looking west, ca. 1863–65.

fishes for the water snake. Whatever is got will not be lost as the alligator will soon dispose of them."[18] "The salamander," he added later, "will eat earth worms freely and has been fed twice this week. The alligator is ravenous as a wolf and eats everything that is put in to him."[19] When an animal died in this peaceable kingdom, it was simply bottled in alcohol to become a specimen in the museum collections.[20]

A model of the Washington Monument and a collection box had been placed in the museum hall in 1858 at the request of the Washington Monument Society, a group of prominent citizens determined to fund construction of the monument through private donations. The obelisk, begun in 1848, remained in an unfinished state until the government took over and completed it in 1885.[21] A photograph showing Henry Horan, the watchman, standing next to the model of the monument also includes Henry M. Bannister and Henry W. Elliott, who were Smithsonian employees as well as roommates in one of the high North Tower rooms.[22] In front of them is a large circular meteorite, which came to the Institution in 1863 (see page 107).

The Arctic explorer Elisha Kent Kane (1820–57) was a national hero described at the time of his death in 1857 as having combined the "energy and courage, the chivalry, piety and abnegation of self so renowned in the knights of the olden times." An Eskimo garment, worn on his last expedition to the North Pole, was meant to sustain a human at temperatures of minus 90 degrees Fahrenheit or more. The Smithsonian's guidebook

John Varden, the first caretaker of the Smithsonian collections, ca. 1860.

A DUTIFUL CARETAKER

John Varden (ca. 1789–1865) was the owner and proprietor of a large collection of curiosities called the Washington Museum. He described his establishment, opened in 1829, as a "rational place of amusement" that compared favorably with any of its kind in the United States in its "comprehension and variety."[23] The museum was actually a room in his house on Fifth Street, N.W., across from City Hall. He invited all to visit, stating that "donations of specimens in the Arts and Sciences [would] be thankfully received."[24] In 1841 Varden's collection was purchased by the newly formed National Institute. In lieu of payment outright, he was given the position of caretaker of the collections in the Patent Office, where he worked for the next sixteen years.[25] When the National Institute was dissolved in 1857, the collection and its sixty-eight-year-old caretaker were transferred to the Smithsonian Institution.[26]

The relocation of objects from the Patent Office to the Smithsonian Building continued over the next five years. Taking orders directly from Assistant Secretary Spencer F. Baird and Secretary Joseph Henry, Varden dutifully cared for the museum's specimens and attended to every detail of their transfer. Henry, in his rush to have the museum opened for visitors in April 1859, directed Varden to arrange the specimens for visual appeal only, saying, "[L]et their scientific arrangement alone for the present."[27] As Henry explained in the 1860 Smithsonian guidebook, "Catalogues which will give descriptions and scientific names of all the articles of natural history, will be published in due time by the Institution."[28]

quoted Kane's description of the image he presented while wearing this outfit as "a lump of deformity, waddling over the ice, unpicturesque, uncouth, and seemingly helpless . . . furs and woolens, layer upon layer, inside, like the shards of an artichoke, till he was rounded into absolute obesity."[29] Kane personally presented the outfit to the Smithsonian, and it was put on display in the museum hall in late 1858. It remained there in a specially made exhibit case until the early 1870s.[30]

Visitors documented in an 1867 photograph (*see page 27*) posed toward the center of the Lower Main Hall, newly decorated after water damaged the walls during the fire that raged through the building's upper floor in 1865. The Lower Hall was relatively untouched as a result of the fireproof construction adopted after the collapse in 1850. Repairing the water damage, the architect Adolf Cluss enhanced the walls and ceiling with delicate stencil work.[31] Because Renwick's original radiant wall hot-air system proved insufficient, two large portable stoves were installed at each end of the hall.[32]

The validity of Joseph Henry's earlier assessment that the museum hall was "quite large enough to contain all the collections hitherto made, as well as such others as may be assigned to it," was soon tested as the museum's collections rapidly expanded to fill

Opposite, top: Elisha Kent Kane's Eskimo garment in the museum hall. Stereograph by Langenheim, Lloyd & Company, Philadelphia, ca. 1858–72. Opposite, bottom: The stoves at the far ends of the Lower Main Hall, 1867. Right: The cast Hadrosaurus skeleton in the Lower Main Hall. Stereograph by J. F. Jarvis, 1874–82.

all available space in the hall. By late 1867 two tiers of cases had to be erected across the space's east end to house the burgeoning items. Late in 1874 the old slant-top cases were modified to serve as bases for massive plaster models of extinct animals, which were moved from the Upper Main Hall to the Lower Main Hall.[33] A stereograph from the time shows the model of Hadrosaurus, created by Benjamin Waterhouse Hawkins and installed in the hall early in 1875, from behind; barely visible at the hall's opposite end is the cast of Megatherium, an extinct giant ground sloth.[34] Beyond Hadrosaurus are models of a gigantic Himalayan tortoise and an Irish elk, which remained in the hall until the mid-1880s, when they were moved to the National Museum (Arts and Industries Building).

THE MEGATHERIUM CLUB

Beginning in 1852, Assistant Secretary Baird enlisted the assistance of young naturalists to label and arrange the natural history specimens for public view. In exchange for their services, they were given sleeping quarters in cold and drafty rooms in the upper reaches of the principal towers. Supplying their own furniture and linen, they formed what was described as an "interesting and somewhat unique household."[35] The group banded together, adopting the moniker the Megatherium Club—the name of the giant sloth whose plaster skeletal cast was later exhibited in the museum. Among the first members of the club were the Arctic explorer Robert Kennicott and the zoologist William Stimpson.

Stimpson (1832–72) had been a student in 1850 of the eminent naturalist Jean Louis Agassiz of Harvard University. He arrived in Washington in November 1852 after completing an expedition in New Brunswick. Making use of the books and the instruments in the Smithsonian's Laboratory of Natural History, Stimpson cataloged the specimens of marine invertebrates he had collected.[36] Following a subsequent expedition that lasted three years, Stimpson returned to the Smithsonian in 1856. It was then that he met Robert Kennicott and struck up an enduring friendship.

Kennicott (1835–66) was described as "jolly, warm-hearted, and zealous."[37] It was said that he handled poisonous snakes as if they were eels, while boasting that no rattlesnake had venom for him.[38] Kennicott lived and worked in the building during the winter months between 1857 and 1863.[39] While at the Smithsonian he became one of the most prominent and valued members of the Megatherium Club. He considered William Stimpson his best friend, affectionately referring to him as "Glorious Stimpson." Summing up his friendship, Kennicott remarked: "Stim is one of the best fellows I know, a perfect gentleman and honest and honorable. Of *course*, being a naturalist, he is a jolly good fellow. . . . Stims witticisms are brighter than sunlight."[40]

Meetings of the Megatherium Club were the scene of much "laughing and animated discussion," and mischief no doubt, as evidenced by Kennicott's description of the club:

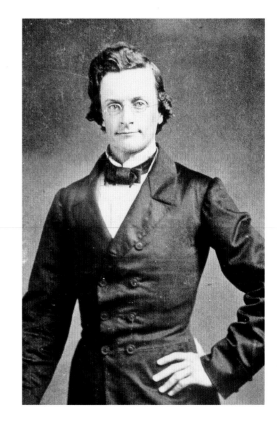

It is at five o'clock, when the Megatherium takes up its prey, that the most interesting character of the animal are seen—Then it roars with delight and makes up for the hard work of the day by much fun and conduction. . . . Vulgar outsiders who think the Megatheria must be rather dry sticks . . . are caused to open their eyes very wide when they are allowed to see the Megatheria taking its prey or on a frolic. It is somewhat of a conceited animal . . . Professor Baird is the Keeper of it and allows it full swing—though I can see he keeps one eye always open to its movements and behavior.[41]

Wisely so, for as Kennicott's younger brother Ira once observed, the scientists he met while visiting the Smithsonian were not quite the reserved young men he had expected:

They are the darndest set of fellows here I ever saw—they are Doctors and Professors and all that, and they talk of their books and all that just as if they *was somebody*—and after all they are just like a parcel of boys—Why tonight we all ran races and hopped and jumped in the big museum hall because it was too rainy to go out for a walk. . . . I suppose Stimpson and some of them are big naturalists, but they act mighty like small boys. . . . Judas Priest . . . there is three or four mummies down in the museum hall and Bob . . . gets up behind 'em and keeps a makin eyes and squaks and groans. . . . I'd tell you about how horrid they look, but perhaps you couldn't sleep well nights.[42]

As the years passed, members of the Megatherium Club went on to pursue their careers in earnest and the club gradually dissolved. In 1864 Robert Kennicott was appointed curator (later director) of the newly reorganized Chicago Academy of Sciences. He spent the year transporting his collections from the Smithsonian to the hall of the academy. In 1865 he was put in charge of an expedition to the Yukon River and Russian America for the

Top: William Stimpson, a zoologist who came to the Smithsonian in 1852. Above: Robert Kennicott, an Arctic explorer who also became a member of the Smithsonian's Megatherium Club.

Western Union Telegraph Company. The expedition had a dual purpose: to map an overland telegraph route from Puget Sound to St. Petersburg, Russia, and to collect natural history specimens, which were to be divided between the Smithsonian and the Chicago Academy of Sciences.[43] Accompanying Kennicott on this trip were fellow Megatherium Club members Henry W. Elliott and Henry M. Bannister, as well as William H. Dall, a later resident of the building.[44] Kennicott would not return from this expedition, as he died suddenly of a heart attack in 1866 at the age of thirty-one. Dall, Bannister, and the others successfully completed the expedition following Kennicott's carefully laid out plans.[45]

In 1867 William Stimpson was appointed director of the Chicago Academy of Sciences, succeeding his friend. Stimpson was permitted to take on loan to Chicago most of the Smithsonian's invertebrate collections, but these specimens and Stimpson's life work, including his original notes and drawings, were destroyed when the academy burned in the great Chicago fire of 1871. Stimpson was devastated by the loss. The disaster may have exacerbated his already frail health; he succumbed to tuberculosis at the age of forty on May 26, 1872, less than eight months after the fire.[46]

NEW MUSEUMS, NEW ARRANGEMENTS

Completion in 1881 of the first National Museum (Arts and Industries Building) caused Secretary Baird to again rearrange the collections. Birds, shells, and mollusks shared space in the Lower Main Hall; the large casts of prehistoric animals were moved to the new building. Framed prints from John James Audubon's elephant folio *The Birds of North America*, attached to the balcony railings, were meant to complement the collection

The Department of Birds on the southwest gallery of the Lower Main Hall, with Leonhard Stejneger, assistant curator of birds, in the foreground, ca. 1886.

The Lower Main Hall, with the Audubon prints hung from the mezzanine railings and fish displayed atop the exhibit cases, ca. 1886.

of mounted birds in the cases below.[47] The large crenellated cases that had been on the balconies were moved downstairs to the middle of the hall, freeing the space for use as laboratories by the curators of the divisions exhibiting in the space.

In 1882 the curators cataloguing and arranging the specimens of fishes and marine invertebrates moved their laboratories to the north balcony. They were soon joined on the south balcony by the curators of birds and mollusks. Not all was harmonious among the various curators sharing the balconies, as revealed by an incident related by Robert Ridgway, curator of birds. A young Henry W. Henshaw was engaged in arranging the bird collections, all the while "whistling to beat the band," as Robert E. Stearns, assistant curator of mollusks, was working on the opposite gallery. In a fit of indignation, Stearns descended the stairs, stormed across the museum, ascended the stairs to the bird gallery and, shaking a hammer in Henshaw's face, shouted, "Young man, if you do not stop that whistling there will be a vacancy in the Geological Survey!"[48]

With the completion in 1911 of the National Museum of Natural History, the Castle's natural history specimens were transferred to the new building.

The library stacks at the east end of the Lower Main Hall, shown in a photograph taken for display at the Smithsonian exhibit at the 1914 Panama-Pacific Exposition.

The Lower Main Hall, looking west, with the initial graphic arts exhibits installed, ca. 1913.

BOOKS AND GRAPHIC ARTS MOVE IN

Once the original collections were removed, the Lower Main Hall ceased to be used strictly for museum purposes and was instead reconfigured as a library with related exhibits.[49] The graphic arts collection was relocated to the hall from the Arts and Industries Building in 1912 because, in addition to explaining how prints were made, they complemented the library collections by illustrating the printing and bookbinding processes.[50] The Audubon prints remained in the hall, but now they provided a link between graphic works of art and publications. They were eventually transferred to the Division of Graphic Arts.

Considering the Smithsonian's library "its most valuable single possession," Secretary Samuel Pierpont Langley, who served from 1887 to 1906, inaugurated a major renovation of the Lower Main Hall to improve the library and the graphic arts collection.[51] The galleries that had been built atop the old exhibit cases in 1855 were demolished, after which the hall once again became a single open space, if only briefly. Some of the original iron gallery railings were reused by the architecture firm Hornblower & Marshall for the new steel library book stacks.

The east-end library stacks were finished and filled with books for a photograph taken for display at the Smithsonian exhibit during the 1914 Panama-Pacific Exposition. From the patchy condition of the plaster and paint, it is clear that renovations in the hall were still ongoing. At the time of completion in August 1914, the library comprised 122,113 unique titles.[52]

During World War I, the Lower Main Hall became a lounge for soldiers, especially for those drilling on the Mall. As an annual report noted, "adequate facilities for letter writing were provided, and the room has been filled with soldiers daily during their rest periods."[53] Museum hours were extended to accommodate the increased number of users.

Conference on the Future of the Smithsonian Institution, with attendees including (left to right, front row) Treasury Secretary Andrew Mellon, Secretary of State Frank Kellogg, President Calvin Coolidge, Chief Justice William Howard Taft, and Charles G. Abbot, acting Smithsonian Secretary; visible fourth from the left in the second row is Secretary of Commerce and future President Herbert Hoover, February 1927.

Construction of the new library stacks at each end of the hall continued for almost two years. Their completion in 1916 allowed for the reinstallation of the graphic arts collection, which filled the hall and included examples of the printing arts and newspaper printing processes, as well as those of photography.[54] Joining the graphic arts exhibits in 1919 were ninety-nine watercolor renderings of native wildflowers painted by Mary Vaux Walcott, the new wife of Secretary Charles D. Walcott. A year later, the Secretary's large photographs of Yellowstone National Park were exhibited in three narrow cases in the center of the hall.[55] With no galleries blocking the windows, the lightness of the space was further enhanced by low exhibit cases, light-colored walls, and new neoclassical-style electric light fixtures.[56]

Early in 1927 the graphic arts exhibits were removed temporarily to make way for an important exhibit that showed the variety and scope of Smithsonian research and publication activities and the most "promising directions for the future work of the Smithsonian."[57] The exhibition consisted of a series of booths, tables, and cases displaying specimens, wall charts, and diagrams that touted the accomplishments of the Institution's various departments. The exhibit coincided with the Conference on the Future of the Smithsonian Institution, held on February 11, 1927.

The purpose of the conference was to guide the Smithsonian in future policymaking decisions and to define the role of the Institution's services. Seated in front of an impressive twenty-three-foot-high column of books—containing one of every Smithsonian publication produced to that date[58]—were many prominent citizens. Among them were President Calvin Coolidge, Chief Justice William Howard Taft, Treasury Secretary Andrew Mellon, Secretary of State Frank Kellogg, the Smithsonian's acting Secretary, Charles Greeley Abbot, and future President Herbert Hoover.

When the conference concluded, the graphic arts collection was reinstalled in the hall. It remained until 1940, when the idea for an exhibit presenting the wide range of Smithsonian activities and services was reintroduced to "tell visitors the story of all Smithsonian activities."

THE "AUDUBON OF BOTANY"

Mary Vaux (1860–1940) was in her fifties when she and Charles D. Walcott married in 1914. She accompanied her husband on many expeditions and performed the duties of Smithsonian hostess, as had his second wife, Helena (see page 57). A rugged outdoorswoman and mountain climber, she was also an accomplished artist.[59]

Combining the precision of a scientist with artistry, Mary Vaux Walcott spent her time on these expeditions painting the wildflowers of North America, especially those in the Rocky Mountains. She was dubbed the "Audubon of botany" toward the end of her career. By then the paintings in her portfolio numbered about nine hundred.[60]

After the exhibition of her watercolor paintings locally and in New York, she decided to have selected paintings reproduced and published for sale to benefit the Smithsonian.[61] *The resulting series of portfolios were published in five volumes of plates with accompanying text by the artist. The stated intent was to provide "in permanent form reproductions of wild flowers printed from life for the use of professional and amateur botanists and designers."*[62] *A new four-color printing process, called the "Smithsonian Process," rendered prints that accurately reproduced the effect of the original watercolors.*[63]

Above: "Pink Ladyslipper," from *North American Wildflowers,* by Mary Vaux Walcott, vol. 5, plate 327, Smithsonian Institution, 1925. Below: Mary Vaux Walcott, a wildflower artist, was the wife of Secretary Charles D. Walcott.

BECOMING THE GREAT HALL

Secretary Abbot had commented in 1939 that, as a result of the Smithsonian's tremendous growth in scope and complexity, visitors needed a guide to the Institution. Consequently he appointed a committee to recommend plans for "a series of exhibits in the Smithsonian main hall that would portray in popular form the work of the Institution in many branches of science."[64] The committee's first recommendation was that the hall be completely redecorated.

The old exhibit cases were then removed, and the walls were stripped and resurfaced with thick plasterlike mastic, which was then treated to imitate both the texture and the color of travertine marble, a porous form of limestone often used on buildings in ancient Rome.[65] New walls constructed at each end of the hall to conceal the old steel bookcases restored a sense of order to the room.[66] The result was that the hall was shortened by more than a third of its original length.[67]

Intended to inform visitors in a concise visual manner about all Smithsonian activities using few objects and minimal labels, the exhibition that filled the newly redesigned hall was dubbed the "Index Exhibit." The hall was divided into a series of eight alcoves representing the departments of astronomy, geology, biology, radiation and organisms, physical anthropology, cultural anthropology, engineering and industries, and art. Each section contained brief descriptions of the Smithsonian departments, simply illustrated with a model or a diorama and other supporting artifacts. Another display addressed the history and founding of the Institution, its organizational structure, and the National Zoological Park. A never-realized plan in 1959 to change the focus of the Index Exhibit referred to the Lower Main Hall as the "original Great Hall."[68] The name, implying a communal gathering place, has been in use ever since. Updated in 1962, the Index Exhibit remained in the Great Hall for more than twenty years.[69]

By the time of the appointment of S. Dillon Ripley as Secretary in 1964, the Index Exhibit in the Great Hall was considered outdated and inadequate.[70] In preparation for the observance of the bicentennial of James Smithson's birth the next year, the hall was again redecorated, this time "in the spirit of James Renwick's design." Secretary Ripley proclaimed that "the hall's red and gold carpets, marbleized pillars, and plush settees convey a sense of Victorian elegance of the period." Harmonizing modern exhibit cases displayed objects illustrating the wide range of Smithsonian activities, as had those of the previous Index Exhibit.[71] At the time it was anticipated that the hall could be returned to its original full length of 200 feet, but mounting costs dictated a scaled-down version.[72]

Smithson's bicentennial was celebrated by the Institution he founded with great pageantry from September 16 to 19, 1965. The ceremonies opened with an academic procession of about five hundred scholars from ninety nations that proceeded from the Castle across the Mall to a temporary pavilion in front of the Museum of History and Technology (now the National Museum of American History). There participants heard an address by President Lyndon B. Johnson, in which he declared that "learning respects no geographical boundaries . . . the growth and spreading of learning must be the first

Below: The Lower Main Hall under renovation, looking east, 1940. Bottom: The Index Exhibit, showcasing all facets of the Smithsonian, installed in the Lower Main Hall, looking southwest, ca. 1941–42. Opposite: James Smithson's bicentennial exhibits in the Great Hall, 1965.

work of a nation that seeks to be free." He also announced his support for the creation of a research center at the Smithsonian in which scholars from around the world would come and collaborate.[73] The meetings and seminar that followed addressed the "situation of man's knowledge" and resulted in the publication of twelve commissioned papers.[74]

In 1971 the hall was again reorganized for the celebration of the Institution's 125th anniversary. A program of lectures was followed by a dinner at which birthday cakes in the Smithsonian's colors, blue and gold, were served while messages from around the world were read to guests. The anniversary coincided closely with former Secretary Abbot's one-hundredth birthday, for which Secretary Ripley noted: "All of us concerned rejoiced both in the anniversary of the Institution and in the birthday anniversary of the fifth Secretary."[75]

The grand Smithsonian-wide celebration of the nation's two-hundredth birthday in 1976 presented an opportunity to further feature the Great Hall as a visitor information and orientation center. The exhibition that filled the entire hall, entitled The Federal City: Plans and Realities (*see page 67*), was sponsored by the Smithsonian in cooperation with the National Capital Planning Commission and the U.S. Commission of Fine Arts. It served to inform visitors about the history and planning of Washington, D.C., and to locate the museum buildings of the Smithsonian in relation to the city's monuments. Included were the original models created for the McMillan Commission of 1902, which

The academic procession for the opening of the bicentennial celebration of James Smithson's birth, 1965.

The Great Hall in 1971, during the 125th anniversary of the Smithsonian Institution, with red and gold carpets, marbleized pillars, and reproduction Victorian settees evocative of the Castle's initial period.

depicted Washington as it existed at that time as well as showing the marble neoclassical city envisioned by the plan's architects.

After a six-year plan to improve information and orientation services for visitors, the new Smithsonian Information Center opened in the Castle's Great Hall on November 5, 1989. The extensively renovated hall featured a central information desk, a Smithsonian Associates reception desk, and interactive touch-screens with information on the Smithsonian posted in seven languages. An award-winning orientation video was shown throughout the day in twin theaters located at the hall's east end. Two scale models of Washington's monumental core, two electronic wall maps of Washington, and interactive touch-screens that highlighted popular capital attractions helped orient visitors to the city.[76] The towering brick and plaster columns received a more realistic faux-marble treatment in shades of gray, black, and tan, while the walls were painted in a palette of muted colors (see page 66). The reopening of the long-closed entrance leading from the Enid A. Haupt Garden through the newly renovated Children's Room in the South Tower created greater access to the building—while also serving as a symbolic new doorway to the entire Smithsonian.

A VISIT FROM THE QUEEN

During her visit to the United States for the celebration of the nation's Bicentennial, Queen Elizabeth II visited the Castle to view the exhibit Treasures from London, a collection showcasing five hundred years of British silver and gold. The exhibit was created by the Worshipful Company of Goldsmiths of London for the Smithsonian Institution Traveling Exhibition Service (SITES). On her arrival at the Castle, she was greeted by Secretary Ripley, Smithsonian Chancellor and Chief Justice Warren E. Burger, and members of the Smithsonian Board of Regents, including Vice President Nelson Rockefeller. She was also shown Smithson's tomb and toured The Federal City: Plans and Realities exhibit. During the event, a joint resolution of the Congress of the United States acknowledging Smithson's gift to the country was presented to her.[77]

Above: Queen Elizabeth II in July 1976, viewing the Federal City exhibit, joined by (left to right) Chief Justice Warren E. Burger, Vice President Nelson Rockefeller, and Smithsonian Secretary S. Dillon Ripley. Bottom, left: Queen Elizabeth in the West Range at the Treasures from London exhibit, documenting five hundred years of work by the city's goldsmiths. Bottom, right: The queen, leaving the crypt of James Smithson.

A temporary exhibit in the Great Hall of the prop called "Pile of Loot," from the film *Night at the Museum: Battle of the Smithsonian*. Photograph by Ellen Dorn, 2009.

In 1992 a gift shop was added to the Great Hall's northeast quadrant, followed in 2003 by a cafeteria occupying one of the former theater spaces; its tables and chairs spilled out into the room's southeast quadrant. The visitor center continued to occupy the remaining space, but many of the informational kiosks were removed, as well as the two large electronic wall maps of Washington. The release of *Night at the Museum: Battle of the Smithsonian* in 2009, filmed on sets based on Smithsonian museums, including the Castle, prompted the installation of a temporary exhibit of one of the central props used in the film: the "Pile of Loot." Several stars were on hand to promote its premiere, including Ben Stiller, Robin Williams, and Amy Adams.

The lecture room in the Upper Main Hall. Woodcut from Rhees, *An Account of the Smithsonian Institution,* 1857.

THE UPPER MAIN HALL

The earliest plan for the Smithsonian Building, made by Robert Mills in 1841—five years before the Institution's authorizing act was passed—showed a vast, unobstructed museum hall occupying the entire upper floor. Although this was the preferred use of the space on every subsequent plan, when the building was completed in 1855, the second floor had been divided into three chambers: an enormous lecture hall, an apparatus museum, and a gallery of art. Up to the time of the fire in 1865, which destroyed the entire second floor, these rooms served an important and active role in the Smithsonian's "diffusion of knowledge." It was not until the restoration of the building after the fire that the upper floor was reconstructed as one open room for use as a museum, as first intended. This grand hall, 200 feet long by 50 feet wide and 25 feet high, flourished as a museum for more than forty years.

With the opening of the Smithsonian's new Natural History Museum in 1911, the Castle's Upper Main Hall was cleared of exhibits and the space assigned to the Department of Botany. The hall was gradually decked over and partitioned off to provide space for offices and collections storage. When the Natural History building's new west wing was constructed in 1965, space was provided there for a new home for the Department of Botany, and the last museum-related bureau vacated the Smithsonian Building. The renovation that followed restored the great public spaces of the first floor; however, the Upper Main Hall was divided into two floors, providing numerous offices for a scholarly center. Only one space at the hall's west end was left as an indication of the grandeur of the original space.

THE FINEST LECTURE ROOM

The floor plan of the building from Robert Dale Owen's 1849 treatise, *Hints on Public Architecture*, showed the second floor of the Main Building as one open museum hall unencumbered with columns (*see page 26*). Joseph Henry had objected to the construction of such a large building from the very beginning of his term as Secretary, fearing that it would deplete the funds of the new Institution.[78] When he was unable to prevent the construction from proceeding, Henry set about rearranging the interior spaces that Owen had laid out in *Hints*, stating: "I am making great changes in the building—remodeling interior so that that ass Dr. Owen the chemist who attempted to plan the whole building would not know his rooms."[79]

Instead of having the museum occupy the entire second floor when the building was completed in 1855, Henry divided the 200-by-50-foot space into three chambers, each with a different purpose. The center of the space held a two-tiered lecture hall, flanked on the east by an apparatus museum and on the west by a gallery of art. The two exhibition rooms were intended to serve also as meeting places for associations. Thus, according to Henry, the arrangement of the entire second floor afforded "facilities for meetings of large associations which have for their object the promotion, diffusion, or application of knowledge."[80] With an eye to future needs, the gallery, the seating, and the partition walls (which were not structural) were all designed to be removable, so the whole upper story could be converted into one large space.[81]

The new lecture hall was completed by October 16, 1854, and Henry declared it the finest in the country.[82] He described this room as "somewhat fan-shaped, and the speaker is placed as it were in the mouth of an immense trumpet. The sound directly from his voice, and that from the reflection immediately behind him, is thrown forward

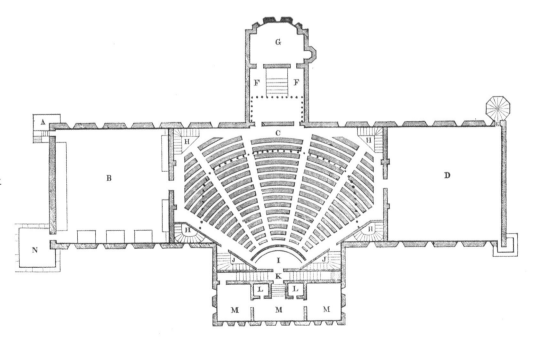

Floor plan of the Upper Main Hall. From Rhees, *An Account of the Smithsonian Institution*, 1857.

upon the audience."[83] The design of the hall was the result of a close collaboration between Joseph Henry and Barton S. Alexander of the U.S. Army Corps of Engineers, the civil engineer who replaced Renwick on the termination of his contract in 1852.[84]

Placement of the lecture hall in the cavernous second-floor space had many advantages over the original location on the first floor. By projecting through the north wall and reducing the width of the grand staircase, an extra 12 feet was added to the room's depth.[85] At 96 feet wide by 62 feet deep and with no columns to obstruct the view of the speaker's platform, the room was better suited for a lecture hall than any other space within the building.[86] The 25-foot ceiling height additionally allowed space for a balcony, increasing the capacity of the lecture hall, which comfortably held 1,500 people and, when crowded, upwards of two thousand.[87] Henry paid particular attention to the room's acoustics, conducting sound experiments with Alexander Dallas Bache in meeting halls and churches of Philadelphia, New York, and Boston; they also examined Montgomery Meigs's plan for the new House and Senate chambers in the U.S. Capitol extensions.[88] The result was that the Smithsonian had a particularly effective, large lecture and meeting hall in which the audience not only could see the experiments performed but could also clearly hear speakers' explanations.[89]

Henry was quite pleased with the success of the lecture hall, stating that "the influence the Institution is having on the character and reputation of the city of Washington is by

"SOIREE MUSICALE"

The first use of the lecture hall in the winter of 1854–55 was by the United States Agricultural Society, which held its sessions and lectures over three days and evenings. This was followed by the American Association for the Advancement of Science, the Association of Medical Superintendents of Hospitals for the Insane, and the meeting of the American Association for the Advancement of Education. The lecture series was equally varied, with topics such as chemistry, astronomy, the art of design, the moral character of Hamlet, and poetry and the practical.[90]

The lecture hall was also used for presentations of visual and musical arts. For the March 20, 1858, meeting of the Artists Convention, Rembrandt Peale (1778–1860), one of the most renowned American painters of the time, delivered a lecture on his famous painting of George Washington to "a large and highly appreciative audience."[91] Musical performances attracted large audiences. The November 8, 1859, "Soiree Musicale" by the Baltimore Beethoven Sextette featured compositions by such composers as Rossini and Verdi, as well as a piece entitled "Artists' Excursion, dedicated to Mr. Smithson," by Bernard Courlaender, professor of music at the Peabody Conservatory.[92] The concert—in which spectators were admonished that "no conversation as loud as a whisper" was permitted during the performance—concluded with a finale, "promiscuous and patriotic," performed by the entire band and full chorus.[93]

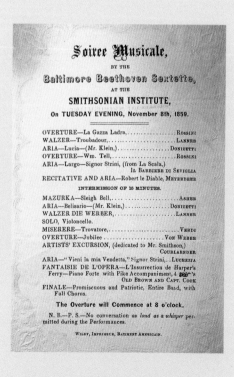

The program for "Soiree Musicale," a concert given by the Baltimore Beethoven Sextette at the Smithsonian Institution, November 8, 1859.

no means small. The free lectures . . . tend to promote the intelligence and morality of the citizens." Although he was concerned that the lecture series, by reaching only a local audience, was too parochial for a national institution, he thought that publishing the content of the lectures in the Smithsonian's annual report fulfilled the Institution's mission to "diffuse knowledge." [94]

APPARATUSES AND ART

The Smithsonian's plan of organization called for the creation of a "museum of physical instruments" for experimental illustration and original research. Two rooms on the first floor of the East Range were dedicated to this use by Robert Dale Owen in his early plans for the building. Secretary Henry, however, instead placed the Apparatus Room on the second floor of the Main Building east of the lecture hall. The apparatuses included Page's Electro-Magnetic instrument; a German-made hydroelectric machine; various instruments for illustrating light, heat, sound, and wave motion; and a large Fresnel lens used in lighthouses. Joining these instruments was a significant collection of instruments donated to the Smithsonian in 1853 by Robert Hare of Philadelphia. The items, many invented by Hare himself, were collected and used by him for research and demonstration during his twenty-nine years as professor of chemistry at the University of Pennsylvania Medical School. The most prominent object on view in the room was Hare's Electrical Machine, which generated static electricity—causing the hair of a person seated below to stand on end. [95]

When opened to the public in 1855, the large room to the west of the lecture hall was designated as a gallery of art. It was intended that the room would both exhibit the Institution's art collection (at the time still in a formative state) and showcase the work of living artists free of charge as a way of encouraging the arts. [96] To that end, the

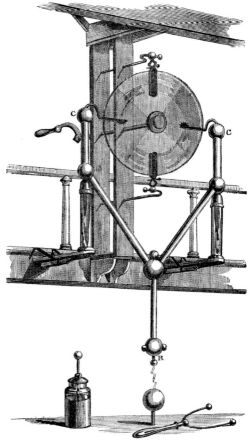

Above: Hare's Electrical Machine. Woodcut from Rhees, *An Account of the Smithsonian Institution*, 1857. Right: The Apparatus Room in the Upper Mail Hall, with Hare's machine visible on the left side of the room, elevated on a platform above a chair. Woodcut from Rhees, *An Account of the Smithsonian Institution*, 1857.

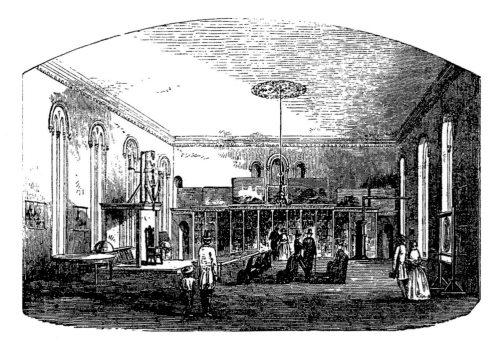

room was filled with more than 150 portraits of American Indians from forty-three tribes, painted by John Mix Stanley (1814–72) over a ten-year period.[97] Joining the Stanley paintings in 1858 was a collection of 147 paintings of American Indians commissioned by the federal government and painted by Charles Bird King (1785–1862) between 1825 and 1837.[98] Believing that the government should also purchase the Stanley collection, Henry stated that "it is a sacred duty which this country owes to the civilized world to collect . . . all that may tend to illustrate the character and history of the original inhabitants of North America."[99]

Also displayed in this gallery was a copy of "one of the most celebrated statues of antiquity," known as the *Dying Gladiator*.[100] Executed in marble, allegedly by the English sculptor Joseph Gott, the statue had been on exhibit at the New York Crystal Palace Exhibition from 1853 to 1854.[101] It and several other statues from the exhibition were offered for sale at auction on November 15, 1854, when it was presumably purchased by Frederick W. Risque, a Georgetown lawyer.[102] The *Gladiator* was exhibited by its owner in Washington beginning in 1854 and then loaned to the Smithsonian in 1857, when it was placed on view in the gallery, free of charge to the public.[103]

THE FIRE OF 1865

By late 1864 Secretary Henry's attitude toward the art collection had changed drastically. He lamented that expending Smithsonian funds to build an art collection worthy of the nation had no advocates, "even among artists." The art gallery, already referred to by Henry as "the former picture gallery," had remained relatively unchanged from 1858. However, early in the winter of 1865 extensive work was begun to change the hall's focus from art to ethnology by adding American Indian artifacts to the portraits and scenes by John Mix Stanley and Charles Bird King. New artifact cases were constructed to encircle the fifty-foot-square room on all four sides, forming a second tier.[104]

January 15, 1865, was a bitterly cold day as work progressed in the former picture gallery—so cold that the caretaker John Varden complained that he could not work in the room without heat. William DeBeust and Tobias N. Woltz, the Institution's machinist and carpenter, respectively, together moved a large stove from the Apparatus Room into the gallery space. Inserting the stovepipe into what they believed was a flue—but which instead was an air space in the building's brick lining—they lighted a fire in the stove. For the next week the three men worked to rehang the portraits of American Indians, all the while smoke and embers collected in the space under the roof.[105] The pictures were hung and the cases, although still empty of artifacts, were completed on January 24, when disaster struck.

At about 2:45 P.M., Secretary Henry was working in his office, located on the third floor between the two front towers on the north, when he heard a crackling noise above the ceiling. He looked into the lecture room from the arched opening above and behind the speaker's platform. On seeing the smoke-darkened room, he exclaimed, "The house is on fire, sound the fire alarm!"[106] The building was so cold that ice had

Top: The picture gallery, documenting the Indian portraits by Charles Bird King and John Mix Stanley. Stereograph by the American Stereoscopic Company, Langenheim, Lloyd & Company, Philadelphia, 1858. Above: *The Dying Gladiator* (or *Gaul*) in the picture gallery. Stereograph by the American Stereoscopic Company, Langenheim, Lloyd & Company, Philadelphia, 1858.

formed around the telegraph alarm box, making it difficult to open. Several of the water barrels that had been placed around the building were also frozen solid, rendering them completely useless.[107] Henry, Spencer Baird, William J. Rhees, and a host of others hurried about the building in a futile attempt to save the Institution's property, but little was rescued from the flames. During the brief period before the roof began to fall into the building, DeBeust began removing pictures, while the night watchman, Henry Horan, carried them out of the room to safety. When a six-foot-square section of the ceiling fell—revealing that the entire roof was in flames—DeBeust fled the room with only two more pictures.[108]

The *Evening Star* in Washington reported on the chaos that day: "[A] man arrested in Henry's room had under his arm a pair of the professor's boots, on his person a number of mathematical instruments . . . and much damage was done to articles removed in consequence of the crazy manner in which they were thrown from the windows by excited individuals."[109] The fire caught everyone off guard because a rigid set of rules had been established expressly to safeguard the building from fire. Residents were forbidden from carrying open lanterns or using matches in their rooms.[110] Henry had further directed that no smoking was allowed in the building, that no person should carry a naked candle from one area to another, that chimneys and flues were to be examined in the autumn, and that a watch was to be kept every night.[111] Horan routinely made an hourly inspection of all the rooms, including those of Henry's residence, except the bedrooms. He maintained twenty-four buckets and two barrels filled with water and located them in different parts of the building, along with hoses to reach the laboratory, the document room, the offices, the lecture room, and the upper rooms in the East Wing.[112]

The South Tower and the two North Towers—in which the dormitory rooms, Henry's offices, and the meteorological offices were located—were also gutted from the top all the way to the second-floor level. The fire totally destroyed the Main Building's second floor but left unscathed the wings, the ranges, and the Lower Main Hall, with its natural

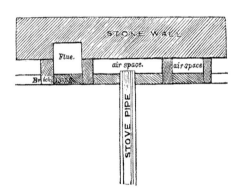

Below: The west wall of the Upper Main Hall, showing the location of the flue and the air passage into which the stove pipe was inserted. Drawing by Barton S. Alexander, from "Origin of the Fire at the Smithsonian Institution, February 21, 1865." Bottom: The fire of 1865, picturing the entire building engulfed in flames, although the fire was confined to the second floor and the upper levels of the towers. Woodcut from *Harper's Weekly*, 1865.

"A GRAND SIGHT AS WELL AS A SAD ONE"

Mary Henry, Joseph Henry's eldest daughter, was deeply moved by the fire. She filled more than five pages in her diary, describing it as "one of the saddest events of our lives."[113] The Henry living quarters had for a time been in great danger of burning but were spared, and only minor damage was incurred. Mary's account of the fire was vivid, at times almost poetic:

One of the gentlemen from the Institution met me saying "the building is on fire, you have but five minutes to save your property." We immediately went to work packing books etc, first clothing and then father's library. The furniture was soon removed and placed under military guard outside of the Institution. Truly it was a grand sight as well as a sad one, the flames bursting from the windows of the towers rose high above, a beautiful fiend, tasting to the utmost the pleasure of destruction. Thousands of spectators had collected in the grounds and a body of men kept mounted guard around the building driving them back as they approached too near. The fire mounted to the upper room of the tower where father's papers were kept—it was very hard to see them come floating down—to feel that in the space of an hour was thus destroyed the labor of years. When the east end of the building was pronounced entirely out of danger, the furniture was restored to our carpet-less, disordered rooms.[114]

The loss of Henry's papers and many of his books caused Mary to lament, "It seems so very hard to save our furniture and other things which are so valueless in comparison with them."[115]

While standing in the fire-ravaged picture gallery the day after the fire, Mary remarked that "the dismantled walls and towers rose high above us reminding us of the ruins of some English Abbey—we picked our way over the cinders and burnt bricks—the remains of 'The Dying Gladiator' lay scattered about—we picked up a few pieces but they crumbled in our fingers."[116]

The Smithsonian Building after the fire of 1865.
Photograph by George D. Wakely, 1865.

history specimens. The museum was protected from destruction by the ceiling's iron beams and its brick construction, although one of the beams cracked from the intense heat and had been perilously close to crashing into the museum below before it was later replaced. Had the beam failed during the fire, the conflagration surely would have spread to the rest of the building, and all would have been lost.[117]

Miraculously no deaths or serious injuries were incurred during the fire. However, even after contracting a severe illness before the fire, John Varden insisted on coming to the building the day after the fire to inspect the damage to the museum, further exacerbating his condition. He never recovered and died on February 10, 1865.[118]

RECONSTRUCTION CHANGES

Within three days after the fire, a temporary roof was constructed in the burned-out space to protect the exhibits in the Lower Main Hall.[119] This roof was built low within the room to avoid impeding construction of the permanent roof. It remained in place until May 31, 1867, when a new iron and slate roof designed by Adolf Cluss was completed.[120] Cluss came to the Smithsonian "warmly recommended" by the mayor of the District of Columbia for his work designing local schools.[121] As the Institution's primary architect until 1890, Cluss was responsible not only for the reconstruction of the building's fire-damaged parts but also for the eventual reconstruction of the two wings and the ranges in fireproof materials. Therefore, by the time his contract was over, many interior spaces of the Castle became the products of Cluss's hand, with the exception of the Lower Main Hall and the West Wing. (Barton S. Alexander completed the Lower Main Hall after Renwick's contract was terminated; and although Cluss renovated the West Wing in 1871 by raising the floor to accommodate the laboratories below, the rest of the space remained as Renwick had designed it.)

Believing that the lecture series did not form an essential part of the Smithsonian's operations and that it had engendered bad relations with Congress, Secretary Henry decided not to reconstruct the lecture room in the Upper Main Hall after the fire.[122] He further argued that the government should purchase the building and assume responsibility for running the Smithsonian's museum facilities or that Congress should increase funding for the purpose.[123] Although Henry's objections to a public museum and the building itself had not abated during the twenty-two years he had served as Secretary, he had resigned himself to their inevitable existence: "Our principal incumbrance [*sic*], however, is the Museum and the building connected with it. Could I succeed in transferring these to the Government, my mission in regard to the Institution would be fulfilled. In this, however, I find considerable opposition."[124]

The result was that the space lay dormant and unfinished for nearly six years. Congress eventually appropriated $20,000 for the care of the collections and reconstruction of the hall in 1870.[125] The hall was then rebuilt as one large open space—realizing for the first time Owen's original plan for the second floor. Even before it was occupied with collections, Henry praised the hall as a near-perfect exhibition space.[126]

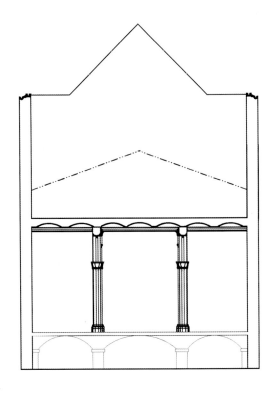

The temporary roof, shown by the dotted line, constructed inside the ruined Upper Main Hall, January 1865. Artist's rendering based on a sketch by Joseph Henry.

FROM ANIMAL CURIOSITIES TO HUMAN ARTIFACTS

The Secretary's plan for the newly reconfigured space was to exhibit archeology, anthropology, and paleontology specimens.[127] To this end, he commissioned designs for the new museum from Benjamin Waterhouse Hawkins, an English artist who had made his reputation as a modeler of casts of prehistoric mammals.[128] Hawkins's elaborate, highly decorative scheme featured galleries around the room's perimeter, which, while providing additional exhibition space, would have compromised the unobstructed open space that Henry had praised. The walls were to be decorated with illustrations of extinct animals, portrait medallions of American Indians, and paintings of their daily life.[129] Hawkins's decorative treatment supported Henry's belief that for "museums to be effective as means of adult education [they] must be attractive and the articles of purely scientific interest put away in drawers for special exhibition."[130]

The congressional appropriation was sufficient only to allow for a simple reconstruction of the room, so Hawkins's plan was never carried out.[131] Instead a skeletal cast of Megatherium, a giant extinct South American ground sloth, was installed in the middle of the hall early in February 1872.[132] Made by Henry A. Ward and given by him to the Institution, the model measured 17 feet long and almost 11 feet from the base to the top of its head. Ward was the proprietor of Ward's Natural Science Establishment in Rochester, New York. Joining Megatherium were casts of a giant tortoise and Glyptodon, an extinct relative of the present-day armadillo.

The hall was still relatively empty, but a portion was given over to an exhibition of about six hundred paintings and sketches of American Indians by George Catlin

Above, left: "Animal Curiosities in the Smithsonian Institution," documenting the mammal collection in the Upper Main Hall. Stereograph by Bell & Brother, 1872. Above, right: A bear, an elk, a deer, a leopard, and a large fish at the hall's far west end, with possibly the Institution's first permanent taxidermist, Joseph Palmer. Stereograph by Bell & Brother, 1872. Opposite, left: "Interiors of the Smithsonian Institution," showing more of the mammal collection. Stereograph by Bell & Brother, 1872. Opposite, right: Cases being assembled among the mammal specimens in the Upper Main Hall. Stereograph, 1873.

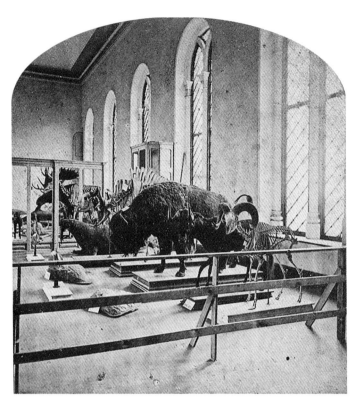

(1796–1872). With the recent destruction of the Stanley and King portraits in mind, this exhibition was an attempt by Henry to persuade Congress to purchase Catlin's entire collection of 1,200 paintings, representing more than forty years of work.[133] Catlin died before any action was taken, and the paintings were packed and stored in the building's basement until they were loaned by his heirs to the Philadelphia Centennial Exhibition in 1876.[134]

Throughout 1872 several large skeletons and mounted mammal specimens were added to the casts of Megatherium and Glyptodon in the hall. Three stereographs by Bell & Brother show the initial installation of the mammal collection. An unlikely herd consisting of a bear, an elk, a deer, a leopard, and, inexplicably, a large fish congregate at the hall's far west end. The collection was overseen by the Institution's first permanent taxidermist, Joseph Palmer. After he was sent to the Smithsonian that year to install the giant Irish elk in the hall, as an employee of Benjamin Waterhouse Hawkins, he was subsequently hired by the Smithsonian in 1873.[135]

Within the year, Henry and Baird were planning to devote the entire hall to the ethnological collections.[136] New exhibit cases, designed by Henry Ward and modified by Adolf Cluss, were constructed by John W. McKnight, a local cabinetmaker. Pine with walnut veneer and bird's-eye maple, these large cases had panes of English plate glass and were clad top, bottom, and back with zinc to render them dustproof.[137] Although they were perfect in most ways, Henry thought that the cases were "almost too elaborate to be in keeping with the size and plainness of the hall."[138] When the cases were completed, the prehistoric casts and mammals were moved to the Lower Main Hall, and then the entire Upper Main Hall was filled with the ethnological collections.[139]

By the end of 1874, Henry reported that almost all the ethnological specimens had been placed in the Upper Main Hall and that it was filled to almost overflowing.[140] He was so pleased with this arrangement of the hall and the interest it generated among the public that he predicted that it would be "even more attractive than the museum of natural history underneath."[141] By 1880 the collections spilled from the more than 160 exhibit cases to fill every available surface of the walls, the case tops, and even the open spaces under the cases. The visual appeal of the immense room was enhanced by the artful arrangements of spears from various tribes on the walls above the cases. The busts of prominent Americans from the National Institute that had been on exhibit in the West Range in the early 1860s were now prominently displayed atop the cases purely for aesthetic effect, along with those representing the races of humankind.[142] An immense painted Tsimshian house front, acquired from the Northwest Coastal Indians for display at the Centennial Exhibition of 1876, towered over the exhibit cases on the hall's west wall.[143]

ANTIQUITIES AND ANTHROPOLOGY

A major reclassification of the departments and staff of the museum, begun early in 1882, resulted in the removal of all ethnological collections from the Upper Main Hall to the new National Museum (Arts and Industries Building), with the exception of those relating to prehistoric archaeology.[144] The spears and busts were also taken down, and the hall was rearranged as the Department of Antiquities by its curator, Charles Rau. He grouped the

The Tsimshian house front made by the Northwest Coastal Indians, behind the displays in the earlier Upper Main Hall, looking west, ca. 1879–85.

Top, left: Model of Zuni Pueblo from New Mexico in the southwest corner of the museum in the Upper Main Hall. Wood engraving from *Frank Leslie's Monthly,* February 1890. Top, right: The Department of Prehistoric Anthropology in the Upper Main Hall, ca. 1895.

artifacts into seven classifications, based on material and similarity of shape: stone, copper, bone and horn, shell, clay, wood and fiber, and methods of attaching handles (hafting).[145] Prominently displayed on the room's wall was a plaster cast of a large Aztec calendar stone; a gigantic Aztec head dominated one of the hall's central cases.[146] These casts were created by Eufemio Abadiano from artifacts of ancient Mexico and Yucatan and donated by him to the museum in 1885, after they had been on exhibit at the 1884–85 World's Industrial and Cotton Centennial Exposition at New Orleans.[147]

In 1891 the prehistoric archaeology collection, then numbering in excess of 160,000 items and renamed the Department of Prehistoric Anthropology, underwent a complete reorganization. Thomas Wilson, appointed curator after Rau's death in 1887, arranged the collections according to geographical location and historical period.[148] Rather than challenge his predecessor's classification system, he stated: "This classification undoubtedly served a good purpose in its beginning, but it had wrought out that purpose, and Dr. Rau declares in his last report (1886) that the collection would be ultimately arranged geographically. Such, therefore, was his intention at the time of his death, and I do but carry it out."[149]

Seeing ancient objects as both "the texts of history as well as its illustrations," the new arrangement put the museum's artifacts in context to explain the people who created them.[150] Wilson introduced an innovation in the exhibit that he termed "synoptical cases." These were placed at the entrance to the hall to provide a general overview of all the specimens on view. A subsequent rearrangement of the hall occurred in 1895, further refining the new classification system. At the far end of the hall on top of the cases was the reclining Pre-Columbian figure Chac-Mool, and occupying the space above it, where the Tsimshian house front had once been, was a painting depicting the Cliff Ruins of Rio Mancos, Colorado.[151]

At the hall's west end, a model of the Pueblo Zuni from New Mexico, measuring 20 by 12 feet, occupied a large section of the newly reorganized Department of Prehistoric

Anthropology in 1891. Several other scale models of pueblos were grouped together with it. The models were the work of the brothers Victor and Cosmos Mindeleff. Victor Mindeleff (1860–1948), an architect and an artist, made detailed measured drawings and studied the pueblos of New Mexico and Arizona with his brother Cosmos (1863–1938) for nine field seasons between 1881 and 1889.[152] First modeled in clay, the models were then covered in papier-mâché, forming a mold from which a plaster cast was created, painted, and mounted on a solid base. Several copies of these models were made by the brothers in the Smithsonian's workrooms, including in a shed in the South Yard, for the many expositions of the late nineteenth and early twentieth centuries (*see page 168*).[153]

THE NATIONAL HERBARIUM TAKES ROOT

Beginning in 1910 the collections in the Upper Main Hall were moved to the nearly completed building for the newest National Museum (National Museum of Natural History). Before the hall was vacated, however, plans were in the works to devote the entire space to a National Gallery of Art. After an appropriation from Congress did not materialize, the plans were shelved.[154]

Instead the hall was converted into office, storage, and laboratory space for the National Herbarium, which had been located in the Arts and Industries Building.[155] The room was then filled with 643 steel specimen cases housing more than 69,000 dried plant specimens, all mounted and systematically arranged for reference.[156] A large two-story deck at the hall's east end enclosed the offices and laboratories. By 1928 the west

The Department of Botany in the Upper Main Hall, looking west, ca. 1965.

"THE MOST FASCINATING THING IN THE WORLD"

Mary Agnes Chase (1869–1963) was as passionate about her field of study—botany—as she was about women's rights. The world-renowned botanist was twice arrested and jailed during suffragist protests in front of the White House during the Wilson Administration. There she was reported to have tended a fire in which to burn all presidential speeches that mentioned "liberty" or "freedom" until women were given the vote.[157]

After retiring as senior botanist for the U.S. Department of Agriculture, where she had worked since 1903, Chase was appointed in 1939 to the position of research associate in the Smithsonian's Division of Plants.[158] *The leading expert in the study of grasses (agrostology), she worked five or sometimes six days a week for twenty-four years at the Smithsonian, without pay, in an office in the Herbarium.*

Chase summed up her dedication by declaring, "Grass is the most fascinating thing in the world."[159] *"If it were not for grasses," she later stated, "the world would never have been civilized. Your bread is made from the seeds of grass. And wheat, which is a grass, was the beginning of civilization."*[160] *Chase published a three-volume index to grass species a year before her death, culminating a sixty-year career.*[161]

Mary Agnes Chase, sitting at her desk with plant specimens, ca. 1960.

The west wall of the Upper Main Hall during the 1968 reconstruction, revealing the outline of the temporary roof constructed immediately after the 1865 fire.

end of the hall was decked over, and by 1954 the remaining portion of the once-cavernous space was essentially divided into two floors.[162]

The plant collections continued to grow through the 1950s and the early 1960s, to the point that the cases were stacked three high on the upper level. In 1965 the Herbarium was transferred to the newly constructed west wing of the Natural History Museum. The collections were removed from the hall through a window and transported to the ground on a temporary elevator set up outside the building.[163] Afterward the steel decking was dismantled in preparation for a full renovation of the second floor.

SCHOLARS IN THE HALL

The Upper Main Hall remained empty for about three years after the Herbarium moved to the Natural History Museum. In 1968 construction began for a proposed Smithsonian Center for Advanced Studies. The walls were stripped down to the bare brick and stone, and most of the ceiling was removed, revealing on the west wall the outline of the low temporary roof constructed immediately after the fire of 1865.[164] Steel beams and columns were inserted into the walls' brick inner lining to form a more permanent floor level than before.

Left: The library of the Woodrow Wilson International Center for Scholars at the west end of the Upper Main Hall, 1972. Opposite: The Castle library, looking toward the southwest corner. Photograph by Eric Long, 2011.

The Center for Advanced Studies was not realized, and instead the space was turned over to the Woodrow Wilson International Center for Scholars. Created by Congress in 1968 and designated to be housed in the Castle until a permanent headquarters could be constructed,[165] the center was envisioned as "a living institution expressing the ideals and concerns of Woodrow Wilson . . . symbolizing and strengthening the fruitful relation between the world of learning and the world of public affairs."[166] Announcing the arrival of the center in 1970, a *Washington Post* editorial stated that "the whimsical Norman castle on the Mall seems to us a most appropriate place to get the center off to a good start. . . . [T]he dignified informality and humble flamboyance of its recently renovated rooms and halls ought to inspire just the right atmosphere and the kind of lively and productive intellectual community."[167]

A labyrinth of offices and meeting rooms designed by the local architecture firm Chatelain, Gauger & Nolan was constructed in the once-grand space. At the direction of the Smithsonian, the west end of the original museum hall was preserved during the renovation for use as a meeting room and a library.[168] The library, which by 1998 held some thirty thousand titles, was also the site of countless seminars, colloquia, noon discussions, and banquets. Speakers and honored guests included the political figures

Richard M. Nixon (who as president dedicated the center's offices on February 18, 1971), Hubert H. Humphrey, Gerald Ford, George H. W. Bush, Barry Goldwater, Daniel Patrick Moynihan, Dean Rusk, Elliot Richardson, Averill Harriman, and Zbigniew Brzezinski. Foreign dignitaries and statesmen who lectured ranged from Harold MacMillan, the former prime minister of the United Kingdom, to Helmut Schmidt, the chancellor of West Germany, as well as the former Israeli diplomat, politician, and historian Shlomo Ben-Ami and the eminent Soviet nuclear physicist, dissident, and human rights activist Andrei Sakharov. Cultural figures included the cartoonist Herb Block, the historian John Hope Franklin, and the feminists Betty Friedan and Gloria Steinem.

After twenty-eight years in the Castle, the Woodrow Wilson Center moved into new space in the Ronald Reagan Building at the Federal Triangle on Pennsylvania Avenue, N.W. Its move opened up approximately eighty rooms on the third and fourth floors of the Main Building, as well as offices in the South Tower, the Campanile, and the fourth through the seventh floors of the North Towers.[169] Those spaces were converted into administrative offices, and the center's former library became a meeting and lecture room and a gathering space for staff.

Four of the large walnut and bird's-eye maple exhibit cases designed by Henry Ward for the hall in 1872 were then returned to their original location. The cases had been grouped together in 1975 for the exhibition 1876, A Centennial Exhibition, forming a representation of the Women's Pavilion, which a century earlier had exhibited objects demonstrating the capabilities and accomplishments of women. Added to the cases were panels inscribed with a Biblical quotation in four languages praising the work of women: "Give her of the fruit of her hands, and let her works praise her in the gates."[170] Of the approximately 284 exhibit cases that occupied the Upper Main Hall at its height in 1891, only the four now returned to the hall and four others in storage are known to remain.[171]

Original 1872 exhibit cases with French, Japanese, Italian, and English porcelain in the Castle library. Photographs by Eric Long, 2011.

Tapestry in the former Woodrow Wilson Center library, documenting the murder of King Priam of Troy. Photograph by Eric Long, 2011.

A TEXTILE MYSTERY

Long thought to depict the beheading of Saint Paul, a large seventeenth-century Flemish tapestry (measuring 11 feet, 3 inches by 10 feet, 10 inches) was hung prominently on the west wall of the Woodrow Wilson Center's library in late 1970.[172] The subject matter of the scene, however, had always been problematic, as no religious symbols, such as halos or crucifixes, are visible. Past directors of the Wilson Center had challenged visitors and scholars to provide a more plausible explanation, all to no avail until 1993.

During a conference that summer dealing with atrocities in the former Yugoslavia, one of the attendees suggested that the tapestry's subject was a scene from the capture of Troy, depicting the aged King Priam's last effort to defend the city from the invading Greek army.[173] During the city's total destruction, Priam was slaughtered by Achilles' son Neoptolemos. In the scene in the tapestry, Priam is at the altar, bending over Polites, one of his sons who already lies dead in the foreground. Priam's wife, Hecuba, and his daughter, Cassandra, despair in the background at the carnage. At the right is Neoptolemos, grasping the kneeling Priam and preparing for the kill. As told in the Roman version of the story by Virgil, Achilles' son dragged Priam "to the very altar-stones . . . raised high the flashing sword and buried it to the hilt in his side."[174]

THE WEST WING
AND THE WEST RANGE

The West Wing and the West Range, both soaring single-story spaces flooded with abundant natural light, were ideal for the needs of a gallery of art, as designated in the 1849 plan for the building. However, when the Castle's west end was completed, the West Wing instead housed the Smithsonian library and the adjoining range was furnished as a reading room. It was not until after the fire of 1865, when the Smithsonian's library collections were transferred to Congress, that the West Wing and the West Range were wholly dedicated to use as exhibition spaces.

Beginning with displays of mineralogy and concluding with those of graphic arts, the two spaces provided educational exhibits for more than one hundred years. With the completion of the Museum of History and Technology (now the National Museum of American History) across the Mall in 1964, the last museum exhibits remaining in the Castle were removed. The building's subsequent renovation in the late 1960s allocated the grand Gothic spaces of the West Wing and the West Range for use as communal gathering places for scholars, staff, and visitors.

MORE BOOKS THAN ART

The West Wing, originally intended to serve as an art gallery, was turned over temporarily for use as the Smithsonian library in early 1850 while the library's permanent home in the Main Building was still under construction.[1] The as-yet-nonexistent art collections were expected to occupy the building's west end. Charles Coffin Jewett, the Smithsonian's librarian and intended supervisor of the artworks, believed that acquiring a proper art collection for the Institution would be impossible: "Engraving seems to be the only branch of the fine arts, which we can, for the present, cultivate. . . . The formation of a gallery of the best paintings is, in this country, almost hopeless."[2]

To that end, a large collection of prints and engravings was purchased from the diplomat and Regent George Perkins Marsh in 1850 for inclusion in the library. In addition, portraits and scenes of the everyday life of American Indians by John Mix Stanley were hung salon style in the West Wing's apse and above the bookshelves. They were part of the Institution's mandate to encourage art by providing a suitable room in which to exhibit pictures free of expense to the artist.[3] The paintings remained the property of the artist while they were on view in the Castle, although he offered to sell the entire collection of 152 canvases to the Smithsonian in 1855 and again in 1858. Both offers were declined by the Board of Regents.[4]

The library increased at such a rapid rate that by 1853 books were shelved two deep in most of the cases.[5] When the building was at last completed in 1855, Secretary Joseph

Opposite: The Commons in the West Wing. Below: The Smithsonian library, sheltered beneath the West Wing's groin-vaulted ceiling. Woodblock print from *The Illustrated News,* New York, November 12, 1853.

Henry decided to devote the entire Lower Main Hall to museum use instead of dividing it between the library and the lecture hall. The library was then assigned permanently to the West Wing and underwent extensive alterations, which included moving the Stanley paintings to the newly completed art gallery on the Main Building's second floor. The library cases were rearranged into two stories of alcoves, thereby doubling the space. An "indiscriminate access" to the books led to what Henry termed "a lamentable want of honesty," requiring restrictive measures. The lower alcoves were secured behind locked doors, for as Henry reported, "Not only are the works in many cases mutilated, merely to avoid the labor of copying a few pages, but valuable sets are sometimes broken by actual theft."[6]

Immediately adjoining the West Wing, a separate reading room was created in the West Range. Stocked with an extensive collection of periodicals and scientific and literary journals from the United States and Europe, it proved to be well used by visitors to the Smithsonian and was popular among young and old.[7] Fourteen-year-old Francis Ormand French (1837–93), son of Benjamin Brown French (1800–70), the grand master of Masons for the District of Columbia (who presided over the laying of the Castle's cornerstone), wrote in his diary in 1851: "Today I went to the Smithsonian Institution where for some hours I read, having an excelent [*sic*] time, for a good book is truly a companion and I know of nothing which is more entertaining. I hope to repeat this visit frequently."[8]

While the library continued to grow in the West Wing, a major change was under way in the West Range. Beginning in 1859 it was converted from a reading room into a gallery of art and a sculpture hall. Paintings, busts, and copies of classical sculpture that had been transferred from the collections of the defunct National Institute for the Promotion of Science were cleaned, repaired, and installed in the hall. By early 1863 the transformation was complete.[9] A plaster replica of the famous *Venus de Medici* and a seated figure entitled *Girl Fishing* were placed in front of the southern windows, behind an iron railing. On the opposite side, a row of busts and sculptural groups rested on pedestals beneath oil portraits of famous statesmen and scientists.[10] In a period photograph documenting the space's north side, the presence of a dog is a mystery; considering that a long exposure time was needed to capture the image and that the tail of the dog is not blurred, it may have been the handiwork of C. Drexler, the taxidermist who worked in the building's preparation room. The Smithsonian's 1863 guidebook directed visitors to that room, stating, "Any persons having a pet bird or animal which they desire to preserve, can have it beautifully mounted by Mr. Drexler at a moderate charge."[11]

A TURN TO SCIENCE

The 1865 fire that destroyed the Castle's Upper Main Hall prompted Joseph Henry to send the Smithsonian's books to the Library of Congress for safekeeping in 1866; many of the prints, sculptures, and paintings were later loaned to the Corcoran Gallery of Art.[12] The West Wing was then used to store natural history specimens preserved in alcohol, including duplicate specimens for distribution, until 1871, when the hall was renovated to make it fireproof.[13] The mineral collections installed in the Lower Main

Below: Francis Ormand French, who as a teenager made use of the Smithsonian's library. Bottom: Sculpted busts and portraits on the north side of the West Range, with a canine visitor, ca. 1863. Opposite: Mineralogical specimens on display in the West Wing. Stereograph by J. F. Jarvis, ca. 1871.

Hall in 1858 were moved to the West Wing, filling specially built cases that completely encircled the 84-by-40-foot room.

Centrally displayed in the hall was the so-called Ainsa Meteorite, found south of Tucson, Arizona, and named for its donor, Jesus Ainsa. At the time it was considered one of the largest known meteorites, weighing 1,400 pounds and described in the Smithsonian's annual report as resembling "an immense signet ring." The meteorite, since renamed the Tucson Meteor, has remained on public view almost continuously since it was received by the Smithsonian in 1863.[14]

The mineralogical exhibits in the West Wing hall formed the backdrop for the April 1874 meeting of the National Academy of Sciences.[15] Henry presided over the meeting from a raised platform in the apse. Although he was initially displeased with the secretive manner in which the academy was established by Congress in 1863 and the selective appointment of its first members, the Secretary nevertheless was a member from the beginning and served as its secretary from 1868 to 1878.[16] The academy was not connected to the Smithsonian, but offices in the Castle were provided for it for more than fifty years, until its own building was dedicated in 1924.[17]

A constant source of annoyance to Secretary Henry and his family were the foul odors emanating from the Laboratory of Natural History, located directly below the family's East Wing living quarters. The 1871 renovation of the West Wing provided an opportunity to remedy the problem. The wing's floor was raised to create more space in the basement for the workrooms used for preserving in alcohol the fishes, reptiles, and invertebrates in the museum's natural history collections.[18] The laboratory's relocation to the opposite end of the building did not entirely solve the problem, however, as Henry soon after noted the continuance of a "very pungent stench."[19]

Meeting of the National Academy of Sciences in the West Wing, with Mary Henry (no. 2) at the far right, April 1874.

Mary Henry, daughter of Secretary Joseph Henry, October 20, 1882.

A DEVOTED DAUGHTER

One of those present at the 1874 meeting of the National Academy of Sciences in the West Wing was Mary Henry (1834–1903), the Secretary's oldest daughter and constant companion. She once noted in her diary that she was "[d]readfully jealous of Henry Elliot who is his assistant instead of myself."[20] Her devotion to her father is further evident in a "poetical inscription" she wrote to accompany her Christmas gift to him (a pot of pomatum):

> Twixt the head & the heart the Philosophers say
> Is a telegraph line or a public highway
> Some mode of communion so swift & direct
> That what one may feel must the other reflect
> So I hope that in touching the roots of the hair
> I may make a more permanent impress elsewhere
> In smoothing your hair use my pomade and water
> And think of your loving & dutiful daughter.[21]

Never married, she was prominent in Washington society and at the time of her death in 1903 was writing a biography of her father.[22]

ETHNOLOGY EXHIBITS

The ethnology collections occupied the West Range from 1868 until 1874, sharing space with vestiges of the earlier gallery of art. Exhibit cases were filled with North American Indian artifacts, while objects from other cultures—including China, Japan, and prehistoric France—were also displayed for comparison.[23] Along the arcades hung portraits of American Indian delegates who had visited Washington between 1858 and 1869, painted by Antonio Zeno Shindler (ca. 1823–99), an artist employed by the National Museum.[24] The portrait of the celebrated author and George Washington biographer François Pierre Guillaume Guizot (1787–1874) hung at the hall's west end.[25] Directly opposite Guizot's portrait, above the entrance to the Lower Main Hall, was one of the full-length portraits depicting George Washington after the Battle of Trenton, painted by Charles Willson Peale (1741–1827). Below the portrait of Washington was a panoramic view of Constantinople, the work of an unknown artist, which measured sixteen feet long.[26] At the bases of the columns were "spit boxes," a cheap alternative to metal spittoons, made by the Institution's carpenter in 1861.[27]

As originally constructed, the East and West Ranges had open, cloistered walkways along their north facades to connect the wings with the Main Building. Because they were ill suited to the purpose and let in the cold north wind, both were enclosed with windows within a few years of the Castle's completion.[28] The sculpture that had been exhibited in the West Range was moved to a room at the west end of the cloister in 1868, when the ethnological displays were installed.[29] In 1871 the room adjoining this was made into the

In the West Range, looking east toward the Lower Main Hall, ca. 1871

photography studio of the Smithsonian's photographer, Thomas W. Smillie.[30] The northern light provided by the wall of windows was ideal for photographing the museum's specimens.

A mannequin dressed as a Japanese warrior was photographed in the west cloister studio in 1873. The armor is either Do-Maru or Haramaki; both types became widely used in the Genpei Wars (1180–85). Japanese armor was constructed with small scales of steel or iron covered with lacquered paper or leather and laced together with cord.[31] A photograph taken in the west cloister between 1872 and 1875 also shows a mannequin representing Chief Red Cloud, a well-known Oglala Teton Sioux warrior and statesman during the 1870s. Although the mannequin no longer exists, the shirt, headdress, feather trail, drum, moccasins, leggings, and earrings are all preserved in the Smithsonian's Department of Anthropology.[32]

In 1873 the Arctic explorer Elisha Kent Kane's suit *(see also page 72)* was again photographed, this time by Thomas Smillie. For unknown reasons, the mannequin dressed in Kane's clothing was photographed with mannequins representing "Joe" (Inuktitut name: Ebierbing) and his wife, "Hanna" (Inuktitut name: Tookoolito), neither of whom was associated with Kane.[33] Kane's clothing consisted of a loose-fitting fox-skin shirt attached to an almost air-tight hood. Underneath the shirt was a similar one made of bird skins, chewed by Eskimo women until they were perfectly soft; the skins of more than five hundred Auks were reportedly used to make a garment of this type. The lower extremities were protected by a pair of bear-skin breeches and boots, which consisted of bird-skin socks padded with grass and topped by bear-skin uppers.[34]

Above left: A model of a Japanese warrior in the west cloister. Photograph by C. Seaver Jr., 1873. Above right: A model of Red Cloud in the west cloister, ca. 1873. Opposite: The Elisha Kent Kane mannequin, posed with an Inuktitut husband and wife given the names "Joe" and "Hanna." Photograph by Thomas W. Smillie, 1873.

FIREPROOFING THE WEST RANGE

As early as 1882 the West Wing had been assigned to marine invertebrates (corals and sea creatures without backbones) in anticipation of the removal of the ceramic collections to the new National Museum, opened in 1881. With cases in the West Range already filled with marine specimens, the walls of the hall were repainted and decorated with floral and geometric stencils that complemented the ceramic tiles filling the three blind niches above the door to the West Wing.[35] Henry Horan, the building superintendent, commented that the artist's work had added "a freshness and beauty to that Hall which it could never boast of before."[36]

Appearances aside, the West Range was in grave danger. What seemed to be a solid stone floor was in fact just thin flagging laid atop wood beams supported by wood columns in the basement, both rotted and highly flammable. The rest of the interior consisted of "a complicated system of decorative hollow columns and vaults, framed of wooden scantlings, boards, and lathed plastering," all of which was considered flammable and structurally unsound as well.[37] Adding urgency to the situation was the fact that the volatile "alcoholic" specimens were stored in the basement below.

The West Range redecorated, with *America* framed by the arched door leading from the West Range to the West Wing, ca. 1882.

CENTENNIAL ARTIFACTS

Some three-fourths of the objects exhibited at the 1876 Centennial Exhibition in Philadelphia were given to the United States and transferred to the Smithsonian by congressional authorization. A large work force labored for more than two months, moving and crating the cache of objects; they were then loaded into forty freight-train cars and shipped to Washington (along with twenty more carloads returning the exhibits sent by the Institution to the fair). Until a new National Museum building could be constructed, the artifacts and specimens occupied twenty thousand square feet of space—stored floor to ceiling on four levels—at the nearby Washington Armory.[38]

Ceramic collections that came to the Smithsonian primarily from the 1876 exhibition took their place in the West Wing after the minerals there were moved to the West Range in 1879–80. Dominating the hall directly in front of the entrance was the sculpture group America, *modeled by John Bell for Henry Doulton & Company in England. This monumental terra-cotta group, which depicted the "United States Directing the Onward Course of America," was a full-sized reproduction of one of the marble corner pieces of the Albert Memorial in Hyde Park, London.[39] That sculpture group was lauded at the time as "probably the largest work of this nature ever attempted."[40] The ceramic collections remained in the West Wing only until 1885, when they were moved to the new National Museum with other centennial artifacts and replaced by exhibits of marine invertebrates.[41] However, the* America *group remained in the hall amid the marine specimens until 1891, probably because of its great weight and the difficulty of moving it.[42]*

Above: The Washington Armory, between Sixth and Seventh Streets at B Street, S.W. (Independence Avenue), on the site now occupied by the National Air and Space Museum, ca. 1890. Opposite: The sculpture group *America* in the West Wing, ca. 1880.

In 1887 Congress appropriated $15,000 to fireproof the West Range. However, the appropriation was insufficient to replicate the Gothic columns and groin-vaulted ceilings with fireproof materials. Instead the architect Adolf Cluss and his partner, Paul Schulze, designed simplified octagonal columns topped with capitals of stylized leaves and scrolls. A plain barrel-vaulted main ceiling and flat aisle ceilings with recessed panels replaced the groined and ribbed Gothic ceilings throughout. The stripped-down aesthetic of the fireproofed hall nonetheless comported with the "the Romanesque general character of the building."[43] Perhaps to soften the stark architecture, Cluss and Schulze proposed an elaborate decorative scheme consisting of selective gilding and multicolored stenciling.

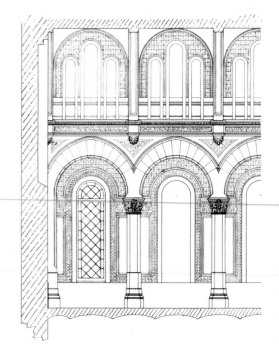

The decor presented by Cluss & Schulze for the West Range was much in keeping with the period's Aesthetic movement, noted for its rich artistic style. A letter to Secretary Samuel P. Langley accompanying these drawings painted a vivid portrait of the room:

The piers separating the naves with the surmounting arches to be treated in gray, as stone, architecture, with the capitels [*sic*] of the piers in light marble tint with gilding of prominent parts. The side walls to have a base of maroon and to be done in a tasty green-gray tint with ornaments kept more brilliant but raised from the same tint. The window framings to be in warmer and more brilliant tints, as implied by the Romanesque style. The panels of the ceiling to be in a pale bluish tint with brilliantly decorated warmer moldings, etc.[44]

Sadly this decorative scheme, which was Cluss & Schulze's last project for the Smithsonian, was never carried out.

WELL-SELECTED SPECIMENS

The West Wing was closed for two years beginning in 1891 while it was rebuilt with fireproof materials, which, unlike the West Range's fireproofing, exactly replicated its original appearance. Early in 1893 the wing reopened with a newly refurbished exhibition of marine invertebrates.[45] Huge plaster casts of an octopus and a giant squid, sculpted for the Tennessee Exposition of 1897, were suspended from the ceiling at the conclusion of the fair.[46] The use of plaster casts instead of actual specimens was explained in the report of the Department of Biology in 1901:

Painted casts can never be actual facsimiles of the animals as they appear in life, and for that reason are less valuable than preparations of specimens. The painting of casts in life colors by competent artists involves very large expense. Furthermore, such casts are rather art objects than natural history specimens. On the other hand, there is no known method of retaining life colors in specimens preserved in liquids, and such specimens are therefore less attractive to the public than they should be.[47]

Although the insect collections were moved into the Castle in 1898, no permanent exhibition space was immediately arranged for them. By 1903, after the fish specimens had been moved to the National Museum and exhibited with reptiles, the entire West Range was given over to the Department of Insects.[48] Behind the sign announcing the hall's new tenants, a gigantic fish cast still hung in the blind niche alongside the newly installed insect exhibits.

Top: Longitudinal section through the end of the West Range, showing the proposed decoration scheme. Drawing by Cluss & Schulze, May 1888. Above: Insects exhibited in the West Range, ca. 1902.

Marine invertebrates on display in the West Wing, ca. 1901.

Before taking possession of the exhibit hall, the insects staff developed innovative techniques for the display. Specially prepared cork and blotting paper were used as a clean, nonwarping background on which to pin the specimens.[49] Descriptive labels were written in language that the average visitor could readily understand.[50] Although the collection numbered nearly 1.5 million insects, only about 2,700 of these, representing the most unusual species, were put on exhibit. The new techniques signaled a break from the museum of the past—once described as "a cemetery of bric-a-brac"—and supported the theory that "[a]n efficient educational museum may be described as a collection of instructive labels, each illustrated by a well-selected specimen."[51]

GRAPHIC ARTS ON DISPLAY

With the completion in 1911 of the newest National Museum (National Museum of Natural History), most of the exhibits and collections in the Smithsonian Building were moved there. This reorganization allowed the Division of Graphic Arts to leave the Arts and Industries Building in 1912, filling the three major exhibit halls on the Smithsonian Building's first floor: the West Wing, the West Range, and the Lower Main Hall. The graphic arts exhibits were left partially unfinished when all three halls were closed to the public from 1914 to 1916 because of extensive renovations in the Lower Main Hall.[52]

The closing of the West Wing allowed the hall to be used as a workroom to repair the iconic Star-Spangled Banner, the garrison flag that flew over Fort McHenry during the Battle of Baltimore in 1814. Originally measuring 30 by 42 feet, the flag had been shortened by eight feet in the years before its arrival at the Smithsonian—cuttings from the flag had been given out as souvenirs.[53] The flag was received on loan from its owner, Eben Appleton of New York, on July 21, 1907. It was unfurled and suspended from the Castle's East Range, photographed, and put on exhibit in the Arts and Industries Building.[54]

CLASSICAL CONTROVERSY

Above: The statue of George Washington in the West Wing. Photograph by B. Anthony Stewart, July 1959. Opposite: Removal of "Greenough's Washington" from the Castle. Photograph by George F. Mobley, September 1962.

Horatio Greenough's neoclassical statue of George Washington was monumental but famously controversial. Created in Italy by the Boston sculptor, it was installed in the Rotunda of the U.S. Capitol in 1841. Only two years later, it was moved to the Capitol's east plaza.[55] Ridiculed as "the one great mistake of a really great artist," the bare-chested statue draped in a Roman toga—with one hand holding a sword and the other raised and pointing to the heavens—was met with both derision and praise. Greenough (1805–52) defended his choice of costume by asserting that it served to identify Washington as a man for the ages, rather than a man from a particular period in time.[56]

By 1908 the statue's deteriorating condition was cause for alarm. On May 22 of that year Congress authorized its transfer to the Smithsonian at the Institution's request.[57] On November 20, 1908, the nearly twenty-ton statue was loaded onto a wagon drawn by twelve horses to be relocated to the apse end of the West Wing "until it shall find a place in the National Gallery of Art where it belongs."[58] Legislation to establish a national gallery finally passed on July 1, 1920.

The Smithsonian's growing art collections were then housed in the Natural History Museum, awaiting a permanent home. However, "Greenough's Washington," as it came to be known, remained in the West Wing until 1962. That year it was moved to the Museum of History and Technology (National Museum of American History), at the time still under construction.[59] With the floor reinforced from below, the massive statue—partially crated and its arm braced—was rolled across the room to an opening in the south wall, prepared by removing the middle window and a stone column.[60] It remains there today.

The iconic flag was subsequently given to the museum in 1913, after which its preservation was undertaken in anticipation of the centennial commemoration of the bombardment of Fort McHenry. With the flag rolled out on a long table that covered half of the West Wing's length, Amelia Fowler of Boston and a team of assistants set to work during the summer of 1914. They meticulously stitched the flag to a backing of specially prepared Irish linen, using an overall net stitch to evenly support its great weight. The silk thread was dyed to match the color of each section, making the thread essentially disappear when seen from a short distance.[61] Fowler further explained: "We do not 'restore' the war banners, but put them in shape to defy the test of time. No effort is made to patch in missing pieces, but only to render the remainder of the flags durable and to bring out all the original colors and designs with silk thread sewing."[62]

With the flag sent back to the Arts and Industries Building and the first floor reopened in 1916, the graphic arts exhibits were finally completed to represent the history of the

Opposite, top: Women repairing the Star-Spangled Banner in the West Wing, 1914. Opposite, bottom: The Star-Spangled Banner hanging from the roof of the East Range, July 21, 1907. Top: The graphic arts studio in the west cloister, with Robert Mooney (foreground) preparing a mat, overseen by the curator, Ruel Tolman, ca. 1933. Above: Graphic arts exhibits on the West Range's north side, showing the suspended "schoolhouse" lights, ca. 1943.

printing arts from "Chaldean cuneiform and Egyptian pepyrus [sic] . . . to the most modern forms of depicting on paper."[63] In the West Wing, rows of glass exhibit cases, augmenting the 1871 wall cases that encircled the room, were neatly arranged along a central aisle leading to Greenough's statue of Washington; some of the new displays enclosed storage units in their bases. Most of the cases dated to the mid-1890s, when many advances in case design and museum methods were perfected. Graphic items were arranged in the cases to fit within the frames of glass, so that "each panel or door stands for itself, like the page of a book, the arrangement being without exception from left to right, as in a book."[64] The large case in the center of the hall opposite the door, installed in 1919, contained a pair of life-sized mannequins representing Japanese woodcut printers at work.[65]

On July 21, 1920, a major change occurred in the Division of Graphic Arts when it and the photography section were transferred from the Department of Anthropology to the Department of Arts and Industries. Ruel Pardee Tolman (1878–1954) was made assistant curator in charge of the division, serving until 1946. Tolman, an artist and an art instructor at the Corcoran School of Art, immediately began a total reorganization of the exhibits "to bring both historical and technical material of a kind together in a chronological order."[66] Under his direction, the collections were refined, increased, and maintained. For the next twenty years, they occupied the three main halls on the Castle's first floor.

The division's studio—used for matting, framing, and mounting specimens for exhibition—was located in what had been the photography studio in the early 1870s.[67] Tolman initiated an ambitious series of temporary exhibits, many featuring the work of living artists, on almost a monthly basis. These shows were seen as a way of encouraging the arts in much the same way that Joseph Henry had done more than sixty years before. Tolman took the concept one step further by allowing the artists to sell their work to visitors, with the division often acting as sales agent.[68] The artists in turn would often donate their prints to the collection. A remarkable 234 temporary exhibits were installed between 1923 and 1946.[69]

In preparation for a major repurposing of the Lower Main Hall as the Index Exhibit, the division in 1939 relinquished a third of its former exhibition space. Only a year earlier, Tolman had replaced many of the West Range's late-nineteenth-century exhibit cases with modern ones to give a "more dignified appearance."[70] After the collections were consolidated, the hall was lighted with new electric schoolhouse-style fixtures hanging from the high vaulted ceiling; rows of lights were suspended above the cases from conduits in the alcoves.[71]

By the early 1950s, the Smithsonian's exhibits—characterized in its own 1954 annual report as "entirely outmoded, inadequate, and all too often uninstructive [sic]"—were in dire need of refurbishing. A long-contemplated program for institution-wide exhibit modernization was begun with a congressional appropriation of $360,000 in 1954.[72] Jacob Kainen (1909–2001), an exhibiting artist who was appointed curator of the Division of Graphic Arts in 1946, stated in his 1955 report that he had started on the exhibits in the West Wing. A year later, with twenty-six of the thirty-five cases finished, the displays illustrating mechanical printing processes were partially opened to the public and were finally

"BOXES OF VISUAL EDUCATION"

The Smithsonian's mission "to diffuse knowledge" often inspires invention by its employees. *Ralph Clifton Smith, a twenty-four-year-old aide in the Graphics Arts Division, created an innovative traveling exhibit in 1922. Entitled How Prints Are Made, it explained the various processes and techniques of printmaking. What started out as a set of panels that could be easily crated and shipped to the convention of the Richmond Printers Association became a series of crated exhibits sent on loan to schools, colleges, public libraries, and museums throughout the country; the only cost to the institution was for shipping.*

Smith developed two exhibits: a large one, consisting of twelve unglazed framed panels measuring 48 by 32 inches and weighing four hundred pounds when crated, and a smaller set for institutions of more modest means that included twenty-five cardboard mats 12½ by 20 inches in size and weighing a mere thirty pounds. Both sets were illustrated with specimens of etchings, engravings, or lithographs, as well as photographs. The large unglazed panels could accommodate actual printmaking tools. Readable, nontechnical labels described the processes. These "boxes of visual education" provided "the student of art or of printing with an object lesson in his craft," revealing the "relationship of the commercial and artistic branches of the graphic arts."[73]

Ralph C. Smith, a graphic arts aide, unpacking a temporary exhibit in the West Wing, ca. 1924.

completed in June 1958.[74] The vintage 1871 wall cases were painted light gray and further modernized by replacing the double doors in each case with a single-paned door. Electric lighting was installed in the West Wing for the first time in its history, with special attention paid to illuminating Greenough's statue of Washington from the ceiling above.[75] With the exception of a low platform in the center of the room, on which three printing presses were displayed, the hall's floor was almost completely unencumbered by exhibit cases—which had not happened since it was the Smithsonian's library.

New exhibits in the West Range were opened with an evening reception on July 10, 1958.[76] This installation, called the Hall of Hand Processes, focused on etching, engraving, lithography, and silkscreen printing. Fine prints by Dürer, Delacroix, Rembrandt, and Matisse were used as illustrations for these various techniques. The history of printing from the invention of the alphabet to printed books was documented with an ancient Chinese block book and a page from the original Gutenberg Bible.[77] The sleek, modern freestanding panels and specially designed table cases were intended for future use in the new Museum of History and Technology (National Museum of American History) and were subsequently transferred there in 1963 when the building was completed.

Top: Modern display cases in the West Range's redesigned graphic arts exhibit, July 1958. Above: The Commons dining room in the West Wing, looking toward the churchlike apse, 1974.

THE COMMONS

With all exhibits removed from the Castle's west end, a major renovation of the entire structure was begun in the mid-1960s and continued in stages until 1970–71. Then the Woodrow Wilson International Center for Scholars moved into the Main Building's upper floors, and the West Wing and the West Range were designated as a dining room and a lounge, respectively, reserved for use by the scholars as a social center.[78] The dining space was renamed the Commons, a term used for dining halls in English medieval colleges.

The West Wing's vaulted ceiling was embellished with gold stars set against a deep blue background, patterned after Sainte Chappelle in Paris, the Gothic chapel of the French kings.[79] Plaster escutcheons (shields) were mounted above cases to represent the coats of arms of famous men of letters and science in England, Scotland, Ireland, and Wales—among them Horace Walpole, William Penn, William Pitt, William Shakespeare, Sir Francis Drake, Edmund Burke, William Laud, Benjamin Disraeli, Isaac Newton, Robert Blake, Geoffrey Chaucer, and Charles Darwin.[80] The shields had decorated the British Pavilion at the 1939 New York World's Fair but were left behind at the outset of World War II and were eventually given to the Smithsonian.

In addition to daily buffet lunches, the room served as a grand setting for symposia, seminars, dinners, and receptions. Perhaps the most prestigious and important use of the Commons was as the site of the 1971 economic summit of the finance ministers of the world's ten leading noncommunist countries, called the Group of Ten (G-10). The meeting was hastily arranged by Treasury Secretary John B. Connally "to attempt to stabilize the world's currencies in the worst international monetary crisis since the end of World War II." The Castle was chosen as the gathering's site in part because of "its architecturally distinguished meeting halls"—but, more important, because the apolitical Smithsonian

was viewed as neutral ground on which the foreign ministers would not feel that the United States was "running the whole show."[81] The so-called Smithsonian Agreement, the result of the three-day conference, was touted by President Richard M. Nixon as "the most significant monetary agreement in the history of the world."[82] Smithsonian Secretary S. Dillon Ripley simply hoped that "the benign influence of the Castle Building was useful in promoting a community of financial interests among the nations concerned."[83]

The West Wing continued as the Commons dining room for the next thirty-three years, but in 2003 a new purpose was found for this Gothic hall. The space's nineteenth-century exhibit cases were refurbished, retrofitted with new microclimate features that included state-of-the-art fiber-optic lighting, filled with artifacts from all the Smithsonian's museums, and reopened to the public in 2004 (*see page 104*). A new exhibition, entitled America's Treasure Chest, augmented the nearby visitors center with a glimpse of the Smithsonian's vast holdings and provided an introduction to its research activities. Visitors with little time could then plan their visits to the Smithsonian museums that most appealed to them.

Treasury Secretary John B. Connally (far left center), presiding over the Group of Ten meeting in the Commons, December 1971.

THE WEST RANGE

When the Commons was opened in 1970, the West Range not only provided additional seating for the dining room but also accommodated large lectures and evening receptions. During a state visit to Washington to discuss deteriorating relations between India and Pakistan with President Nixon, Indian Prime Minister Indira Gandhi in

November 1971 addressed about a hundred prominent Washingtonians in a lecture sponsored by the Woodrow Wilson Center and the Smithsonian. Among those present at the lecture in the West Range were Smithsonian Secretary Ripley, Supreme Court Justice William O. Douglas, Senator Hubert H. Humphrey, and General William C. Westmorland, the U.S. Army chief of staff.

The West Range became a reception center for members in 1972, when the Smithsonian Associates' functions were consolidated.[84] In 1974, two years before the nation's Bicentennial celebration, the Smithsonian prepared to accommodate a great influx of visitors "with guidance, information, food, protection, and a sense of welcome and enthusiastic reception."[85] The West Range was furnished with nineteenth-century furniture from the Castle Collection to fill its new function as a lounge for visiting Smithsonian Associates.[86] Sofas and chairs for relaxing and tables for writing postcards were provided, along with historically significant pieces of furniture. Among these was a pair of mahogany arm chairs in the Renaissance Revival style that had belonged to Edwin M. Stanton (1814–69), secretary of war from 1862 to 1867 under Presidents Lincoln and Grant.

When the West Wing was converted back into an exhibition hall in 2004, the West Range also received a makeover. No longer serving as a lounge for members, the hall was used increasingly for special events and temporary exhibits. Its fresh "new" paint scheme

Prime Minister Indira Gandhi of India, delivering a lecture in the West Range, November 4, 1971.

PAINTING AS A PASTIME

Sir Winston Churchill (1874–1965), perhaps the world's most famous amateur painter, did not start painting until after the age of forty. He produced more than five hundred canvases during the fifty years he pursued his muse, mostly in his studio at Chartwell, his home in the Surrey countryside. Churchill took up oil painting in 1915 during a particularly trying time in his life, after being forced to retire from the British government. Soon afterward he published an essay, "Painting as a Pastime," extolling the virtues of painting as a physical activity for repairing the brain's fatigue.[87] *In it he said: "[P]ainting is a friend who makes no undue demands, excites to no exhausting pursuits, keeps faithful pace even with feeble steps, and holds her canvas as a screen between us and the envious eyes of Time or the surly advance of Decrepitude. Happy are the painters, for they shall not be lonely."*[88]

Winston S. Churchill: Painting as a Pastime, an exhibit of fifty-one paintings that was organized by the Royal Oak Foundation (an American affiliate of the English National Trust) was put on view in the Castle's West Range from September to November 1983.[89] *This show was not the first time that the British prime minister's paintings had traveled to this country; his first solo exhibition came in 1958 at the urging of his personal friend President Dwight D. Eisenhower. That collection of thirty pictures, circulated throughout the United States and Canada by the Smithsonian's Traveling Exhibition Service (SITES), made stops in Kansas City, Missouri; Detroit, New York, and Toronto before arriving at the Smithsonian's Natural History Museum as its final venue.*[90] *The show was seen by more than 223,000 people during its three-week stay in Washington.*[91]

The opening exhibition reception for the paintings of Winston Churchill in the West Range, September 1983.

The Smithsonian Associates' reception area in the West Range, furnished with one of Edwin Stanton's mahogany arm chairs (far right, behind the column), 1976.

(see page 24) was actually based on Adolf Cluss's 1887 decorative proposal, which had never been carried out. An in-depth paint analysis of Cluss's Arts and Industries Building revealed under multiple layers of twentieth-century coatings several shades of his self-described "tasty green-gray tint" that appear to match his written decorative proposal.

Specially designed exhibit cases, constructed in 2006 for a temporary exhibit, Legends of Numismatics, then filled the spaces between the columns of the northern arcade and were put to use for rotating exhibits. One of the most popular of these opened in June 2010: a display of jewelry from the personal collection of Madeleine Albright, the first woman secretary of state. Albright began her collection after the Iraqi press corps referred to her as a serpent; she then wore a golden snake brooch pinned to her suit for a meeting on Iraq. Many of the brooches were worn by Albright to communicate special messages: "I found that jewelry had become part of my personal diplomatic arsenal. While President George H. W. Bush had been known for saying 'Read my lips,' I began urging colleagues and reporters to 'Read my pins.'"[92]

THE TOWERS

Secretary Joseph Henry—fearful that James Smithson's gift was being consumed by the erection of a large and ornate edifice—unsuccessfully pushed to have the building completed with fewer towers.[1] Viewing the planned towers as the epitome of architectural excess, Henry had complained that "the buttresses, turrets, and towers, while they add very little to the accommodation of the building, greatly increased the cost."[2] Sharing Henry's view was the prominent American sculptor Horatio Greenough, whose statue of George Washington was given to the Smithsonian by Congress. On seeing the building for the first time in 1851, silhouetted against the U.S. Capitol in the distance, he wrote: "Tower and battlement, and all that medieval confusion, stamped itself on the halls of Congress, as ink on paper! Dark on that whiteness—complication on that simplicity!" Speaking of the towers in particular, he went on: "This is a practical land. They must be here for something. Is no coup d'etat lurking there? Can they be merely ornaments, like the tassels to a University cap?"[3]

The towers, nine in all, did have practical purposes. Some were intended to house staircases and elevators to raise books and freight, while others were destined to provide spaces for offices, laboratories, and storage. A room in the South Tower serves as the meeting room for the Smithsonian's Board of Regents and also once provided a temporary resting place for the remains of the Institution's benefactor and namesake, James Smithson; a more permanent crypt for Smithson was created in yet another tower room.

Rooms in the upper levels of the towers were used as sleeping quarters for young scientists in exchange for their services cataloguing the Smithsonian's collections.[4] Others were occupied by owls. The roof of the South Tower became an aviary for falcons, and the room below served as a dormitory for their caretakers. The roof of the tall North Tower provided a perfect perch for observation during the Civil War. The northern light that poured into one of this tower's lower rooms proved to be ideal for the temporary studio of a famous painter of American Indians and Indian life. In the late twentieth century the towers continued to furnish offices for many Smithsonian employees and scholars, but currently for fire-safety reasons only the rooms of the lower levels are occupied as offices.

THE SOUTH TOWER

Located at the center of the Castle's south facade, the South Tower—with its solid massing and roofline crenellation—is the only part of the building truly reminiscent of a castle. Its interior was originally divided into three floors delineated on the exterior by the large arched door of the first floor, the oriel window of the second floor, and the tall double window, under the crenellation, of the third floor. The first-floor room was intended by James Renwick as a vestibule but became instead part of the Lower Main Hall's museum

Opposite: The restored Children's Room in the South Tower as it has looked in recent years. Photograph by Eric Long, 2011. Above: The Octagonal Tower (left) and the crenellated South Tower with its adjacent Chimney Tower (right). Photograph by Ken Rahaim, 2008.

127

when it was completed. The room above, with its protruding bay window, was the Regents' Room, while the uppermost room was used by Secretary Henry as an office from 1852 to 1861.[5] The tower's interior and exterior configuration remained unchanged until after the fire of 1865, when three additional floors were inserted.

Perhaps the most distinctive feature of the South Tower is its small attached Octagonal Tower, entered separately at ground level.[6] It originally served as a private staircase to the Regents' Room and the room above. The architect's building specifications paint a vivid picture of these hidden stairs: "They will wind around a column from 8 to 12 inches in diameter, and will have treads and risers of yellow pine, and a handsome moulded hand rail 3 by 4 inches, of black walnut. . . . the walls will be wainscoted [*sic*] on end with black walnut . . . to the height of hand railing."[7]

RECONFIGURATION AFTER THE FIRE

Reconstruction of the South Tower as a result of the fire on January 24, 1865, had a profound effect on the configuration of the interior spaces. The upper third of the tower was so heavily damaged that it was pulled down immediately, but by March 8 a temporary wooden roof was installed above the remains.[8] Both the main South Tower and the Octagonal Tower were left windowless for a time. Seventeen months into the reconstruction, Henry reported that "repair of the larger south tower has been a more laborious work than was anticipated."[9] However, by September 15, 1866, the stonework had been finished, by October 20 the tower's roof was complete, and by November 16 round porthole windows were cut into the tower walls to light three newly created floor levels that Adolf Cluss had inserted, thereby doubling the amount of usable space.[10]

When the rebuilding was complete in mid-1867, the exterior of the South Tower appeared very much the same, although the interior was altered considerably by the insertion of the three additional floors. On the tower's east and west sides, Cluss had inserted small circular windows whose form and size were carefully chosen to provide adequate light, while only subtly altering Renwick's design.[11] Renwick's logical division of the exterior architecture—announcing the interior's three distinct levels—was nonetheless lost during the renovation.

The Regents' Room was restored to its original function, and the other rooms in the tower were occupied. The South Tower Room on the first floor, considered an extension of the Lower Main Hall museum, remained filled with an eclectic mix of objects that escaped the fire: a California Redwood tree plank, an enormous piece of copper from mines near Lake Superior, several statues and idols from Nicaragua, a live alligator from Georgia, and a marble sarcophagus from Syria.[12] In the newly created second-floor room, shelves, bins, and other fixtures for the International Exchange Service were constructed. Three floors above the Regents' Room were used for general storage and other unspecified purposes. Amenities included water closets and an elevator for hauling books and specimens from the basement to four of the six stories above (a staircase was built to reach the top two floors). Fire hoses used water supplied directly from the Potomac River.[13]

Below: Cutaway rendering of the South Tower as it appeared before the 1865 fire. Bottom: The tower after three floors were added during its post-fire reconfiguration, completed in 1867. Drawings by Richard E. Stamm, 2005.

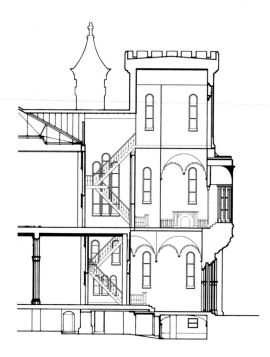

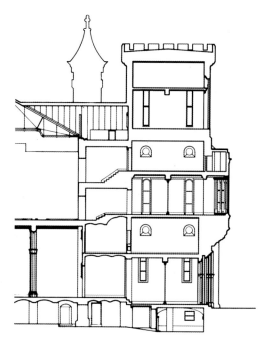

THE SYRIAN SARCOPHAGUS

The Syrian sarcophagus in the South Tower Room. Photograph by F. H. Bell, 1867.

Prominently displayed in the center of the South Tower Room was the Syrian sarcophagus. This marble sarcophagus, erroneously thought to have held the remains of a Roman emperor, had been brought to the United States in 1839 from Syria on board the U.S. Frigate Constitution *by Commodore Jesse Duncan Elliott and offered to former President Andrew Jackson (1767–1845) as a tomb for his remains. In a letter to Elliott written shortly before his death, Jackson graciously declined the gift, stating that, "whilst from debility and affliction, I am gasping for breath . . . I cannot consent that my mortal body shall be laid in a repository prepared for an emperor or a king. My republican feelings and principles forbid it; the simplicity of our system of Government forbids it. True virtue cannot exist where pomp and parade are the governing passions."[14]*

Respecting Jackson's wishes, Elliott instead gave the sarcophagus to the National Institute for the Promotion of Science and the Useful Arts "as their own and sole property, exempt from any condition."[15] After the institute's dissolution, it was transferred to the Smithsonian in 1860 and placed in the South Tower Room.[16] The sarcophagus, the collection of large ethnology specimens, and the stone images from Nicaragua that were exhibited in the room all survived the 1865 fire.[17] To support these weighty objects, the sagging floor had to be braced from the basement by a brick pier in 1871.[18] This remote coal cellar, which provided a safe hiding place under the stone floor for valuables during the dark days of the Civil War, was used in 1895 for the building's first dynamo, which supplied electricity for offices in the East Wing.[19] The sarcophagus is now in storage.

THE CHILDREN'S ROOM

By 1883 the Syrian sarcophagus had been moved to the Arts and Industries Building, after which the South Tower Room was devoted to exhibits of birds. But in 1899 a new purpose was found for the first-floor chamber. Secretary Samuel P. Langley began preparations to convert the entire room for the "purpose of bringing together there, in a simple and attractive manner, objects which may be of interest to children."[20] Langley explained his intent plainly: "It must be a cozy, pleasant room, with plenty of light and pretty things, as well as a collection of specimens not many in number, but each object chosen just to give the child pleasure."[21]

The architecture firm Hornblower & Marshall was chosen to make structural changes to the room to increase its light and cheerfulness, as well as to design the room's furnishings.[22] The architects suggested a mosaic floor of red, blue, green, yellow, black, and white tiles inspired by Celtic designs. Low glass-front exhibit cases framed with light maple were constructed, encircling the room at a child's eye level.[23] A massive table in the center held a large aquarium with colorful fish, which, like the exotic birds in the cages above, were meant to inspire in a child the wonder of the beauty of nature.[24] Exhibit labels with Latin inscriptions, commonly found in other parts of the museum, were banned

because, as Langley explained, taking the child's perspective: "We are not very much interested in the Latin names, and however much they may mean to grown-up people, we do not want to have our entertainment spoiled by its being made a lesson."[25]

For the artistic design of the Children's Room, the prominent local interior designer and artist Grace Lincoln Temple (1864–1953) was selected.[26] She chose luminous shades of green for the walls, which were sectioned off by gilded moldings. A unique stenciled frieze with highly stylized birds, scrolls, and feathers encircled the room just above the exhibit cases. In an article describing the newly completed room, the author and Mark Twain biographer Albert Bigelow Paine wrote: "The ceiling is painted to represent a vine-clad arbor, with sky spaces through which birds of gayest plumage seem to look down on friends and relatives below. Indeed, a number of living relatives are just below, where four gilt cages of song supply a never ending chorus of nations, the little singers having been chosen from the many far and near corners of the whole earth."[27]

Above: The Children's Room in the South Tower Room. Color lithograph from the *Annual Report for 1901*. Opposite, top: The decorator Grace Lincoln Temple with the ceiling stencils for the Children's Room, ca. 1901. Opposite, center: William Duncan Strong, director of the Ethnogeographic Board, in the South Tower Room, July 1943. Opposite, bottom: The Smithsonian Associates' reception center in the South Tower Room, 1972.

Situated beneath the birdcages were two aquariums, one filled with live saltwater fish and the other with freshwater fish and baby turtles. To pique children's interest, the cases had simple titles, among them "Some Curious Birds," "Birds with Curious Nests and Eggs," "Bright-colored Birds," "Pretty Shells," "Strange Insects," and "How Creatures Hide." Other cases held such wonders as the largest and smallest birds of prey, the smallest and largest eggs in the world, the largest lump of gold ever found, and the largest diamond ever cut. Propped against the wall above the low cases were several of the Smithsonian's Audubon prints, displayed to show birds in action.

All the objects were chosen to support the theme of the room, which was painted on the transom above the south entrance: "Knowledge Begins in Wonder."[28] The hope was that after a visit to this special place, "the child goes home at last, glad, and with knowledge, and the love of knowledge, in his heart. He is happy, and, because his wonder has been aroused, he has learned."[29]

SOUTH TOWER ROOM CHANGES

By 1941 the Children's Room, emptied of specimens and its decorative scheme painted over, was used as an adjunct to the new Index Exhibit in the Lower Main Hall. The old Children's Room exhibit cases were modified as bookcases in which to display bound copies of all the Institution's publications from 1846 to 1941. An important new feature of the room was a staffed desk where visitors could receive information on all Smithsonian exhibits and events.[30]

With the outbreak of World War II, this information center was converted into an office in 1942 for the newly formed nongovernmental Ethnogeographic Board, established by the Smithsonian in tandem with the American Council of Learned Societies, the Social Science Research Council, and the National Research Council. The function of this wartime board was "to act as a clearinghouse between the above institutions and other scientific and educational organizations throughout the country, and the Army, Navy, and war agencies within the government."[31] William Duncan Strong (1899–1962) of Columbia University, formerly an anthropologist for the Smithsonian's Bureau of American Ethnology from 1931 to 1937, returned as director of the board.[32] Scientific staff members of the bureau were detailed to the board, joining liaison officers from the War and Navy Departments. The board provided strategic information on the people, geography, and related features of areas involved in the war. Research conducted on behalf of the board was all of "a strictly confidential character . . . concerned with many different branches of science, including anthropology, biology, geology, physics, and meteorology."[33]

After the war, the Ethnogeographic Board was disbanded and the South Tower Room was again used as an information center. By 1966 it also included a sales shop that provided visitors with "attractive and educational remembrances of their visit."[34] After the Smithsonian Associates' functions were consolidated in 1972, a reception center for members was created in the South Tower Room and the West Range.[35] The center's success was evident when more than 13,000 pieces of mail were answered and 125,000 phone inquiries were channeled through it by 1974. It was also responsible for recruiting, training, and placing information volunteers throughout the Institution.[36]

An office for the reception center's new director, Mary Grace Potter, was created in the former Children's Room. Period antiques from the Castle Collection used there included a Colonial Revival five-light chandelier, dating from about 1900. It was hung in front of a pair of massive oak doors that filled the archway and replaced the 1900 glass-paneled doors and transom. A pair of gilt mirrors was moved into the blind arches on each side of the door; the mirrors, once owned by Simon Cameron, President Lincoln's first secretary of war from 1860 to 1862, were a gift to the collection by Cameron's granddaughter. A large-scale copy of a photograph of the earlier Children's Room served as a reminder of the room's former grandeur.

A major renovation of the Castle's Great Hall for a new Smithsonian visitor information and Associates' reception center presented an opportunity to include a decorative restoration of the Children's Room. Preliminary analysis of the ceiling revealed that Grace Lincoln Temple's stenciled design was largely intact beneath multiple layers of paint. Removal of forty-seven years' worth of paint and restoration of the decorative elements of the room was completed under the direction of the Smithsonian's Office of Architectural History and Historic Preservation, with funding from the Pew Memorial Trust.

When the new visitors center opened to the public on November 15, 1989, the newly restored Children's Room served as a grand entryway from the Enid A. Haupt Garden.[37] Although a complete re-creation of the Children's Room cases and exhibits was not feasible at the time, the restoration in a small way brought back its original connection to the outdoors, as Albert Paine had poetically alluded to in 1901: "[I]t is a sunny little spot, with doors and windows opening to clambering vines, grass plots, and happy trees, where in summer are birds that build and sing."[38]

A room located directly above the Children's Room had also been modified at the turn of the twentieth century. In observance of the centennial of Joseph Henry's birth, Secretary Langley in 1899 created a museum here "for the care of the valuable collection of physical apparatus used by Professor Henry and others in various investigations."[39] Among the displays was a set of tuning forks used by Henry for his acoustics experiments in 1854.[40] The results of that research were applied to the design of the Smithsonian's lecture hall, whose acoustics Henry believed were unsurpassed by any in the country. The terrazzo floor, with its geometric tile border, was probably the work of Hornblower & Marshall, who at the time were contracted to make structural changes in the Children's Room.

THE REGENTS' ROOM

The 1846 plan for the Smithsonian Building envisioned a committee room for the Board of Regents in a style compatible with the building's medieval revival architecture. James Renwick designed a small but lofty vaulted room on the original second floor of the South Tower (which became the third level after the fire-related changes). Completed in

Top: The Children's Room upon reopening in 1989. Above: The second-floor room in the South Tower dedicated to Joseph Henry's apparatus collection, with his acoustical tuning forks visible on the shelving unit at the back, ca. 1899. Opposite: A Regents' chair designed in 1848 by James Renwick, ca. 1900.

SÉANCES IN THE REGENTS' ROOM

The original Regents' Room. Woodcut from Rhees, *An Account of the Smithsonian Institution*, 1857.

Soon after the Regents' Room was reconstructed, two séances were held there early in 1868. A well-known spiritualist, Charles H. Foster (1838–85)—described by Joseph Henry's daughter Mary as "a dreamy, sympathetic individual"—was both praised as "the most gifted and remarkable Spiritual Medium since Swedenborg" and excoriated as a fraud and a swindler.[41] Foster had been warned that Secretary Henry was not a believer.[42] Ignorance about the nature of electricity and its use in telegraph systems gave rise to the belief that mediums could communicate with spirits from beyond the grave through a "spiritual telegraph."[43]

Henry was keenly aware that science was being misused to prove the validity of spiritualism. An ever-skeptical Secretary stated that his purpose in holding the séances was to "investigate this whole matter of spiritualism which is environed with so much charlatanism and delusion and to sift out the psychological principles by which so many minds were thrown into an abnormal condition."[44] The spiritualist's performances failed to impress Henry, who afterwards pronounced him "a most consummate actor." Mary Henry's reaction was even more incredulous: "[I]t would take a great deal to make me believe that spirits from beyond the grave are coming back for such trivial child's play as picking out names and telling what is written in folded papers."[45] The Henrys were joined by an ever-growing list of disbelievers, including Mark Twain, Henry James, and P. T. Barnum, whose delight in exposing fake mediums would eventually help bring down the movement.

December 1852, the Regents' Room measured approximately 14 feet long by 23 feet wide and soared 20 feet high to a groin-vaulted ceiling.[46] A black walnut wainscot with round-headed arches ran around the entire room, punctuated by a mantel on one wall. Light was provided by a gas chandelier and the tall windows in the oriel alcove. The oriel was reached by three steps and set off by an arched colonnade.

In the center of the room was a long table surrounded by stately armchairs specially designed by Renwick, which he described as "heavily carved in the Norman style . . . from the best black walnut, varnished four coats and polished."[47] The chairs were embellished with distinctive details reflecting the building's exterior stonework; the seats were covered with maroon-colored leather.[48] Although the table was destroyed in the 1865 fire, nine of the original eighteen Renwick chairs survived.

The Regents' Room was also the repository of some of the personal possessions of the Institution's founder. James Smithson's effects had been stored at the U.S. Custom House in New York from the time of their arrival in 1838 until June 1841, when they were transferred to the National Institute.[49] After being displayed in the Patent Office until 1857, they were moved to the Smithsonian Building—finally fulfilling the mandate of the 1846 act creating the Smithsonian, which required that Smithson's possessions be "preserved separate and apart from other property of the Institution.[50]

The more than 180 Smithson objects were for the most part mundane, with the exception of a small chemical laboratory, a marble head of St. Cecilia by the noted sculptor Bertel Thorwalsden, a rural scene painted by the seventeenth-century Dutch painter Nicolaas Berghem, and the benefactor's small library of 115 volumes.[51] The library and two portraits of Smithson, one as a student at Oxford and the other a bronze medallion by Pierre Joseph Toilier that served as the model for the Smithsonian's first official seal,[52] survived the fire because they had been placed on exhibit in the West Wing and the West Range. Inexplicably the Berghem painting also withstood the fire, even though it had been on display in the Regents' Room at the time.[53]

Henry dismissed the loss of the Smithson artifacts, indicating that they were "of little value, except as mementos."[54] However, several other Smithson-related mementos came to the Smithsonian soon after, including a small portrait of him painted on ivory by the Dutch miniaturist Henri Joseph Johns in 1816.[55] By 1880 the Regents' Room once again housed a collection of Smithson-related objects, arranged in a shallow walnut display case, along with a small glass-front bookcase with Smithson's library.[56]

Remodeling of the Regents' Room began in 1899 by Hornblower & Marshall and continued throughout 1900. The architects designed an enormous brick fireplace surround made of what they called "old gold" brick, with two shelves of red stone.[57] Other architect-designed furnishings were two long exhibit cases on the north wall to house the Smithson-related objects as well as the founder's library, plus a classically inspired trestle table made of quarter-sawn oak. A pair of chandeliers equipped with patented Welsbach burners and incandescent gas mantles provided light in the room to rival the brilliance and efficiency of the period's electric light.[58]

The newly refurbished Regents' Room was in use for little more than four years when it had an unexpected "visitor"—forcing the Regents to meet elsewhere. In 1901 the Regents were notified by the British consul that by 1905 the cemetery in which James

Opposite: James Smithson's library in the Regents' Room, ca. 1899. Right: The remodeled Regents' Room, with its massive brick fireplace. Photograph attributed to Thomas W. Smillie, ca. 1900.

Smithson was interred in Genoa, Italy, would be relocated to accommodate expansion of the stone quarry at the foot of the hill on which the cemetery rested.[59] Regent Alexander Graham Bell strongly urged his fellow board members to bring Smithson's remains to this country.[60] Finally winning approval late in 1903, he and his wife, Mabel, sailed for Italy and arrived in Genoa on Christmas Day. Smithson's remains were exhumed during a pelting winter storm on December 31, throughout which Mrs. Bell "pluckily took a great variety of photographs of the place and ceremonies."[61]

Soon after, the Bells set sail with Smithson's remains on board, arriving in Washington on January 25, 1904.[62] The coffin, wrapped in the British Union Jack, was loaded onto a horse-drawn caisson and, after brief ceremonies on the dock, was escorted through the streets of Southwest Washington by a squadron of the U.S. Cavalry. On arrival at the Smithsonian Building, Bell symbolically handed over Smithson's remains to the Institution, saying, "And now . . . my mission is ended and I deliver into your hands . . . the remains of this great benefactor of the United States."[63]

The coffin was then symbolically draped with both the U.S. and the British flags and placed in the center of the Lower Main Hall for short but impressive ceremonies. While the Regents considered plans for the erection of "a proper memorial" to Smithson, the coffin, then covered with the U.S. flag alone, was placed temporarily in the Regents' Room, which soon after opened to the public. The coffin remained in the Regents' Room for only a year, until it was transferred to the benefactor's newly finished crypt (*see page 157*). Smithson's personal effects, however, remained in the room until 1911, when they were moved and made more accessible to the public in the Lower Main Hall.[64]

In 1911 the Regents' Room became a library and a reference room for the Division of Plants.[65] It served as an adjunct to the Herbarium, located in the nearby Upper Main Hall, until both were relocated to the new west wing of the Natural History Museum in 1965. To help sort, catalogue, and care for the collections during the Great Depression, the Smithsonian benefitted from the services of highly trained and educated men and women as part of the Civil Works Administration effort to provide temporary jobs for millions of unemployed Americans during the hard winter months of 1933–34.[66] The Division of Plants, then part of the Department of Biology, was aided by thirty CWA workers, including a botanist, a translator, a steno-typist, eight typists, seven cataloguers, and twelve workers who mounted plant specimens.[67] In the short time the program was in effect, a remarkable 37,380 specimens were mounted in the botanical library, under the direct supervision of Eleanor C. White, an assistant scientist in the division.[68]

During the 1968 renovation of the building, the Regents' Room was restored to its original function as the meeting space for the Smithsonian's governing board. Secretary S. Dillon Ripley's vision to restore the Castle's interior spaces to reflect the building's mid-nineteenth-century exterior was also realized at that time. The Hornblower & Marshall fireplace was replaced with a Renaissance Revival mantelpiece and a mirror from the 1870s, while on the opposite wall a monumental eleven-foot-tall mirror of the same period loomed over the antique conference table and chairs.[69] Other period antiques were added, and the James Renwick–designed chairs were refurbished and returned to the room.

The period decor of the Regents' Room was again refreshed in 1987: repainted, recarpeted, and slightly refurnished. A Gothic Revival chandelier dating to about 1855, attributed to the Archer & Warner Company of Philadelphia, was hung from the beam in the middle of the room, and a girandole set entitled "Paul and Virginia," attributed to Cornelius & Company, graced the mantel.[70] Placed over it was a large portrait of Representative William Jervis Hough (1795–1869) and his family.[71] Hough, a one-term congressman from Cazenovia, New York, served on the Smithsonian's first Board of Regents; it was his version of the final bill establishing the Smithsonian that used the term *Regents* in relation to the Smithsonian's governing board.[72] As a member of the Institution's Building Committee, Hough was influential in the choice of building materials, as well as methods of heating, lighting, and ventilating the new building. He was elected interim Secretary and served in that capacity from September to December 1846, when Joseph Henry was appointed the Institution's first Secretary.[73]

Opposite, top: The procession with James Smithson's remains at the U.S. Navy Yard, Washington, D.C., January 25, 1904. Opposite, bottom: James Smithson's coffin in the Regents' Room, 1904.

With the new millennium came an increased demand for a more modern conference facility for the Board of Regents. Several changes were undertaken to accommodate new technologies for conducting business meetings, while still maintaining a period ambiance in the historic room. A remote-controlled motorized projection screen was permanently installed on the ceiling of the oriel window, hidden behind the decorative frieze. New oak doors were constructed in the entrance at the opposite side of the room, with a specially designed shelf built in to hold a projector high above head level. Perhaps the most striking change in the room was the replacement of the sixteen-foot-long antique table with a round table. The Regents and the Secretary had complained that because of the extreme length of the old table, eye contact among those seated at opposite ends was difficult, if not impossible, and a round table would remedy that. Built in pie-shaped sections, the custom-designed thirteen-foot circular table featured the Institution's official seal stenciled in gold leaf in the center. African mahogany, bird's-eye maple, and tiger maple veneers and solids used on the table blended with the antique furniture that remained around the room's perimeter. The newly reconfigured space was completed in time for Smithsonian board meetings on May 6 and 7, 2001.[74]

The updated Regents' Room, with its new round conference table. Photograph by Eric Long, 2011.

Robert Ridgway, an ornithologist, in his office on the fifth floor of the South Tower, August 1884.

THE FIFTH FLOOR

The fifth-floor room in the reconstructed South Tower was used for various purposes. By 1879 it was the office of Robert Ridgway (1850–1929).[75] The ornithologist had first come to the attention of Spencer Baird at an early age, when the two corresponded about the identification of birds. Ridgway would enclose a carefully colored drawing of the bird in question, sometimes including specimens as well.[76] Baird praised the young Ridgway's efforts as showing "an unusual degree of ability as an artist, and of intelligent attention to a scientific subject."[77]

Luncheon with Margaret Mead (right, at the head of the table) in the South Tower office of Wilton Dillon. Among those also shown are E. Richard Sorenson (to Mead's right), Nuala O'Donnell Pell (to Sorenson's right), and Dillon (to her right), 1976.

Ridgway's office was reached by a steep flight of eighty-seven stone steps, which he delighted in bounding up two at a time. The climb proved much more daunting to visitors: "... a very large man, a burly German, opening the door and stepping inside. Breathing heavily, in fact audibly he stopped, mopped his face, then placing his right hand over his heart, as his chest heaved visibly, exclaimed: 'Shentlemens, my heart bleeds for you.'"[78] The time that Ridgway spent in this South Tower office was an extremely prolific period for him, as he published more than three hundred articles on birds.[79] His lifetime legacy of 550 articles and books—combined with the twenty-three species, ten subspecies, and two genera of birds named for him—will ensure that his name is perpetuated in the field of ornithology.[80]

In September 1886 a major earthquake devastated Charleston, South Carolina, and violently shook Washington, terrifying many residents. The Smithsonian collaborator Lucien M. Turner (1848–1909) related his experience while sitting in Robert Ridgway's office:

I was sitting in the south tower of the Smithsonian building, with my chair tilted back and my heels resting on the table, certainly an excellent position to enable me to detect the least tremor. I recognized the cause, and looked at my watch. An old gas fixture, shaped like an inverted T suspended from the ceiling and not more than two feet from my head, served admirably as a seismometer. Its height from the floor is six feet six inches and sixty-six feet six inches from the surface of the ground. The disturbance was so great as to cause the fixture to swing five inches.[81]

Just under one hundred years after Robert Ridgway first occupied the fifth-floor South Tower room, the Smithsonian's Office of Symposia and Seminars, headed by Wilton Dillon, was established there. For more than two decades, Dillon organized the Smithsonian's symposia, playing host to senators, university presidents, foreign dignitaries, Native American tribal leaders, school groups, and other notables. Dillon recounted that the setting, with its eclectic mix of antiques and twentieth-century furnishings, "excited people's poetry" and became the Smithsonian's intellectual and "cultural crossroads of the world."[82]

In 1978 Dillon convened a luncheon meeting with the distinguished anthropologist Margaret Mead (1901–78) to discuss her concerns about global environmental issues and how scholars and activists could work together. Mead and E. Richard Sorenson, the founding director of the National Anthropological Film Center, had done independent fieldwork in Papua New Guinea. Also in attendance was Nuala O'Donnell Pell, an environmentalist and the wife of Senator Claiborne Pell of Rhode Island; Alexander Crary of the National Endowment for the Humanities; Helen Garland, who worked with Margaret Mead at the United Nations in establishing Earth Day; Wilton Dillon; and Carla Borden, a staff member. That same year Mead served as chairman of Kin and Communities: The Peopling of America, Dillon's symposium on exploring family history.

Describing his fifth-floor South Tower office, Dillon mused: "Visitors to the tower, famous or otherwise, all seem struck by the magic of emerging from a shadowy spiral [staircase] to encounter a blaze of sunlight pouring in from high windows on three sides of a room hoary with Smithsonian history."[83] So it was when the American actress Elizabeth Taylor (1932–2011) visited Dillon to discuss her participation in an upcoming symposium. Her first words on entering the office were, "[W]hy this is a stage set!" Dillon recounted that her eyes then caught sight of the portrait of Kate Hyde Scully Bowman by Howard Chandler Christy (1872–1952),[84] which hung for many years in his office:

"Who is this darling woman?" Elizabeth asked as her own eyes locked into a gaze from Kate, who managed to see everything going on in the room at the same time. I fell in love with her at first sight, I confessed, explaining that the frame was lower on the wall than usual pictures because I wanted to look at her eye level while seated at my desk and always on the phone. "I don't blame you a bit," replied the appreciative Elizabeth, still mesmerized by Kate's eyes which were almost identical to hers. It was difficult for me to avoid thinking about how Christy might paint Elizabeth Taylor as another manifestation of sensuality and respectability.[85]

Up past the fifth floor, the roof of the South Tower became an aviary during the hot summer of 1980 as part of the Peregrine Fund, a program begun in 1970 at Cornell University to reestablish a wild-breeding population of peregrine falcons on the East Coast. On the roof a wooden castlelike birdhouse, complete with crenellations matching those of the tower, was built as a home for six young falcons, three males and three

Portrait of Kate Hyde Scully Bowman, by Howard Chandler Christy. Oil on canvas, ca. 1928.

females. The sixth floor was again put into service as a dormitory room for two Cornell students who handfed the young birds until they were mature enough to fly off on their own and cruise for food, snaring pigeons and starlings "on the wing."[86]

OWLS IN THE TOWERS

Owls frequently entered unused rooms in the upper floors of the towers through gaps above windows or other convenient openings. The earliest observations of such owls were recorded in 1861 and again in 1865.[87] By 1913 owl sightings in the towers were common and even encouraged by Smithsonian scientists as a means of repelling the hordes of pesky starlings that plagued the Mall.[88] The owls not only attacked and devoured their intended prey, they also swooped down on the heads of night watchmen, who petitioned Secretary Alexander Wetmore (1945–52), an ornithologist who served from 1945 to 1952, to "shut them out" of the towers. Unmoved, his response was that "our guards must remain dauntless to any and all attacks!"[89]

In 1947 Wetmore noted that three young barn owls had been discovered in one of the top floors of the lower North Tower, attracting the attention of local birders as well as Smithsonian staff.[90] Louis J. Halle Jr. (1910–98)—international scholar, State Department officer, naturalist, and author—paid a visit to the owls on September 4, 1947. That same year Halle published *Spring in Washington*, a poetical collection of philosophical observations of migratory birds, wildflowers, sunrises, sunsets, and clouds of Washington's spring that had begun as a journal in 1945.[91]

After Wetmore retired as secretary, owl sightings in the towers abated. Then in 1974 Secretary Ripley, also an ornithologist, reintroduced a pair he named Athena and Alex, after Wetmore, to the small tower attached to the West Wing (called the "single

Top left: Young peregrine falcons in their roost on the South Tower roof. Photograph by Richard Hofmeister, 1980. Top right: Larry Morrisette, a Cornell University student, holding one of six peregrine falcons on the roof of the South Tower, 1980. Photograph by Richard Hofmeister, 1980.

Right: Louis J. Halle with owls in the lower North Tower, 1947. Bottom left: The owls named Increase and Diffusion in the West Tower, ca. 1977. Bottom right: Smithsonian staff member Amy Ballard on her way to feed the owls in the West Tower, 1977.

UNSAVORY CREATURES

In 1881 a spiral staircase was constructed in the small tower attached to the northwest corner of the Main Building to give access to the building's basement, where specimens in alcohol were stored by scientists working in the balcony laboratories of the Lower Main Hall. As related by Mary Jane Rathbun (1860–1943), who joined the marine invertebrates staff in 1886: "Many of the alcoholic specimens were arranged in the dark cellar. The door was made with slats widely separated. I soon learned to make a loud noise at the door, else the rats would jump out upon me."[92] Retrieving the division's specimens from the storeroom, the diminutive Rathbun, at four feet, six inches tall, had to maneuver the narrow spiral staircase up three levels to the balcony, all the while balancing large alcohol-filled glass specimen jars.

Mary Jane Rathbun at work in 1930 (then at the Natural History Museum).

Campanile" in Renwick's specifications). The curator of the Birds Unit of the National Zoo, Guy A. Greenwell, laid out plans for the "S.I. Barn Owl Re-Establishment Research Project." From "preparation of the loft" ("loft floor must *not* be cleaned") to "care of owls" ("food will be in picnic type cooler delivered by SI mail truck"), every detail was specified. If one of the owls died, the corpse was to be sent to the zoo's Birds Unit for autopsy.[93] The pair produced seven owlets, but eventually all "flew the coop," never to return.[94]

A second try in spring 1977 enlisted a corps of volunteers to care for new avian residents of the tower, this time named Increase and Diffusion. Donning overalls, helmets, and face masks, the volunteers climbed to the top floor of the tower on shaky wooden ladders a hundred feet above ground every Tuesday, Thursday, and Saturday to leave either four to six rats or six to ten mice (freshly killed) for the sequestered owls to eat.[95] A log book kept throughout the summer revealed that by September, the second brood, like the first, had flown away: "Fresh 'food' and water left. Based upon the disposition of the remains (fur and bones), I remain convinced that we are only feeding the bugs, of which there is a plentiful supply. No sign of recent occupancy by the owls."[96] The owls never returned, and the small tower remains unoccupied today, effectively shut off by tightly fitting windows.

THE NORTH TOWERS

The multiple levels of the two central North Towers, the tallest of the building's nine towers, served a variety of functions: as offices, laboratories, dormitories, an artist's studio, a watchman's room, a janitor's closet, and even a crypt for the Institution's benefactor. When completed, the taller of the two towers was the highest structure in this part of Washington. From its top one could see all the way across the Potomac River to Alexandria, Virginia.

Its roof as well as the lower tower's upper rooms were perfect observation decks during the Civil War. When the Southern Army advanced close to the city in 1864, Mary Henry, the Secretary's oldest daughter, climbed to the top of the lower tower to

Opposite: The North Towers, ca. 1870. Below: Repairing the finial on the Northwest Tower, 1923.

observe the Union troops cross over Long Bridge into Alexandria. After watching for some time, she said: "[T]he sun is sinking lower now and shedding its last beams over a scene of such quiet beauty that it seems to mock our excitement. The shadows of the towers stretch longer and longer over the green pasture below us, we look towards the distant Capitol and White House and wonder if they can be in danger."[97]

The view from the tall North Tower, looking southwest, with Long Bridge in the distance. Photograph by Titian Ramsay Peale, 1863.

THE WEATHERVANE

In addition to its commanding view of the entire city, the tall North Tower roof provided an excellent place to mount an anemometer, a device like a weathervane that has long been one of the building's distinctive features. Part of Joseph Henry's project of predicting weather changes by collecting meteorological observations, it recorded the direction and time of changes in the wind.[98] Henry mounted the first anemometer low, directly on the tower's roof, in 1858. Measuring about twenty feet tall, it was clearly visible above the parapet wall from the ground.

The anemometer was connected to a recording device in the meteorological office on the tower's second floor. Records were maintained by William Quereau Force (1820–80) in offices on the second floor.[99] Force lived in the building and was on hand to take nighttime readings of the anemometer, which on one occasion caused the concern of a nearby resident that the Smithsonian tower was being used to signal the Confederate Army. The man urgently sought an audience with President Abraham Lincoln, who was at the time meeting with Secretary Henry. The visitor

announced that for several evenings past he had observed a light exhibited on the highest of the Smithsonian towers, for a few minutes about nine o'clock, with mysterious movements, which he felt satisfied were designed as signals to the rebels encamped on Munson's Hill in Virginia. Having gravely listened to this information with raised eyebrows, but a subdued twinkle of the eye, the

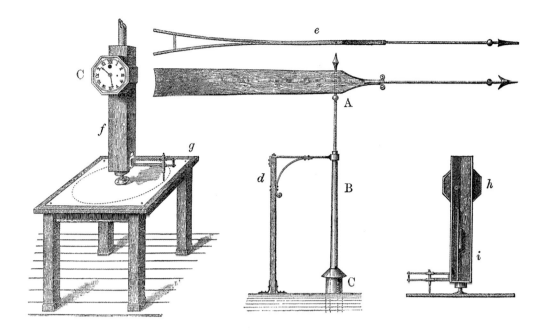

Right: Drawing of the anemometer, from the *Annual Report for 1860*. Below: Eric Gaardsmoe remounting the weathervane on the tall North Tower's flagpole, 1981.

President turned to his companion, saying "What do you think of that, Professor Henry?" Rising with a smile, the person addressed replied, that from the time mentioned, he presumed the mysterious light shone from the lantern of a watchman who was required at nine o'clock each evening to observe and record the indications of the meteorological instruments placed on the tower.[100]

The story as related by Carl Sandburg (1878–1967) in his biography of Lincoln differed considerably:

One dark night Lincoln with four other men climbed up the tower of the Smithsonian Institution. Toward hills encircling Washington they flashed signals. Next day an army officer marched into Lincoln's office a prisoner, Professor Joseph Henry, secretary and director of the Smithsonian Institution, the most eminent man of learning in the employ of the U.S. Government. "Mr. President," said the officer, "I told you a month ago Professor Henry is a rebel. Last night at midnight he flashed red lights from the top of his building, signaling to the Secesh. I saw them myself." Lincoln turned. "Now you're caught! What have you to say, Professor Henry, why sentence of death should not immediately be pronounced upon you?" Then, turning to the army officer, Lincoln explained that on the previous evening he and others had accompanied Henry to the Smithsonian tower and experimented with new army signals. The officer thereupon released from his custody a physicist of international repute.[101]

As the 1865 fire destroyed the upper parts of the Castle, the Secretary's daughter Mary noted: "Farther on the highest tower still stood mantled with flames while above it the anemometer turned, steadily recording the wind which fanned into greater fury the fires beneath. Faithful in its dumb creation."[102] Destroyed in the fire, the tower was without an anemometer until 1884, when a weathervane was mounted to a new fifty-foot flagpole.[103]

Constant exposure to harsh weather conditions and lightning strikes required periodic maintenance of both the flagpole and the weathervane; twice, in 1929 and 1947, the wooden flagpole was completely destroyed. The weathervane's absences did not go unnoticed by nearby residents and merchants: "Since the destruction of the former pole this office has received numerous inquiries as to what happened to the flagpole on the 'old building' and 'when are you going to put back the flagpole on the Smithsonian.' Most of these persons indicated they made a daily practice of looking at the weather vane in order to judge what the weather was going to be."[104] The present forty-five-foot-tall iron flagpole was erected on the roof in 1948, with the restored 1884 weathervane mounted on top.[105] By 1981, with the wooden parts of the weathervane again in need of attention, it was removed by one of the Smithsonian's intrepid rigging crew, Eric Gaardsmoe, and restored in the Institution's craft shop in the Natural History Museum.

BOARDERS AND THEIR SUCCESSORS

William Q. Force was only one of the many young men who lived in the North Towers. Throughout the 1850s and early 1860s, the number of people residing there increased to the point that Joseph Henry threatened to stop the practice entirely in 1863, stating: "I have created quite a stir in the Institution by requesting all who have slept in the building except Mr. Meek and DeBeust to find lodgings elsewhere. . . . [I]ndeed I have concluded that making the Smithsonian Building a caravansary has been carried a little too far. I have ordered the gas to be stopped off at the end of the present month. I wish to impress some of the gentlemen with the fact that sunlight is cheaper than gaslight and answers all the purposes equally."[106]

The Secretary's mandate, if it was ever carried out, was short lived, for in 1865 there were still at least seven boarders in the building.[107] Among the young scientists still in residence were the Megatherium Club members Robert Kennicott and William Stimpson. While classifying material he had collected on the North Pacific Exploring Expedition (1853–56), Stimpson lived on the second floor of the Campanile, the tower at the Main Building's northeast corner.[108]

During the 1865 fire, firemen broke into his room to gain access to the Apparatus Room on the building's upper floor. In his desk diary, Secretary Henry wrote:

The firemen on the night of the accident behaved badly. They broke open a room in the NE tower [the Campanile] in which the effects of Mr. Stimpson were stowned [sic], plundered his chest drawers and made free use of a quantity of whiskey which had been kept for preserving specimens. They were however repaid for the use of this by the effect of the sulphate of copper which had been dissolved in it. Several of them became deadly sick and would have died had they not vomited freely.[109]

The fire destroyed most of the dormitory rooms in the North Towers, effectively accomplishing what Henry could not, if only temporarily. When restoration of the towers was completed late in 1867, most of the rooms were designated for office or storage use. It is not clear whether any were immediately assigned as sleeping quarters. However, by 1872, at least five rooms were again used as dormitories, and by 1878 no fewer than seven naturalists and scientists were living in the building. [110]

Above the porte cochère that marks the Castle's north entrance, a large circular window dominates the space between the two North Towers and floods the large room behind it with ample northern light, making it a perfect artist's studio. Although the

Robert Kennicott and Henry Ulke (standing, left to right), with William Stimpson and Henry Bryant (seated, left to right).

The North Towers and the prominent circular window above the porte cochère, ca. 1872.

room had been Joseph Henry's office at the time of the 1865 fire, when the towers were rebuilt he chose not to return there. The room later served for about six months in 1872 as a studio for the celebrated painter George Catlin while his sketches of American Indian life were on exhibit in the Upper Main Hall.[111]

Late in the summer of that year, Catlin fell ill and was attended to for several months by Henry Horan, Horan's young nephew, and Secretary Henry's personal servants.[112] A Washington reporter related a story told to him by Horan's nephew fifty years after his encounter with Catlin:

A little boy brought him his meals in the high tower and attended to his simple wants. The old artist had no money to pay the little boy. Instead every now and then he gave him a picture. The child had no use for the pictures. He accepted them rather than hurt the old gentleman's feelings. As soon as he was out of sight, down the winding stairs of the tower, he would leave them and month after month they accumulated. By and by the old man, very sick and discouraged, left the brick tower and went away to live with relatives. The boy never saw him again.[113]

(This is all the family I have)

Henry recounted Catlin's last months: "Unfortunately, in passing between the Institution and his boarding place which were separated by the distance of more than a mile, he exposed himself to the heat of the unusually warm summer, and was seized with a malady which terminated his eventful life on the 23rd of December, 1872."

The paleontologist Fielding Bradford Meek (1817–76) resided in the Castle from 1858 until his death in 1876, almost as long as Joseph Henry. Like many of the Institution's first scientists, Meek was given lodging in the building in lieu of pay.[114] At the time of the 1865 fire, he occupied a pitifully small room beneath the stairs leading up to the balcony in the lecture hall.[115] After the fire, he moved to one of six dormitory rooms in the towers, possibly the one called the "Tin Room" on the fifth floor of the lower North Tower.[116] Meek, an accomplished artist who at one time supported himself as a portrait painter, illustrated many of his own scientific reports.[117]

He had no family at the time of his death, as evidenced by the finely drawn picture of his cat, plaintively inscribed, "This is all the family I have." Henry wrote that in his last years, "Meek gradually lost his hearing, and could only be communicated with by means of writing. He gradually withdrew from social intercourse, and devoted his life exclusively to the prosecution of science. He was in correspondence with the principal investigators of the world and although scarcely known in this city his name was familiar to the cultivators of geology everywhere."[118]

By 1881 only one room in the lower North Tower was designated as a dormitory, and the practice of lodging scientists in the building ceased completely by 1884. In the taller North Tower, space above the seventh floor was an empty cavern, with only a wooden ladder to access the roof, until 1929. That year Secretary Charles G. Abbot established the Division of Radiation and Organisms to study the effects of radiation on plant life.

Above: The Division of Radiation and Organisms office in the higher North Tower, December 1929. Below: Raising the roof onto the lower North Tower. Photograph by Al Robinson, 1970.

The laboratories of the new division were located in the basement of the West Wing and the West Range, while five new floors were inserted into the tall tower for the division's office, creating a total of twelve levels.[119]

Abbot vividly remembered climbing the wooden ladder to the roof one day in 1903, carrying a long telescope to witness the aborted flight over the Potomac of the "Aero-drome," Secretary Samuel P. Langley's flying machine.[120] "I saw the front wings lift and the rear wings flop. It turned a somersault and crashed into the river."[121]

As part of the tower renovation, Abbot ordered the installation of a new electric elevator manufactured by the A. B. See Elevator Company.[122] Only three-foot-square inside, the elevator was prone to breaking down—forcing tower occupants to descend the emergency exit (an iron ladder) and to open trap doors at each level. In 1937 his coworker Florence Meier Chase fell through an open trap door on the eleventh floor to the office below. She broke her back, but the Secretary quipped that it was not as bad as it sounded: she ended up marrying the physician who "fixed her up."[123] When Abbot retired in 1944, he chose the eleventh-floor room as his emeritus office and continued to occupy it until 1968, when he had to relocate because of the major building renovations then under way.

TOPPING OFF THE TOWERS

The peaked roof of the lower North Tower, destroyed in the fire of 1865, was not rebuilt afterward but was instead replaced by a flat roof. While planning for the major building renovation during the mid-1960s, Secretary Ripley called for the restoration of the tower roof to its original appearance.[124] In May 1970 a new thirty-two-foot-high spire was hoisted to the top of the tower—ending a 105-year-long architectural disfigurement.[125]

Although James Renwick designed the tall North Tower with four clock faces carved into the stone and the Regents approved a resolution authorizing the Secretary to purchase a clock and a bell for the tower in 1851, neither was installed at the time. The

Opposite: Lifting the bell up to the roof of the higher North Tower. Photograph by Richard Strauss, August 10, 1996. Top: Casting the Smithsonian bell for the tall North Tower. Photograph by David Shayt, 1995. Above: The porte cochère, looking out to the Smithsonian Park in the late nineteenth century.

planning committee for the 1960s building renovation called for the installation of a clock on the tall North Tower and bells to ring out the hour, stating that "the sweet tones of these bells would have a soothing effect upon the foreign scholars in residence behind the brownstone walls."[126] A clock was installed in July 1966,[127] but still no bell rang out. The Smithsonian's 150th anniversary year presented an opportunity to finally fulfill both proposals.

An 821-pound bronze bell was commissioned from the Whitechapel Bell Foundry of London, with funds donated by the A. T. Cross Company, which shares the Smithsonian's year of origin, 1846. The foundry, in continuous operation since 1420, also cast Big Ben, the Liberty Bell, and several other working bells in Washington, D.C., including those at the Old Post Office and the Washington National Cathedral. Casting took place on September 21, 1995, and was witnessed by several Smithsonian officials. On an otherwise gloomy London day, a beam of sunlight broke through the foundry's clerestory window, touching down on the molten metal at the precise moment it was poured into the mold. Bearing an inscription proclaiming the Smithsonian's mission, "for the increase and diffusion of knowledge," the bell on August 10, 1996, was lifted into its position on the roof of the tower, where it rang out its B-flat tones for the first time during the Smithsonian's birthday celebration.

THE NORTH ENTRANCE

Visitors could enter the Castle by any of three doors in the North Towers. A porte cochère (carriage porch) announced the main entrance, while other doors brought visitors in from the east and the west. A prominent architectural feature on the Castle's north facade, the porte cochère provided protection from inclement weather for visitors arriving originally in horse-drawn carriages.[128] Its square shape, projecting away from the building, its bold battlements, and its tall arched openings framed with Romanesque-style cable (ropework) moldings echoed somewhat the details of the massive South Tower. But unlike the two North Towers themselves—with their strikingly different forms recalling religious structures—the covered porch proclaimed that this edifice was not a church. It offered shelter more typical of domestic architecture, rather than the ecclesiastical visions conjured up by the towers on either side.

AT THE PORTE COCHÈRE

In 1888 a different type of "carriage" arrived at the porte cochère. Promoting his newly patented steam tricycle,[129] the inventor Lucius D. Copeland visited the Castle and met with the vehicle's builder and promoter, Sandford Northrop, and the Smithsonian curator of transportation and engineering, Edwin H. Hawley.[130] Steam to propel the cycle was generated by a boiler fueled by a pair of kerosene lamps, a set of foot pedals at the ready in case of engine failure. Copeland's invention was immediately met with skepticism in the press: "[T]here is one feature of it that strikes us as a trifle inconvenient, to say the

least. We refer to the boiler being placed directly beneath the rider's seat, where in case of explosion it would probably do him considerable damage," suggested the *Boston Daily Globe*.[131] Copeland's steam tricycle never caught on with the public and not long after it was manufactured in limited quantities, it ceased to exist.[132]

THE SMITHSON CRYPT

A grand central vestibule at the Castle's north entrance was flanked on either side by two small but lofty rooms, one for the janitor and the other for the librarian.[133] All three rooms on the first floor of the North Towers terminated in groin-vaulted ceilings rising twenty-five feet high. To provide additional offices in the towers after the fire of 1865, these rooms were reconstructed at half their original height; they then served as offices for the building superintendent and the watchman throughout the rest of the nineteenth century.

While James Smithson's coffin was on public view in the Regents' Room, a year-long endeavor to find a fitting final resting place for his remains began on a modest scale in

Above: The inventor Lucius D. Copeland at the controls of his steam tricycle in front of the porte cochère, ca. 1888. Also pictured are the photographer Frances Benjamin Johnston (the passenger), with the vehicle's builder, Sandford Northrop (at left, with cane) and the Smithsonian curator of transportation and engineering, Edwin H. Hawley (at right, with cane). Opposite, top: One of Totten and Rogers's proposals for a Smithson memorial, 1904. Opposite, center: One of Henry Bacon's proposals for a Smithson memorial, 1904. Opposite, bottom: A model for the seated statue of James Smithson, by Gutzon Borglum, 1904.

February 1904 and eventually selected the left entrance room. Assistant Secretary Richard Rathbun (1852–1918) at first had suggested two suitable sites on the grounds for a simple tomb. However, the scope of the project broadened considerably when the Board of Regents formally recommended that Congress provide funds for a grand Smithson memorial.[134] Secretary Langley was directed to contact renowned artists to prepare monument designs, but he was not alone in his search; individual Regents had also begun to solicit designs from artists and architects. Proposals were received, reviewed, and dismissed one by one throughout 1904. As funding became scarce, the designs were scaled down accordingly.

Of the designers contacted, some were only locally known, while others were nationally prominent. Those approached included Augustus Saint-Gaudens (1848–1907), the most noted American sculptor of the day; his brother Louis Saint-Gaudens (1854–1913); and Gutzon Borglum (1867–1941). Architects included the Washington, D.C., firm Totten & Rogers; the New York architect Henry Bacon (1866–1924), designer of the Lincoln Memorial; and Hornblower & Marshall, the Washington firm employed at the time by the Smithsonian to plan the Natural History Museum.

Totten & Rogers submitted two designs of monumental proportions. The first no doubt drew its inspiration from both the ancient Greek Mausoleum at Halicarnasus and Grant's Tomb in New York City, built in 1897. The architects' second design was much less detailed, making it harder to discern a possible source of inspiration; however, both drawings depicted structures that, if built, would dwarf the Lincoln Memorial. Henry Bacon's scaled-down proposals were both garden structures—one a pergola and the other an excedra (a semicircular stone bench). Each was to be erected over an underground tomb, with sculptural elements provided by Louis Saint-Gaudens.

At Alexander Graham Bell's request, the emerging New York artist Gutzon Borglum, later the sculptor of Mount Rushmore, submitted two proposals: a sculptural treatment of James Smithson and a mausoleum to replace the just-completed Children's Room (perhaps Borglum was unaware that it was Langley's pet project). Borglum depicted Smithson contemplating a mineral, presumably Smithsonite, which had been posthumously named for him in 1832. Once completed, the bronze sculpture was to sit on a five-foot-tall marble base positioned above an underground tomb. Borglum's estimated cost of $10,000 was the lowest of the estimates then received, but it was still more than the Smithsonian was able to spend.[135]

The limited funding available for the memorial persuaded Secretary Langley instead to retrieve the original sarcophagus-shaped grave marker that had been erected over Smithson's Italian grave in 1829 and the memorial plaque that the Smithsonian installed at the grave site in the late nineteenth century. Designs for a simple, dignified room to the left of the north entrance were prepared by Hornblower & Marshall. Featuring three nonecclesiastical stained-glass windows, a plaster ceiling with a deep cove molding, and a floor made of dark Tennessee marble, the room was sealed off by a heavy iron gate fashioned from pieces of the fence that had surrounded the Italian grave site. The room, whose mood was somber and contemplative, was further enhanced

for the dedication ceremony by two large palm and laurel-wreath arrangements flanking the Italian marble monument. The palm, symbol of eternal peace, and the laurel wreath, emblematic of glory, made these appropriate adornments for the neoclassical tomb.

Entombment took place on March 6, 1905, in a small ceremony following the Regents' meeting. Smithson's casket was carried downstairs from the Regents' Room in the presence of the Regents and was sealed in a vault specially built at floor level. The austere Mortuary Chapel, as it was then called, was intended to be a temporary resting place until funds for a "proper memorial" could be provided by Congress.

To make the room more welcoming to visitors, significant changes to Hornblower & Marshall's design were carried out in 1973. The iron gate was removed to allow people into the room for the first time, the plaster ceiling and cove molding were taken down to reveal the original nineteenth-century vaulted ceiling, and the marble plaque was moved to the opposite side of the room. A modern exhibit case was mounted to the wall to display the Smithsonian mace, a copy of Smithson's will, a portrait of Smithson as a student at Pembroke College, and several other related items.[136]

Believing that Smithson's coffin might hold documents or manuscripts that would shed some light on the Institution's somewhat mysterious donor, James M. Goode, curator of the Smithsonian Building, decided to exhume the remains. On October 3, 1973, shielded behind heavy screens to maintain privacy, the 1904 vintage coffin was removed from the base of the Italian grave marker and opened, revealing an inner metal box soldered shut. Goode recounted the event:

At 10:45 A.M. the workmen melted the solder and the lid to the copper box was removed. . . . The blow torches quickly melted the solder but in doing so set the silk lining (then in a dilapidated condition) on fire. The foreman sent the laborers into the hall to fill their mouths with water so as to extinguish the small fire as quickly as possible without disturbing the skeleton. Unfortunately, no manuscripts or documents of any kind were found within the copper box.[137]

Top: James Smithson's Italian grave site, May 1897. Above: Exhumation of Smithson's remains, with the Smithsonian officials Robert Brooks, Charles Blitzer, and Paul Perrot (left to right) peering over the coffin. Photograph by Richard Farrar, 1973.

What was discovered was that the skeleton was in a state of disarray amid dirt, nails, and fragments of rotted wood and silk.

The coffin was then unceremoniously draped in a tablecloth from the Commons dining room and carried across the Mall to the Natural History Museum's Department of Anthropology laboratory. There Smithson's remains were examined by Lawrence J. Angel (1915–86), curator of the department and the nation's leading forensic authority. After the bones were cleaned, x-rayed, and photographed, a complete examination was conducted. The report detailed that Smithson had a "low head," was slightly over five feet, six inches tall, had bad teeth, perhaps smoked a pipe (evident from the way one tooth was worn down), and had "nice young looking joints" (no arthritis).[179]

More than one hundred years have passed since James Smithson's remains were delivered to the Institution bearing his name, in a country he never visited in life, to be interred in this "temporary" resting place. As the Smithsonian has literally grown up around him—far exceeding anything he could ever have envisioned—it has become in itself the most splendid and fitting Smithson memorial.

James Smithson's crypt to the left of the north entrance. Photograph by Eric Long, 2011.

THE GROUNDS

Opposite: The South Yard's Enid A. Haupt Garden, with the Downing Urn at left. Photograph by Eric Long, 2010. Above: Andrew Jackson Downing, the noted horticulturist hired in 1851 to landscape the Mall. Below: The Smithsonian Building from the southwest, its towers rising above the fledgling tree-lined park, with the U.S. Capitol still under construction in the distance. Photograph by Mathew Brady, ca. 1862–63.

The 1846 act establishing the Smithsonian Institution authorized the Regents to select a suitable site, specifying that government-owned land between the Patent Office and Seventh Street be chosen with the consent of the president, the secretaries of state, the treasury, war, and the navy; and the commissioner of the Patent Office. The act contained this proviso: "but, if the persons last named shall not consent, then such location may be made upon any other of the public grounds within the city of Washington, belonging to the United States, which said regents may select."[1] With this authority, the Regents instead selected a site on the Mall that extended from Seventh Street, N.W., to the Potomac River and totaled more than one hundred acres.[2] This site was later reduced to nineteen acres.[3]

Early on, the site's northern portion in front of the building was considered part of the Mall, while the quadrant to the south was thought of as the building's back yard. Landscaping of the Smithsonian's grounds turned what had been an open field into a serene wooded park. Soon, however, as space in the building became more and more scarce, the Smithsonian began constructing small buildings for laboratories, workrooms, and storage on the south. By the late nineteenth and early twentieth centuries, this area abutting a bustling thoroughfare (now Independence Avenue) was then called the South Yard and resembled a small village. Added to this collection of wooden structures were rockets and spacecraft put on exhibit outdoors until a new museum could be constructed to house them properly. Although a partial clearing of the South Yard allowed for the planting of a Victorian Garden to complement the Castle's architecture, a large parking lot was allowed to remain.

With the construction of a new underground museum complex filling the entire space, topped with a new garden at turns lush and manicured, peace and tranquility finally returned to the South Yard during the late twentieth century.

LAYING THE CORNERSTONE

May 1, 1847, was declared a holiday and "a day of public rejoicing" for the laying of the Smithsonian's cornerstone. A grand procession, reported to have been a mile long, formed at City Hall (Fifth and D Streets, N.W.) and proceeded to the White House and then onto the Smithsonian grounds. Masonic ceremonies followed on a specially built grandstand "beautifully arched with festoons and wreaths of flowers and evergreens.⁴ Many articles commemorating the day were put into a leaden casket inside the cornerstone's cavity; an engraved metal plate, properly inscribed, was placed beneath the stone.⁵ After a prayer by the grand chaplain of the Grand Lodge of Maryland came the symbolic pouring of corn, wine, and oil on the stone by the grand master of the District of Columbia, Benjamin Brown French. To conclude the Masonic ceremony, three raps were delivered to the stone with the same gavel that George Washington had used for the laying of the cornerstone of the U.S. Capitol in 1793.⁶ Six to seven thousand people were reported in attendance.⁷

Several attempts to locate the cornerstone have been made over the years, but its exact location on the building remains a mystery. The stone's face was not engraved, and the account of the ceremony did not specify its location. It is assumed to be somewhere in the East Wing, as that was the first section of the building to be built. Although it is now Masonic custom to locate the cornerstone at a building's northeast corner, the cornerstone of the Capitol, also laid with a Masonic ceremony, was placed at the building's southeast corner. This may also have been the case with the Castle's stone.⁸ As the account of the Smithsonian's ceremony stated: "The military was then formed in line on the south side of the site and the President, heads of departments, diplomatic corps, Regents, mayor and corporation of Washington &c., passed in front, receiving their salute, and repaired to an elevated platform erected for the occasion near the cornerstone." Newspaper stories about the Smithsonian's losing its own cornerstone have provided a snicker or two in the press at the expense of the Institution—the "collector and cataloguer of all things."⁹

An unproductive search in 1975 for the Castle cornerstone, thought to be in the East Wing.

DOWNING'S "PLEASURE GROUNDS"

The site selected for the Smithsonian Building in 1847 extended east to west from Ninth Street to Twelfth Street, N.W., and from south to north from B Street (Independence Avenue) 750 feet to the center of the Mall. The Board of Regents expended Smithsonian funds for fencing and care of the grounds until 1851, when President Millard Fillmore hired the widely esteemed horticulturist Andrew Jackson Downing (1815–52), the author of several popular books on landscaping and rural architecture, to design and execute a master plan for the improvement of the Mall. Downing's plan was literally to create a tree museum: "a collection of all the trees that will grow in the climate of Washington, and, by having these trees plainly labeled with their popular and scientific names, to form a public museum of living trees and shrubs where every person visiting Washington could become familiar with the habits and growth of all the hardy trees."¹⁰

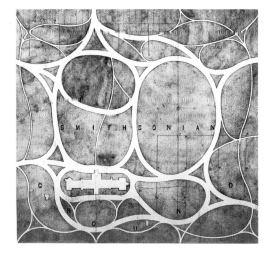

Downing named the area immediately surrounding the Castle the "Smithsonian Pleasure Grounds."[11] His plan comported perfectly with the views of Smithsonian Secretary Joseph Henry, who was enthusiastic about the entire proposal:

I allude to the improvement of the grounds of the city on a general plan under the direction of a gentleman of taste and science; I refer to Mr. Downing whose plans have been adopted and are now in the process of being carried out. From the capitol to the Potomac the whole space is to be laid out in a park with several miles of carriage roads and walks. The fields between 7th street and 12th streets have been thrown into one—traversed by under drains and are now adorned with trees of considerable size that have been brought from a distance by Mr. Downing.[12]

Without surrendering the right to use the grounds appropriated to the Institution, Henry directed the removal of the fence separating the Smithsonian from the rest of the Mall to the north, but he retained the fence to the south along B Street. To facilitate the approach to the Smithsonian from Pennsylvania Avenue, the city appropriated funds for the construction of an iron foot bridge across the canal at Tenth Street, and Downing laid a gravel walk from the bridge to the building's front door. Henry believed that when completed the Mall would be "a beautiful park adorned with evergreen and other ornamental trees, and traversed with carriage drives and gravel walks. In the midst of this variegated landscape the Smithsonian building will occupy a prominent position, and with its picturesque architecture will produce a harmonious effect."[13]

Downing was at the height of his career when he was killed in a senseless accident involving a race between two riverboat steamers on the Hudson River on July 28, 1852. Only thirty-seven years old, he had just begun to carry out his grand plan for the Mall. The "Smithsonian Pleasure Grounds" was the only one of the six major sections of the plan to be completed.

By 1867 Henry was concerned that the Smithsonian grounds were becoming thick with wild undergrowth, endangering many of the valuable trees originally planted by Downing.[14] Access to the building was often made difficult by the deplorable condition of the gravel paths crossing the Mall, which turned to mud during inclement weather. Henry remedied that condition by having boards laid out on the paths that led to the Castle from the canal at Tenth Street.

Stretching from the Potomac River to the foot of Capitol Hill, the canal further isolated the building from downtown Washington and proved to be a persistent problem. The fact that by 1868 it was no more than an open sewer prompted Henry to complain to the Board of Regents that visitors to the Institution were

shocked and their olfactory nerves outraged, in approaching the building from the city, by having to cross that most disgusting object known as the 'canal,' though for years it has done no service of any value in that capacity. It is, in fact, a Stygian pool, from which are constantly ascending in bubbles, as from a caldron, mephitic vapors. That part of it which bounds the Smithsonian grounds and those of the Agricultural Department, on the north, consists of a basin 150 feet wide, extending from Seventh Street to Fourteenth street. Into this is poured most of the excrementitious matter of the city, which is suffered to decompose into offensive gases, and exposes with each ebb of the tide a mass of the most offensive matter conceivable.[15]

Finally, after Henry was called to testify before Congress against the canal in April 1872, the offensive ditch was filled in and paved over later in the year, becoming what is now Constitution Avenue.[16]

COMMEMORATIVE SCULPTURE

Placed throughout the grounds near the Castle are sculptural works that commemorate key people in the Institution's history. The first of these, a classical urn dedicated to Andrew Jackson Downing, was erected in 1856 by the American Pomological Society, of which Downing was a member. After his untimely death, the designer was eulogized as one who had "done more than any man to introduce ideas of taste and beauty, and adaptation into suburban and rustic gardening."[17] Designed by the architect and Downing collaborator Calvert Vaux (1824–95) and carved from Italian marble by the sculptor Robert Launitz (1806–70), the urn was described in the 1857 guidebook as "ornamented with rich arabesque; acanthus leaves surround the lower parts. The handles rest on the heads of satyrs, (the tutelary gods of groves and woods)." The base was inscribed on all four sides; however, the most apt inscription, given its location, was on the southern face, which read in part: "Build halls where knowledge shall be freely diffused among men and not shut up within the narrow walls of narrower institutions."[18] The Downing Urn has been relocated along the Mall many times since it was first erected, and it now resides directly behind the Castle in the Enid A. Haupt Garden.

The bronze statue of Secretary Joseph Henry by William Wetmore Story (1818–95) today looms larger than life on its pedestal in front of the Castle, appearing apropos and timeless; however, its location and orientation have twice been altered since its initial placement facing the Castle. One of Henry's conflicts as Secretary was the very building the statue originally faced. After failing repeatedly to halt construction of the Castle, which he deemed a "gross violation of the trust," Henry became resigned to it, but nevertheless it remained a source of displeasure to him throughout his long tenure.

The unveiling ceremony on April 19, 1883, was a grand affair, with music composed by John Phillip Sousa performed by the U.S. Marine Corps Band before an audience of ten thousand people.[19] The statue's location, on a small triangle of grass formed by the intersection of three carriage paths, harmonized perfectly with the picturesque arrangement of Downing's design of the Mall. Its placement about 150 feet to the northwest of and facing the Castle's West Wing was thought appropriate, as the president of Yale University, Noah Porter, stated in his dedication oration: "[H]ere by day and night, in sunshine and in storm, our honored friend shall ever as in his lifetime keep watch and guard over the scene of his cares and labors, of his conflicts and triumphs."

When the Mall was reconfigured in 1934 to realize the 1901 McMillan Commission design—obliterating Downing's landscaping—the statue was moved to its present location, centered at the front of the Castle, but again facing toward the building. There for the next forty-two years it stood face-to-facade with the building Henry so

Below: The Downing Urn, erected in 1856 to honor Andrew Jackson Downing's plan for the Smithsonian grounds. Stereograph, ca. 1870. Bottom: Relocation of the Joseph Henry statue, after which it still faced the Castle, November 8, 1934. Opposite: The bronze Henry statue in front of the Castle, repositioned to look toward the other Smithsonian museums on the Mall. Photograph by Eric Long, 2010.

disdained. On May 24, 1965, Henry's likeness was rotated to face outward toward the Mall; Secretary S. Dillon Ripley had reasoned that it was high time for him to see the rest of the Smithsonian's ever-expanding museum complex.[20] If facing the building might seem incongruous, it is equally quizzical for the statue to look toward the range of Smithsonian museums along the Mall. From the time he accepted the position as Secretary, Henry was opposed to using Smithsonian funds to support a museum, saying that it was "of local interest and did not comport with the cosmopolitan intentions of the bequest."[21]

The stylized bronze figure portraying the second Smithsonian Secretary, Spencer F. Baird, standing with his hands folded behind his back, was commissioned by the Smithsonian in 1976 from the American sculptor and printmaker Leonard Baskin (1922–2000). The aim was to create a larger-than-life portrait commemorating Baird's achievements as a great naturalist, educator, and builder of institutions. Baird actively charted much of the direction and content of nineteenth-century science and scientific exploration. He was the guiding force behind developing museum collections and exhibits at the Smithsonian, while mentoring a generation of naturalists and developing the scientific method now known as the "Bairdian School." When the bronze was received in 1977 and dedicated on May 4, 1978, it was at the head of the Victorian Garden's parterre and faced the Castle's south entrance.[22] In 1994, several years after completion of the Haupt Garden in that space, it was placed at the west entrance to the Arts and Industries Building.[23]

An ornate stone niche projecting from the east side of the South Tower is presumed to have been intended for a statue of James Smithson; however, the niche remained

Opposite: The life-sized statue of Saint Dunstan, which was relocated in 1980 to the South Tower niche from Westminster Abbey. Photograph by Ken Rahaim, 2008. Above: The bronze of Secretary Spencer F. Baird, by Leonard Baskin, in its original position facing the Castle's south entrance, 1978. Right: The stonecarver Constantine Seferlis and the Castle curator James M. Goode, with the restored statue of Saint Dunstan, 1980.

unoccupied for more than 130 years. In 1977 Secretary Ripley inquired of his special assistant, Richard H. Howland, if there was any possibility of finding among the Smithsonian's collections a statue to fill the niche. "I am thinking," he said, "of something, of course, in the classic Italian tradition ranging from mourning figures to knights of old to Saints."[24]

During a visit to Westminster Abbey in 1979, Howland learned that several deteriorated late-nineteenth-century statues filling niches along the north facade were about to be replaced. Howland secured for the Smithsonian the donation of one of the statues, Saint Dunstan (910–88), archbishop of Canterbury. According to legend, Saint Dunstan

carries those tongs because of his blacksmith days and as a reminder of the time the Devil tried to tempt him by appearing before him as a beautiful maid. Unfortunately for Old Nick, his skirts rode up revealing cloven hoofs. Doughty Dunstan plucked his red-hot tongs from the forge, and with them seized the satanic nose. They say the devil flew off, howling, until he spotted the spa at Tunbridge Wells and plunged in. That's why its water is reddish and tastes of sulphur.[25]

The statue was in poor shape, but Ripley agreed to the donation. It was then shipped to the Institution, arriving in January 1980 after a two-month voyage. In July 1980 a contract to restore the statue was awarded to the master stonecarver Constantine Seferlis (1927–2005), formerly with the Washington National Cathedral. He quickly determined that the head, shoulders, feet, arms, and hands had to be completely recarved. After three months' work, the thousand-pound statue was lifted into the niche in November 1980.

THE SOUTH YARD

In 1853 a small cottagelike building was constructed to house instruments used to determine variations in the direction and intensity of terrestrial magnetism.[26] Located about 150 yards southeast of the South Tower, this wood-framed Magnetic Observatory was designed to correspond to the architecture of the Castle. It sat atop a 12-by-16-foot subterranean instrument room enclosed within two brick walls, one 9 inches and the other 24 inches thick; between them ran a two-foot-wide air passage that maintained a constant air temperature. Because the magnetic readings taken here were almost identical to observations recorded in Philadelphia and Toronto, all but one of the instruments were relocated to Key West, Florida, in 1860.[27] During the early 1870s, the cottage was home to the Institution's building superintedent, Henry Horan, and his mother.[28] It was torn down in 1879 to make way for the new National Museum (Arts and Industries Building).

In 1875 the South Yard gained the Laboratory of Natural History, which was constructed southwest of the Smithsonian Building for use by taxidermists preparing exhibits for the Philadelphia Centennial Exhibition. The original two-story brick building, measuring about 30 by 27½ feet, provided laboratory space for the taxidermists in the basement and on the first floor. A photography studio occupied the skylighted second floor; when the Smithsonian's photographers were moved to the Arts

Top: The small, cottagelike Magnetic Observatory, dwarfed by the Castle, looking west. Photograph attributed to Titian Ramsey Peale, ca. 1862. Above: The Magnetic Observatory, since replaced by the Arts and Industries Building, looking east. Photograph attributed to Titian Ramsey Peale, ca. 1862. Opposite, top: The Laboratory of Natural History, home to Smithsonian taxidermists, November 1, 1918. Opposite, bottom: Nelson R. Wood, the bird taxidermist, in the laboratory's second-floor taxidermy studio, ca. 1916.

and Industries Building in 1881, the studio was then used until 1884 by photographers of the U.S. Geological Survey and the Bureau of American Ethnology.

After two wings were added 1901 and 1902, the lower floors became a stable and a carriage house and the entire second floor was occupied by the bird taxidermists. Among the thousands of bird skins that Nelson R. Wood (1852–1920), one of the country's foremost bird taxidermists,[29] expertly mounted there, perhaps the most poignant example was that of the last passenger pigeon in America. Hatched at the Cincinnati Zoo in 1885, at a time when the birds' numbers were fast declining, the pigeon named Martha died at the zoo on September 1, 1914. Quoting the language of the first game laws enacted by Ohio in 1857—stating that the "wonderfully prolific" passenger pigeon "needs no protection"— Charles W. Richmond, the assistant curator of birds, commented in his annual report that it was "truly the irony of fate that the final extinction of this species should take place in the same State 57 years later."[29] After the taxidermy studio was moved to the new Natural History Museum across the Mall, this small, obsolete building was demolished in 1919.

In 1884 yet another temporary structure was located at the corner of B and Seventh Streets. This small wood-framed building, measuring about 100 by 50 feet, was designed and constructed by the architecture firm Cluss & Schulze.[30] Its sole purpose was to provide space for the preparation of the Smithsonian's specimens and exhibits for three major exhibitions to be held in 1884 in Cincinnati, Louisville, and New Orleans. The structure was to be torn down immediately afterward, and in fact within a year the shed was considered "a serious encumbrance" to the Institution.[30] It was not demolished until 1887, however, instead put to use as storage for the specimens returning from the three expositions.[31]

Three photographs of the shed's interior provide a snapshot of the varied activities conducted inside. In one, Cosmos Mindeleff is seen working on the model of Puebla Shipaneluvi Moki, Arizona, on the upper loft level. Mindeleff's pueblo models, on view in the Castle's Upper Main Hall at the time, were popular with visitors and considered "among the most conspicuous and interesting objects in the National Museum."[32] A second photograph taken in the taxidermist's workroom on the first floor of the temporary shed shows William Temple Hornaday (1854–1937) constructing a model of a tiger from straw and twine, on which the skin in the foreground would eventually be mounted. Hornaday was the Smithsonian's taxidermist from 1882 until 1889, during which time he collected living animals for study, housing them in pens and wooden sheds behind the Castle. The third photograph (*opposite*) shows the master craftsman, artist, and modeler John W. Hendley (1827–99), seated in the foreground of his studio on the first floor of the temporary shed with one of his most famous creations—a wax model of a taxidermist.[33] As the Washington *Evening Star* reported in 1886:

Wayfarers along the road that turns into the Smithsonian grounds from 7th Street, near the southeast corner of the grounds, cannot help noticing, if they have eyes, a large barn-like frame building that stands near the road. If they are observant probably the figure of a man who sits apparently engaged in some work inside the building, near a window, will attract their attention. This seemingly industrious person is always there always intent upon the work before him: never raising his eyes an instant to look upon the scene outside, however attractive; a model public servant surely. If the visitor enters the big building, and turns into the little work-room at his left he will get a view of the figure from the interior. The man sits at a table upon which are strewn some of the tools and materials used by a taxidermist. In his left hand he holds the body of a partridge and his right has a wire, which he is apparently on the point of running into the bird's body. He has his coat off and his working clothes on. His derby hat is tipped a little towards the front to shade his eyes. Upon his nose is perched a pair of glasses. Out of his vest pocket peeps a cigar and at the side of the chair is a spittoon or cuspidor, showing that this taxidermist solaces himself with the weed while at work. Every stranger who comes in waits for the silent, motionless figure to speak or move, but he never speaks or stirs. In fact, the man who made the figure did not supply it with vocal organs or motive power. It is a mere inanimate, voiceless effigy. . . . This is Mr. J. W. Hendley's work-room and that gentleman takes much delight in the amusing perplexity of his visitors over the motionless taxidermist."[34]

Hendley's lifelike fruits, vegetables, and human figures earned him the nickname "Wizard of the National Museum."

Top: Elevation of a temporary shed used to prepare specimens for exhibition. Drawing by Cluss & Schulze, July 1884. Center: Cosmos Mindeleff at work on a pueblo model on the upper level of the temporary shed. Photograph attributed to Thomas W. Smillie, ca. 1884–87. Bottom: William Temple Hornaday making a model of a tiger on the lower level of the temporary shed. Photograph by Thomas W. Smillie, ca. 1884–87.

LIVING SPECIMENS

It is somewhat ironic that a taxidermist whose job it was to mount the skins of dead animals (often killing them himself) would foster a collection that developed into a center for the preservation and conservation of living animals. During the mid- to late 1880s, William Temple Hornaday requested donations of live animals, instead of skins and skeletons, so he could study the form and the habits of the specimens before they were killed and mounted.[35] One of two low sheds constructed south of the Castle in 1887, using material salvaged from the demolished 1884 temporary shed, was put to use to house the increasing number of live animals that began arriving at the museum. The

John W. Hendley (foreground), the "Wizard of the National Museum," in the first floor modeler's studio of the temporary shed with a wax model of a taxidermist near the window, ca. 1884–87.

small shed, then opened to the public, became extremely popular: "The crowds of visitors which daily thronged a small, ill ventilated and highly uncomfortable temporary building, furnished abundant testimony to the eagerness of American people generally to learn more about our American fauna."[36]

The arrival in 1888 of a pair of bison and several other large animals necessitated construction of several additional small buildings and pens, including a bison shed.[37] Public interest created by these new "exhibits" played an important part in the creation of the Department of Living Animals, with Hornaday appointed its curator. The focus of the new department soon changed from study to public education about the plight of endangered animals, especially the American bison, which by that time was seriously in danger of extinction in the wild. Hornaday spent a good deal of time during both sessions of Congress in 1888–89 engaged in urging the establishment of a national zoological garden, citing in part the immense popularity of the museum's collection of living animals. Legislation creating the National Zoological Park was passed by Congress on March 2, 1889.[38] With the animals relocated to the new zoo in Rock Creek Park in 1890–91, the bison shed, the animal pens, and most of the South Yard's other small sheds were torn down.[39]

AIMING SKYWARD

Samuel P. Langley, the Institution's third Secretary, established the Smithsonian Astrophysical Observatory in 1890 to study the energy from the sun that strikes the outer edge of Earth's atmosphere.[40] The observatory's original building was constructed between November 18, 1889, and March 1, 1890,[41] but soon afterward it was considered unsuited for refined physical investigation because of its close proximity to the heavily traveled B Street. However, Langley thought that certain types of investigations could effectively be carried out there by making minor adjustments to the instruments.[42] The original building was enlarged in 1892 with a two-story addition for office and library use, and the complex grew over the next several years to include an instrument shop, a laboratory building, and a darkroom. By 1913 the observatory's fenced area was enlarged to accommodate a horizontal telescope and five small frame buildings, three movable shelters for instruments, and a small brick building serving as an electrical station. The entire complex then occupied approximately 16,000 square feet.[43]

During the summer of 1955, the observatory's scientific headquarters were moved from Washington to Cambridge, Massachusetts, and its buildings were converted into a machine shop.[44] The structures were later used as offices, classrooms, and greenhouses for the Radiation Biology Laboratory.[45] Preparations in 1975 for the upcoming celebration of the nation's Bicentennial presented an opportunity to at least partially restore the South Yard to a more fitting setting for the historic Castle. The old observatory buildings were demolished that year and soon replaced by the Victorian Garden, sharing the space with the employee parking lot.[46]

Top: The bison pen adjacent to the Castle in the South Yard, ca. 1888–91. Above: The expanded Astrophysical Observatory and its fenced complex in the South Yard, ca. 1908. Opposite, top: The South Shed, whose upper floor was the workroom for Secretary Samuel P. Langley's research into manned flight, ca. 1928. Opposite, center: The Aircraft Building, with captured World War I German artillery, ca. 1939.

THE YARD TAKES FLIGHT

The two-story South Shed, constructed in 1898 from designs by the architecture firm Hornblower & Marshall, was intended to serve as a temporary workroom for Smithsonian taxidermists and "various other purposes." Located southwest of the Castle, it was built far enough away to "prevent annoyance," presumably from odors generated by the taxidermists.[47] Within two years of its completion, Secretary Langley, an astronomer, appropriated the upper floor as a workroom to build his experimental "Aerodrome" (a term he coined) to achieve mechanical flight.[48]

Langley's December 8, 1903, manned test flight failed, but a few days later, on December 17, the Wright brothers' flight famously succeeded. Langley's machine was taken back to the South Shed, where it remained untouched until 1914.[49] After Langley's death in 1906, controversy had ensued: some, including Secretary Charles D. Walcott, asserted that Langley did not have a proper chance to prove the airworthiness of his "Aerodrome." It was subsequently refurbished and flown in 1914, which led the Smithsonian to claim that it in fact was "the first man-carrying aeroplane in the history of the world capable of sustained free flight." Because of this assertion, the feud that ensued between the Wright brothers and the Smithsonian was not resolved until 1942, when the Institution officially repudiated the claim and acknowledged that the Wright brothers were the inventors of the airplane.[50]

The 14,000-square-foot Aircraft Building, a temporary metal shed, opened to the public on October 7, 1920.[51] Erected in the South Yard along Independence Avenue in 1917 by the War Department, it was first used by the U.S. Signal Service. In 1919 the shed was transferred to the Smithsonian for a proposed exhibit of aircraft and accessories produced during World War I. In 1927 twenty pieces of German artillery captured during the war were added to the Smithsonian's war collections and exhibited around the Aircraft Building.[52]

As the United States made initial advances in the exploration of outer space, beginning in the late 1950s rockets, space capsules, and satellites were given to the Smithsonian. Space-related artifacts continued to increase, while their popularity soared. Then in 1961

A CALL TO ARMS

Within a year after the outbreak of World War II, Secretary Charles G. Abbot handed over to the U.S. Army thirty-five artifacts from the museum's historic artillery collection, including cannons captured from the Germans in the previous war. Amounting to a hundred tons worth of scrap metal, it was a significant contribution to the war effort—practical yet symbolic, as Abbot eloquently stated:

[T]he steel in these old weapons is needed to be hurled back upon the same world peace disturbers from whom they were seized in gallant action by the fathers of the brave men now fighting in the armies of today.[53]

Secretary Charles G. Abbot giving
Smithsonian artillery to the war effort, 1942.

the metal shed housing the National Air Museum, as the collection had been named in 1946, was renamed the Air and Space Building.[54] Legislation authorizing the Smithsonian to plan and construct a new National Air Museum had been passed and signed into law in 1958, but the museum's plans and focus would change dramatically over the next eight years. Although the museum's advisory board recommended changing its name to the National Air and Space Museum—"to reflect the widening responsibility of the Museum in the field of historic space flight" in December 1959—legislation authorizing the name change was not introduced in Congress for several years, finally passing on June 29, 1966.[55] Plans for the new National Air and Space Museum progressed, with a proposed completion date of 1976 to coincide with the nation's Bicentennial.

After the air and space collections were moved to the new Air and Space Museum, the old "temporary" air shed was demolished. The Astrophysical Observatory and the South Shed were removed as well, leaving only the staff parking lot still occupying the southwest corner of the South Yard. The yard's southeast quadrant was then transformed into a Victorian Garden, which opened in September 1976 as a tranquil retreat from the bustle of nearby Independence Avenue. Complementing the nineteenth-century architecture of the Castle and the Arts and Industries Building, the plantings of the garden's central feature, a formal parterre with geometric flower beds, was modeled after the sunken parterre of the Horticulture Hall at the 1876 Centennial Exhibition in Philadelphia.[56]

THE QUADRANGLE

By November 1979 plans were being developed for a vast museum and study center to be built in the Smithsonian's South Yard, three stories underground.[57] The Center for African, Near Eastern, and Asian Cultures was envisioned by Secretary Ripley as a place "to tell Americans about the history of the rest of the world, especially about those parts and nations of which we are still so woefully ignorant."[58] The design contract was awarded to the Boston architecture firm Shepley, Bulfinch, Richardson and Abbott, which submitted a cross-section rendering of "the imagined inner workings of the quadrangle project."[59] Three underground levels for exhibitions, theater productions, and study were to be accessed by a pair of above-ground pavilions, one for each museum, and a small kiosk for entry to a central concourse level. The original design for the complex was altered considerably during ongoing planning sessions and even during construction, so that the interior spaces of the completed museum complex bear little resemblance to the early cutaway drawing.[60]

The June 21, 1983, groundbreaking ceremony was presided over by Secretary Ripley, Chief Justice Warren Burger, and Vice President George H. W. Bush. Excavation began almost immediately: "Soon after the groundbreaking came the onslaught. A small army of mud-smeared soldiers in hard hats, armed with gigantic weapons for displacing and reshaping sizable chunks of the earth, mounted their formidable attack. In no time the Victorian Garden was gone and the South Yard of the Castle looked like a piece of no man's land."[61]

Top: Demolition of the metal Aircraft Building, 1975. Above: Aerial view of the original Victorian Garden, with its central parterre, planted in the South Yard's southeast corner, 1976.

After four years of construction, a new and improved South Yard was unveiled with the September 28, 1987, opening of the Quadrangle museums. Atop them lay the four-acre Enid A. Haupt Garden—constituting perhaps the country's largest "green" roof. The only evidence of the underground complex visible in the garden are skylights, emergency exits, and the two pavilion entrances to the museums below, all carefully designed to blend with the historic structures that surround the garden. Jean-Paul Carlhian, the Quadrangle's Beaux Arts–trained principal architect, decided that the pavilions had to fit visually between the granite of the Freer, the red brick of the Arts and Industries Building, and the reddish brown sandstone of the Castle. "We were not going to allow the pavilions to look like a baby Freer and a baby A&I, you know, so we needed something different that wouldn't fight with the existing buildings."[62] Carlhian decided on a grayish pink granite called Rockville Beige for the Arthur M. Sackler Gallery pavilion, to complement the Freer Gallery, and a Texas granite called Sunset Red for the National Museum of African Art pavilion, to blend with both the Arts and Industries Building and the Castle.[63]

Below: Construction of the underground museums in the Quadrangle complex, 1984.
Bottom: Aerial view of the Enid A. Haupt Garden between the two pavilions of the Arthur M. Sackler Gallery and the National Museum of African Art. Photograph by Eric Long, 2010.

THE RENWICK GATES

Four months before the late September 1987 ribbon-cutting ceremony for the Quadrangle complex, the installation of an impressive gateway off Independence Avenue realized a never-built feature of the Smithsonian Building. Designed by the building's architect, James Renwick Jr., gates of iron and Seneca sandstone were pictured in Robert Dale Owen's 1849 book, *Hints on Public Architecture (see page 23).*[64] The newly built gateway, named in honor of Renwick, now forms the southern entrance to the Haupt Garden, the Quadrangle, and the Castle itself.

At the start of the design process, full-scale cardboard mockups were made and placed at various locations, both near and offset from the sidewalk, to evaluate the gates' scale and design. Once all the details were worked out on paper, the job of carving the stonework of the tall piers fell to the master stonecarver Constantine Seferlis. The iron gates were cast by the Gichner Iron Works of Beltsville, Maryland. By the time the new Smithsonian museums opened that fall, the Haupt Garden had already provided a cool and shady enclave during the especially hot Washington summer of 1987 for visitors passing through the picturesque Renwick Gates.[65]

Above: Mockup of the proposed Renwick Gates leading into the Quadrangle, 1981. Below: The Renwick Gates as completed in 1987. Photograph by Eric Long, 2010. Opposite: Aerial view of the Haupt Garden's central parterre. Photograph by Harold Dorwin, 2010.

NOTES

Abbreviations:
AHHP: Smithsonian Architectural History and Historic Preservation Division
SIA: Smithsonian Institution Archives
SICC: Smithsonian Institution Castle Collection, AHHP

A Symbol for the Institution

1. Joel R. Poinsett, *Discourse on the Objects and Importance of the National Institution for the Promotion of Science* (Washington, D.C.: Force, 1841), 5–6.
2. Major Richard Delafield to Colonel Joseph G. Totten, 3 June 1839, National Archives, RG 94, D-531: "a style not only pleasing to the eye, but . . . in accordance with Collegiate buildings elsewhere." Colonel Totten, Major Delafield's superior as chief, U.S. Army Corps of Engineers, was to become head of the Smithsonian Institution Building Committee in 1847. Colonel Totten for Secretary of War Joel Poinsett to Major Richard Delafield, 15 June 1839, West Point Archives, no. 164, with the attached letter of Robert Mills to Poinsett, June 1839, endorsing the ogee dome.
3. Robert Mills to Joel R. Poinsett, secretary of war, 27 February 1841, National Archives, Records of the Office of the Chief of Engineers, Civil Works Map File, Construction 90, no. 5, RG 77.
4. Robert Dale Owen to David Dale Owen, 15 August 1845, 5–6, in "Correspondence Explanatory of the Details of a Plan of Buildings for a Smithsonian Institute Prepared by David Dale Owen, M.D., and Robert Dale Owen" (New Harmony, Ind.: Workingmen's Institute, n.d.). As Robert Dale Owen saw it, the Institution would best serve as a teaching establishment, so he directed his brother to "consult utility first, in the various internal arrangements, and let architectural elegance follow as a secondary, though not unimportant, consideration." Robert Dale Owen to David Dale Owen, 15 August 1845, 4–5, in "Correspondence Explanatory."
5. In Robert Dale Owen to David Dale Owen, 15 August 1845, 2, in "Correspondence Explanatory": "I cannot furnish to you an elevation showing the order of architecture proposed; but Mr. Mills writes me that he selected the Anglo Saxon style; a selection which seems to me judicious, as being solid, imposing, & probably the most economical among ornamental styles." This argument reflected Owen's familiarity with the work of the English architecture writers Thomas Hope and J. C. Loudon, whom he would later quote in *Hints on Public Architecture*.
6. David Dale Owen to Robert Dale Owen, 10 October 1845, 6, in "Correspondence Explanatory." The descriptive material in the following paragraphs is from this source. William H. Pierson Jr., in his vol. 3 of *American Architects and Their Buildings*, points out that the wings and ranges were clearly lower than the central building because David Dale Owen described "large" and projecting windows at the east- and west-end walls of the third story, as well as "lofty" windows on the north and south sides.
7. William J. Rhees, ed., *Journals*, 4. A letter, from which the quotation was taken, accompanied this project and was printed in H. M. Pierce Gallagher, *Robert Mills, Architect of the Washington Monument, 1781–1855* (New York: Columbia University Press, 1935), "Mills to Robert Dale Owen," appendix, 189–98. Gallagher gave no date for this letter, but in the text, clearly written after passage of the

bill on 10 August 1846, Mills referred to Christmas as being three months off.
8. Rhees, *Journals*, 4–6. As a means of advertising the upcoming architecture project, the Regents published the resolution creating the Building Committee in Washington newspapers on 22 September 1846. The architects, however, were already aware of the opportunity. One local builder-architect, William Archer, had submitted his plan and drawings with specifications on 9 September. Isaiah Rogers, a highly regarded Boston architect, had come to Washington at the time to obtain the commission if possible. Rogers's presence was recorded in his diaries on 7, 8, and 9 September 1846. We learned of these references through the transcriptions of the diaries, which are in the Avery Architectural and Fine Arts Library, Columbia University. Denys Peter Myers has generously shared the relevant parts of his transcription with the Smithsonian.
9. David Arnot, *Animadversions on the Proceedings of the Regents of the Smithsonian Institution,* 1847, 10.
10. Sketches Renwick made as he was developing his Smithsonian Building entry were kept by him and his heirs until their deposit in the SIA in 1992.
11. William H. Pierson Jr. has identified this drawing as the scheme most closely approximating the final form of Renwick's first submission in November 1846. SIA, Drawings Collection Miscellany, box "Architectural Drawings: Current Files."
12. John Henry Parker, *A Glossary of Terms Used in Grecian, Roman, Italian and Gothic Architecture,* 1838. In the copy purchased for the Smithsonian are notes and marks made by Robert Dale Owen. He marked the oriel window entry as "committee window," noting at the bottom of p. 89, "We want an oriel window in the Norman style."
13. Robert Dale Owen, *Hints on Public Architecture*, 85.
14. Ibid., 42.
15. Ibid., 41. "These were obtained within a bell tower, of the old Norman form."
16. James Renwick Jr., "Specification of the Stone and Cutting for the Smithsonian Institution," 6, SIA, Records of the Office of the Secretary, 1835, 1838, 1846–65, RU 43, box 1.
17. Rhees, *Journals*, 7. The minutes of the Board of Regents recorded that thirteen plans, two of which were by James Renwick, were submitted. Twelve are known to us, primarily through mention in Rhees's *Journals*, 4–5, 23, 671–72: those of William Archer, Howard Daniels, William P. Elliot, John Haviland, Robert Mills, John Notman, David Dale Owen, Isaiah Rogers, Owen Warren, Joseph Wells and David Arnot, and Renwick twice. The drawings of Renwick, Notman, Rogers, and Warren have survived, while the other entries have been lost.
18. Joseph Henry to Harriet Henry, 20 January 1847, SIA, Henry Collection, RU 7001, box 57. The story of the "tempest" is told in detail in Kenneth Hafertepe's *America's Castle,* 39–61.
19. Rhees, *Journals*, 7. "The design includes all the accommodations demanded by the charter, to wit: a museum, 200 feet by 50; a library, 90 feet by 50; a gallery of art, in the form of a T, 125 feet long; two lecture rooms, one of which is capable of containing from 800 to 1,000 persons, and the other is connected with the chemical laboratory; a committee room for the Board of Regents; a Secretary's room; a room for the effects of Mr. Smithson; a janitor's room, &c."
20. Rhees, *Journals*, 12, 17, 18. Henry was elected 3 December 1846 (*Journals*, 12). His acceptance letter of

7 December was read into the record on 14 December 1846 (*Journals*, 17). He took up his duties on 21 December 1846 (*Journals*, 18).
21. Joseph Henry to Harriet Henry, 22 December 1846, SIA, RU 7001, box 57.
22. Joseph Henry to Harriet Henry, 18 December, 1846, SIA, RU 7001, box 57. On 18 January Henry was shown Renwick's reduced plan. Acceptance of that plan on 27 January 1847 was recorded in Rhees, *Journals*, 29. Other cost-cutting measures were introduced, such as the idea to extend the construction phase so that costs could be met from interest only and a move to cut building costs by more than half, which Joseph Henry described to Harriet Henry, 27 January 1847, SIA, RU 7001, box 57.
23. This model was found in the building. According to the catalogue card, Joseph Henry's daughter Caroline gave a daguerreotype of this model, located in the National Museum of American History's collection, to Richard Rathbun for the Smithsonian.
24. Selma Rattner, "Renwick, James," in *Macmillan Encyclopedia of Architects*, vol. 3 (New York: Free Press, 1982), 541–48. William H. Pierson Jr., "James Renwick, St. Patrick's Cathedral, and the Continental Gothic Revival," in *Technology and the Picturesque: The Corporate and the Early Gothic Styles,* vol. 2, *American Buildings and Their Architects* (New York and London: Oxford University Press, 1978), esp. 215–19.
25. William Jervis Hough's report on the specifications is found in Rhees, *Journals*, 611. For the German and Norman design sources, see Renwick, "Specification of the Stone and Cutting," p. 8, SIA, RU 43, box 1.
26. Owen, *Hints*, 42. "It was judged expedient, that the upper story of the main building should be occupied, in its entire length, by a single apartment, to serve the purposes of a museum. This was effected by running up the staircases within central towers, projecting in front and in rear; these towers harmonizing well with the style adopted; affording small apartments, which were indispensable; and lending themselves to the architectural effect of the structure, both by giving it elevation, which, in its somewhat low and flat site overlooked by Capitol Hill, it wanted, and much increasing its breadth, as seen from the east or west; this latter item being important, inasmuch as the internal adaptations of the main building had given to it a width of but fifty to a length of two hundred feet, and that length again had been more than doubled by the addition of the wings and connecting ranges."
27. Rhees, *Journals*, 599–630.
28. Rhees, *Journals*, 7. Meeting minutes of 30 November 1846. See also p. 32 for meeting minutes of 5 February 1847, when the resolution to publish a pamphlet was upgraded to an illustrated treatise.
29. Owen, *Hints*, 85. George L. Hersey, *High Victorian Gothic: A Study in Associationism* (Baltimore: Johns Hopkins University Press, 1972), 1–43, esp. 14. "Loudon believed that 'expression of fitness for the end in view'—i.e., Alison's principal associational test was a supreme architectural law. On this basis he invented specific meanings for architectural elements . . . saying that these expressed truths about the building's interior, its purpose, the nature of its occupants, its relation to the surrounding landscape, and even its role in local and national life."
30. Owen, *Hints*, 93–98.
31. Ibid., 8, 65.
32. Ibid., 109.
33. Ibid., 85.

Changes with the Times

1. The Historic Structure Report for the Smithsonian Castle, completed in 2009, gives a comprehensive history and evolution of the building, along with a condition assessment. Excerpts from the report are available at www.si.edu/ahhp.

2. Periods of significance are established to aid in the discussion of a building's design integrity and as a guide to shape a preservation approach.

The East Wing and the East Range

1. Joseph Henry was elected Secretary of the Smithsonian by the Board of Regents on 3 December 1846 and accepted the appointment on 7 December 1846.

2. Joseph Henry to Harriet Henry, 18 December 1846, SIA, Joseph Henry Papers, 7540.

3. *Annual Report for 1848*, 22. The "Programme of Organization" was adopted by the Board of Regents on 13 December 1847.

4. Joseph Henry to James Alfred Pearce, 21 July 1849, SIA, Joseph Henry Papers, 9375.

5. *Annual Report for 1849*, 22. Possession of the East Wing and the East Range was taken by Henry on 10 April 1849.

6. Joseph Henry Desk Diary, 26 April, 27 April, 28 April, 30 April, 1 May, 2 May (lighting), 4 May (trap door) 1849, SIA, Henry Collection, RU 7001, box 14.

7. Joseph Henry Desk Diary, 3 June 1849. Owen's book, *Hints on Public Architecture,* was published in 1849.

8. Joseph Henry Desk Diary, 4 June 1849.

9. *Annual Report for 1855*, Report of the Building Committee, 73.

10. Joseph Henry Desk Diary, 16 January 1850 (first lecture in the new room), 4 July 1849 (capacity of lecture hall), 1 January 1852 (vaulting). By 1852 the lecture hall had been fitted with gas lights. Desk Diary, 15 April 1852.

11. *Annual Report for 1850*, 25.

12. Joseph Henry Desk Diary, 3 June 1849, discusses the fireproof measures taken. *Annual Report for 1849*, 61, and *Annual Report for 1872*, 42, mark the time frame for the occupation of these rooms.

13. Rhees, *An Account of the Smithsonian*, 31. Research reports for each volume of *Contributions* were printed individually, with separate titles and paging; the reports for the year were later collected and bound into volumes. This method allowed the reports to be distributed to scholars interested in a particular subject almost as soon as they were released from the press, without having to wait for the volume to be completed.

14. William Healey Dall, *Spencer Fullerton Baird: A Biography*, 1915, 287–91.

15. Benjamin Brown French to Joseph Henry, 4 December 1846, SIA, RU 7001, box 8.

16. *The Washington and Georgetown Directory, Stranger's Guidebook for Washington* (Washington: 1853), 48, lists Henry's address as "w[est] side [of] 10th [Street] w[est] between Maryland Ave[nue] & C S[outh]."

17. Joseph Henry to John Torrey, 15 January 1872.

18. Joseph Henry to Asa Gray, 22 February 1856, Harvard University, Peabody Museum of Archeology, Gray Herbarium.

19. Joseph Henry Desk Diary, 10 June 1871. Harriet Henry's injuries were serious enough that although she had recovered by the following March, she still suffered "considerably from pain in her right side and limb." Joseph Henry to William Healey Dall, 13 March 1872, SIA, RU 7001, box 4.

20. No documentation was found to verify if these changes were carried out.

21. The 1879 floor plan also shows two rooms adjoining the two corner bedrooms; their function is not known, but it is assumed that they were bedrooms as well. No photographs of these two inner rooms are known to exist, probably because of insufficient light; there were no windows in one room and only one small window in the other.

22. For use before 1872, see "Origin of the Fire at the Smithsonian Institution, February 21, 1865," 38th Congress, 2d session, Senate Document Rep. Com. No. 129. SIA, RU 7081, box 14. For use after 1872, see "Rules and Regulations of the Smithsonian Institution, January 1872," 19–41, SIA, RU 7081, box 5.

23. "Rules and Regulations of the Smithsonian Institution, January 1872," SICC, SI.1997.017. The three rooms are labeled East Chamber, Middle Chamber, and West Chamber and bear room numbers that correspond to those on the 1879 floor plan.

24. Marc Rothenberg, Kathleen Dorman, John C. Rumm, and Paul H. Theerman, eds., *The Papers of Joseph Henry*, vol. 7 (Washington, D.C.: Smithsonian Institution Press, 1996), 379, n1.

25. Dorothea Dix to President Millard Fillmore, 5 April 1852, Buffalo and Erie County Historical Society, Millard Fillmore Collection.

26. John Varden Diary, 28 August 1861 and 2 October 1861.

27. Miscellaneous Records Collected by the Chief Clerk, Records of the Office of the Secretary of War, 1811–87, RG 107, National Archives.

28. Thomas J. Brown, *Dorothea Dix: New England Reformer* (Cambridge: Harvard University Press, 1998), 305, n400.

29. The stereographs, numbering six in all, were inscribed on the back to the ". . . Misses Henry with compliments of Mrs. T. R. Peale, July 31, '62."

30. Mary Henry Diary, 7, 8, and 24 January 1863; 26 January 1864; and 6 July 1867, SIA, RU 7001, box 51.

31. Joseph Henry to William J. Rhees, 17 August 1865, SIA, RU 7001, box 11.

32. For designation of the rooms, see "Rules and Regulations of the Smithsonian Institution, January 1872." For the cook's name, see Joseph Henry Diary, 30 December 1866.

33. Solomon G. Brown to Spencer F. Baird, 22 September 1856, SIA, RU 7002, box 16, Solomon Brown folder.

34. Solomon G. Brown to Spencer F. Baird, 22 August 1857.

35. William J. Rhees to Spencer F. Baird, 1 September 1857, SIA, RU 7002, box 62.

36. Solomon G. Brown to Spencer F. Baird, 22 August 1857.

37. "Doors & Keys, April 1879," SIA, RU 7081, box 21.

38. Joseph Henry to Mrs. Bache, 5 October 1867, SIA, RU 7001, box 57.

39. Joseph Henry to Harriet Henry, 25 September 1867, SIA, RU 7001, box 57.

40. William J. Rhees to Spencer F. Baird, 28 July 1871, SIA, RU 7002, box 57.

41. Joseph Henry to John Torrey, 15 January 1872.

42. Joseph Henry Desk Diary, 26 February 1872.

43. Joseph Henry Desk Diary, 12 October 1875.

44. Mary Henry Diary, 23 October 1867.

45. Mary Henry Diary, 23 March 1866.

46. Ibid.

47. Mary Henry Diary, 6 December 1862. Will died 17 October 1862.

48. Mary Henry Diary, 13 December 1862.

49. Mary Henry Diary, 25 December 1862.

50. Mary Henry Diary, 1 January 1863.

51. Mary Henry Diary, 3 April 1863.

52. Mary Henry Diary, 13 December 1862; 12 June 1866; 1, 2, 3, 8 August 1866; 6 and 18 July 1867; 23 November 1867; 5, 6, 12 December 1867; 2 and 18 March 1868.

53. Mary Henry Diary, 12 June 1866.

54. *Annual Report for 1858*, 16. The portal windows had originally provided light to the East Range from the open cloister on the building's north side. This cloister (walkway) was enclosed and decked over in 1858 to provide additional space, as well as to insulate the building from the cold northwest wind.

55. Curtis M. Hinsley Jr., *Savages and Scientists*, 1981, 101. By 1871 Mary was taking painting lessons at the school of Theodore Kauffman in Washington.

56. Thomas W. Smillie was the Smithsonian's photographer from 1871 until 1917.

57. John H. Richard's origins are unclear; he is variously referred to as French or German. For the French reference, see *Annual Report for 1881*, 43. For the German reference see *Who Was Who in American History, Arts and Letters* (Chicago: Marquis Who's Who, 1975), 425. After moving to the United States, Richard resided in Philadelphia, working as an engraver for the printing firm Peter S. Duval between 1841 and 1843. Richard experimented with a new process of lithography, "lithotinting," and in collaboration with Duval produced what was said to be the first true lithotint in America, entitled *Grandpapa's Pet*, published in the April 1843 edition of *Miss Leslie's Magazine*. *Who Was Who*, 425.

58. These included the Wilkes Expedition, the Mexican Boundary Survey, and the U.S. Pacific Railroad Expedition and Survey.

59. *Annual Report for 1881*, 43. For reference to Ridgway, see Robert Ridgway to Spencer F. Baird, 16 June 1870, 28 June 1873, 30 July 1875, 27 July and 26 September 1879, Spencer F. Baird Collection, SIA, box 32, Robert Ridgway folder.

60. *Annual Report for 1881*, 43.

61. *Annual Report for 1879*, 61–62. According to the floor plan in the 1883 Smithsonian guidebook, the offices in the old laboratory space were then occupied by the chief clerk, the corresponding clerk, and the bookkeeper. Rhees, *Visitor's Guide*, 1883.

62. Wooten Desk Company to H. O. Towle, 24 January 1876, Records of Assistant Secretary Spencer F. Baird, 1850–77, RU 52, vol. 209. Towle was the Wooten representative in Washington.

63. Betty Lawson Walters, *The King of Desks: Wooten's Patent Secretary* (Washington D.C.: Smithsonian Studies in History and Technology, 1969), 1.

64. Two pieces of furniture visible in the photograph remain in the Smithsonian Building: the swivel desk chair (next to the Wooten desk) and the small writing table (far right), both catalogued in the SICC.

65. Joseph Henry to William Healey Dall, 13 March 1872.

66. *Annual Report for 1884*, xxi.

67. William J. Rhees to Smithsonian staff, memorandum, 1 March 1883, SIA, RU 7081, box 14.

68. *Annual Report for 1884*, 8. An additional $15,000 was appropriated by Congress for completion of the rooms in the upper two floors, which were occupied by the end of June 1884.

69. William J. Rhees, Slate Frame, patented 15 January 1867, U.S. Patent no. 61253.

70. Advertisements for commercial products and services were common in the Smithsonian guidebooks from the first one published in 1857 through the late 1880s.

71. Rhees, *An Account of the Smithsonian Institution,* 1869, 38.

72. "Arrangements for the Occupation of Eastern Portion of Smithsonian Institution Upon Fireproofing," 1 April 1884, SIA, RU 7081, box 5. For the reference to artists' rooms, see *Annual Report for 1884,* 8.

73. *Annual Report for 1884,* xxi.

74. Adolf Cluss, "Specifications for the Reconstruction of the East Wing and Range," 12 January 1885, SIA, RU 7081, box 5.

75. Rhees, *The Smithsonian Institution,* vol. 1, 1901, 466.

76. *Annual Report for 1852,* 20–21.

77. The name derives from the design reformer Charles Locke Eastlake's *Hints on Household Taste* (1868). However, Eastlake decried the use of his name as applied to this class of cheap mass-produced furniture manufactured in America.

78. *Annual Report for 1893,* 5.

79. *Annual Reports for 1932* and *1950–60.* The International Exchange Service report in each volume itemizes the combined total number of incoming and outgoing packages, as well as total weight.

80. *Annual Report for 1966,* 339.

81. *Annual Report for 1958,* 90.

82. Proceedings of the Meeting of the Board of Regents, 19 September 1983, 81–82, SIA, RU 1, box 14. The report cited several reasons for the dissolution of the service, primarily that it had outlived its usefulness and that its continuance would be an unneeded drain on precious resources. The three remaining staff members were assured of other jobs within the Smithsonian.

83. *Washington Post,* 19 April 1911, 5. Reference to a tea hosted by Secretary and Mrs. Charles D. Walcott: ". . . the chief social function of the day in connection with the meeting of the National Academy of Sciences." The tea was held in the Smithsonian's new art gallery.

84. Among the notable women Kronstrand painted during his tour of the United States was Mrs. William Howard Taft, the first lady. *Washington Post,* 31 October 1910, 2.

85. The painting is inscribed with the date and those present in pencil on the back of the canvas. The accident occurred 11 July 1911. *Washington Post,* 12 July 1911, 2.

86. "Another great improvement added during the year is the introduction of electric lights in all offices of east wing (SIB), the electric power being supplied by a special plant, which, with the ventilating apparatus, has been placed in the basement of the south tower, where considerable changes were made for their accommodation." *Annual Report for 1895,* 5.

87. *Report of the National Museum for 1903,* 257–58. Rathbun gave a brief history of the gradual installation of electricity in the building.

88. Montgomery Ward and Company, *Catalogue and Buyers' Guide,* 1895, an unabridged reprint of the original edition with a new introduction by Boris Emmet (New York: Dover, 1969), 438, 535. Reprint of the 1902 edition of the *Sears, Roebuck Catalogue,* introduction by Cleveland Amory (New York: Bounty Books, 1986), 587, 591.

89. Portrait of Robert Hare, oil on canvas, ca. 1856, by Alvan Clark (1804–87), Smithsonian National Portrait Gallery, NPG66.57.

90. *Annual Report for 1914,* 616.

91. *Annual Report for 1881,* 12. The phones communicated through a switchboard in the north tower of the Arts and Industries Building.

92. *Guide to the Smithsonian Institution Archives* (Washington D.C.: Smithsonian Institution Press, 1996), 348.

93. William Howard Taft (1857–1930) was the twenty-seventh president of the United States (1909–13). As chief justice of the United States, Taft served as chancellor of the Smithsonian Institution from 1921 to 1930.

94. Sidney Dillon Ripley was installed as Secretary of the Smithsonian Institution in a private ceremony during the Regents' meeting on 23 January 1964. Ripley, an ornithologist and a wildlife conservationist, served as Secretary until 1984.

95. Dubbed the "tag sale of the century," Warhol's collection was sold at auction after his death by Sotheby's in a sale spanning ten days, 23 April to 3 May 1988. It was reported that the ten thousand objects, which ranged from trash to treasures, brought $25.3 million. *New York Times,* 22 April 1988, B3, and 6 May 1988, A39.

96. *Annual Report for 1900,* 18–19.

97. George Perkins Marsh, representative from Vermont in the U.S. House of Representatives from 1848 to 1849, was appointed to the Board of Regents on 22 December 1847. The collection was described in the *Annual Report for 1850,* 29–30.

98. Before the 1884 renovation, the room had been the Henry family's large parlor and Music Room from 1855 until 1878.

99. The photographs were purchased for the Smithsonian's exhibit at the 1901 Pan American Exposition in Buffalo, New York, and installed in the Art Room at the conclusion of the fair. *Annual Report* for 1902, 98. Adolphe Braun, a French photographer of art history images, became one of the largest publishers of such images. http://www.dictionaryofarthistorians.org/brauna.htm.

100. Hornblower & Marshall's original drawings for these cabinets have been preserved in the SIA.

101. Ground was broken for the new National Air and Space Museum on 20 November 1972. *Annual Report for 1973,* 67. The museum opened 1 July 1976, during the nation's Bicentennial year. *Annual Report* for 1976, 82.

102. *Annual Report for 2000,* 8–9.

103. *Annual Report for 1894,* 20.

104. *Annual Report for 1879,* 12.

105. Records of the Property Clerk, 1882–90, 1900–10, 1925–30, SIA, RU 78, box 15, record no. 1013.

106. The plaque was one of three commissioned from the New York sculptor William Ordway Partridge. After the first two were completed in 1896, one was installed at Smithson's Italian grave, the other in the Protestant church nearby. *Annual Report for 1896,* 16. The third plaque was commissioned a year later and given to Pembroke College, Oxford. *Annual Report for 1898,* 19. Hanging above the plaque in the Archives Room is a small framed photograph of Smithson's grave in Italy, showing the plaque that had been erected there in 1896.

107. *Annual Report for 1884,* xxi.

108. *Annual Report for 1913,* 20.

109. *Annual Report for 1969,* 571, and *Annual Report for 1970,* 111.

110. *Annual Report for 1976,* 236.

111. The Harvard stove was removed and sold at auction on 27 July 1914, Records of the Property Clerk, RU 78, box 15, record no. 1013.

The Main Building

1. George Brown Goode, "The Genesis of the National Museum," *Report of the National Museum for 1891,* 273–380.

2. *Annual Report for 1849,* 61.

3. Joseph Henry Desk Diary, 26 February 1850. The accident occurred in the evening after Louis Agassiz delivered the first of a series of lectures in the East Wing on the "Unity of the Plan of the Animal Creation." Henry wrote in his diary: "I had left the building a few minutes before with Prof. Agassiz and while at dinner was called to the door with the information that Prof. J[ewitt] wished to see me. He appeared in a violent state of excitement as well he might, considering the narrow escape he had made." A workman clearing the rubble from the fallen structure about a month later was not as fortunate as Jewitt and the four others: "accident happened at the building this morning, workman taking down damaged framing fell and was instantly killed." Joseph Henry Desk Diary, 29 March 1850.

4. The investigation was conducted by three outside architects: John R. Nierensee, a well-known Austrian-trained architect practicing in Baltimore; Colonel William Turnbull of the U.S. Topographical Engineers; and Edward B. White, an architect from Charleston, S.C.

5. The Metropolitan Mechanics' Institute was established in 1852; at the time of the request (18 October 1854), Joseph Henry was serving as its president. Joseph Henry to Alexander Dallas Bache, 18 October 1854, William Jones Rhees Collection, Huntington Library, San Marino, Calif.

6. Advertisement for the second exhibition of the Metropolitan Mechanics' Institute, Broadside Collection, Rare Book and Special Collections, Library of Congress, portfolio 202–2. For Henry and the Mechanics' Institute, see Molella, Reingold, Rothenberg, Steiner, Waldenfels, eds., *A Scientist in American Life: Essays and Lectures by Joseph Henry* (Washington, D.C.: Smithsonian Institution Press, 1980), 54–55.

7. *The Washington and Georgetown Directory, Strangers' Guidebook for Washington, and Congressional and Clerks' Register,* compiled and published by Alfred Hunter (Washington, D.C.: Alfred Hunter, 1853). George Hilbus's music store was located on the south side of Pennsylvania Avenue between Tenth and Eleventh Streets, N.W.

8. Smithsonian Polka Sheet Music (Washington, D.C.: Hilbus & Hitz, 1855), SIA, accession 99–031. A gift to the Smithsonian from the Charles D. Walcott family, the sheet music was originally given to them by Mrs. Herbert Hoover.

9. The sheet music for the "Institute Polka and Schottisch" can be seen in the Division of Music, Library of Congress.

10. W. W. Turner to John Russell Bartlett, 31 January 1855, John Russell Bartlett Collection, John Carter Brown Library, Brown University.

11. The engraving was executed before the hall was completed in 1855.

12. Robert R. Hershman and Edward T. Stafford, *The Story of Our First Hundred Years* (Washington, D.C.: Washington Gas Light Company, 1948), 21–23.

13. Marc Rothenberg, Kathleen Dorman, John C. Rumm, and Paul H. Theerman, eds., *The Papers of Joseph Henry,* vol. 7 (Washington, D.C.: Smithsonian Institution Press, 1996), 358–60. Letter from Joseph Henry to Harriet Henry, 14 July 1848. With the Smithsonian Building still under construction, it is assumed that the ball was stored at the Patent Office until after the building was completed.

14. *Annual Report for 1858*, 14–15. Edward Clark, then architect of the Interior Department, supervised the construction. Walter worked closely with Joseph Henry on other aspects of the design of the Main Hall, including helping the Secretary select an appropriate pattern for the iron railing that encircled the room at the balcony level. Joseph Henry Desk Diary, 26 March 1858. A part of this railing exists in the SICC.

15. John Varden Papers, 1829–63, 17 August 1858, SIA, RU 7063, box 1, Diary 1857–63. "Finished bringing 12 large cases from the Pat. Office this day about 12 PM."

16. The reference to the label is found in Rhees, *An Account of the Smithsonian Institution*, 1860, 61. The reference to the ball's installation date is found in John Varden Papers, 1829–63, 20 October 1858.

17. Rhees, *An Account of the Smithsonian*, 1869. The reference to the "Feegee Islands" is on p. 69, that to the snakes on p. 84.

18. John Varden to Spencer F. Baird, 9 August 1862, SIA, Spencer Baird Papers, Incoming Correspondence, 1830–90, RU 7002, box 35, U–W.

19. Ibid., 20 September 1862.

20. Ibid.

21. The Society of Military Engineers, *The Washington Monument* (Washington, D.C.: Thomas McGill, 1923), 5–10.

22. *Annual Report for 1863*, 55–56. Bannister, Elliott, and Horan were identified from photographs in the SIA, Small Print Files.

23. Richard Rathbun, *The National Gallery of Art* (Washington, D.C.: 1909), 30–31.

24. *National Intelligencer*, 4 July 1836.

25. Rathbun, *The National Gallery of Art*, 30–31.

26. John Varden Papers, 1829–63, 10 December 1857: "inspected the new cases in the Smithsonian Building. Secretary Joseph Henry told me that it was his intention that I should go with the collection on the same terms that I am now engaged."

27. John Varden Papers, 1829–63, 5 April 1859.

28. Rhees, *An Account of the Smithsonian Institution*, 1860, 59.

29. Rhees, *Visitor's Guide*, 1863, 68.

30. *Annual Report for 1872*, 51. Beginning in the early 1870s, the museum embarked on a plan of constructing a large number of "effigies" (mannequins) on which to display the clothing of American Indians. It is assumed that a mannequin for Kane's Eskimo dress was also made at that time.

31. *Annual Report for 1867*, 105.

32. Joseph Henry Desk Diary, 11 February 1865.

33. Joseph Henry to Spencer F. Baird, 25 July 1874, SIA, Spencer Baird Papers, RU 7002, box 25.

34. Richard C. Ryder, "Hawkins' Hadrosaurus: The Stereographic Record," *The Mosasaur* (1986): 169–80. The cast of the Hadrosaurus was later considered an inaccurate reconstruction. "The larger casts of extinct animals have been placed in the lower room and their number increased by the restoration of the skeleton of the Hydrosaurus [sic] a very large Legend from the [illegible] pits of New Jersey restored by Mr. Waterhouse Hawkins." Joseph Henry Desk Diary, 10 January 1875.

35. William Healy Dall, *Spencer Fullerton Baird: A Biography*, 1915, 230.

36. William Stimpson, "Marine Invertebrata of Grand Manan," *Smithsonian Contributions to Knowledge* 11, no. 6 (1853), 5–67.

37. Dall, *Spencer Fullerton Baird*, 378.

38. Lucius Eugene Chittenden, *Recollections of President Lincoln and His Administration* (New York: Harper & Brothers, 1901), 241.

39. *Dictionary of American Biography*, vol. 5 (New York: Scribner, 1932–33), 338.

40. Robert Kennicott to Charles Kennicott, 17 February 1863, courtesy the Grove National Historic Landmark, Glenview Park District, Glenview, Ill.

41. Ibid.

42. Ira Kennicott to James Redfield, 14 April 1863, courtesy the Grove National Historic Landmark, Glenview Park District, Glenview, Ill.

43. *Dictionary of American Biography*, 339.

44. Alton James, *The First Scientific Exploration of Russian America and the Purchase of Alaska* (Evanston, Ill.: Northwestern University, 1942), 14.

45. Ibid., xi.

46. Alfred Goldsborough Mayer, *Biographical Memoir of William Stimpson, 1832–1872* (Washington: National Academy of Sciences, March 1918), 425–27.

47. The print closest to the viewer can be identified as *Barn Owl*, painted in 1832.

48. Harry Harris, *Robert Ridgway, with a Bibliography of his Published Writings and Fifty Illustrations* (Washington: Smithsonian Institution, 1928), reprinted from *The Condor* 30 (January 1928): 32–33.

49. *Annual Report for 1911*, 14. The rationale for this use of the hall was founded in the original 1846 plan: "It is hoped that this hall, which was originally planned for library purposes, may in the near future become available for such use."

50. *Annual Report for 1907*, 30–31.

51. *Annual Report for 1914*, 24.

52. *Annual Report for 1915*, 95.

53. *Annual Report for 1918*, 90.

54. *Report of the National Museum for 1915*, 13, 32.

55. *Report of the National Museum for 1919*, 59. Thirty-two more Mary Vaux Walcott watercolors were added to the exhibit in 1920. *Report of the National Museum for 1920*, 63.

56. *Report of the National Museum for 1916*, 14. These neoclassical fixtures were inverted 24-inch glass (holophane) bowls, pale brownish beige in color, and deepening in the thicker parts of the ornamental detail. A great deal of light was brought into the hall by the use of eight 60-watt bulbs in each fixture.

57. *Annual Report for 1927*, 13–17.

58. *Annual Report for 1938*, 112, and *Annual Report for 1928*, 3. The column remained in place until 1938.

59. Hope Ridings Miller, "Local Artist Starts Abroad at 75: Mrs. Walcott Will Visit with Old Japanese Friends." *New York Times*, 2 March 1924, SM10.

60. *Washington Post*, 6 August 1939, S6.

61. "The World of Art: Typographic Art and Other Kinds," *New York Times*, 2 March 1924, SM10. In addition to the exhibition at the Smithsonian, Walcott's watercolors were shown at the Anderson Gallery in New York.

62. Mary Vaux Walcott, introduction, *North American Wildflowers* (Washington, D.C.: Smithsonian Institution, 1925).

63. The "Smithsonian Process" was developed by the printer William Edwin Rudge of New York, to provide reproductions that were in character with the original watercolor drawings. The plates were printed as standard commercial four-color relief halftones on 100 percent rag paper, but the ink was not allowed to dry between printings of each color. The sheets were then dipped in water as a final step to raise the surface fibers of the paper. This water bath provided a rougher surface more nearly approximating the original watercolor paper and somewhat blended the colors. Rudge used the "Smithsonian Process" for other publications, and it was occasionally used by his successors at William E. Rudge's Sons and at the Peter Pauper Press.

64. *Annual Report for 1939*, 14. The committee consisted of Mitman (chairman), Foshay, Friedman, Setzler, and True. They met weekly, beginning in the summer of 1939, according to the *Annual Report for 1940*, 13.

65. *Stones for Building and Decoration* (New York: George P. Merrill, 1891), 116–17. http://www.archive.org/stream/stonesforbuildin00merrrich#page/116/mode/2up/search/travertines. The faux-marble treatment was executed by the master painter Morris L. Haimovicz between 17 January and 25 April 1940. SIA, RU 157, box 3, *Annual Report, Division of Buildings and Labor*, FY 1940, 57–58.

66. *Annual Report for 1940*, 13.

67. The original length was 200 feet; it now measures 125 feet.

68. J. L. Keddy to Leonard Carmichael, 11 December 1959, SIA, Records of the Under Secretary, 1958–73, RU 137, box 3. By late 1959 the Assistant Secretary initiated planning for restoration of the space then referred to as "the original Great Hall."

69. The Index Exhibit opened in January 1941. *Annual Report for 1941*, 1, 12–13. The exhibit was updated in late 1962. *Annual Report for 1963*, 21.

70. G. Carroll Lindsay to S. Dillon Ripley, 19 March 1964, OAHP, Richard Howland Papers.

71. *Annual Report for 1966*, 1–3.

72. Frank Taylor to James Bradley, 17 May 1965, SIA, Office of the Secretary (S. Dillon Ripley), 1964–71, RU 99, box 46.

73. This would eventually become the Woodrow Wilson International Center for Scholars, established by act of Congress on 24 October 1968. *Annual Report for 1969*, 483.

74. *Annual Report for 1966*, 1–3.

75. *Annual Report for 1972*, 13.

76. *Annual Report for 1990*, 161.

77. *Annual Report for 1976*, 13.

78. Rothenberg, Dorman, Rumm, Theerman, *The Papers of Joseph Henry*, vol. 6, 599. Joseph Henry to Harriet Henry, 18 December 1846. Henry had been appointed the first Secretary of the Smithsonian at the 3 December 1846 meeting of the Board of Regents.

79. Ibid., vol. 7, 570. Joseph Henry to John Torrey, Torrey Papers, New York Botanical Garden Library.

80. *Annual Report for 1854*, 70.

81. Ibid.

82. Joseph Henry to Alexander Dallas Bache, 16 October 1854, SIA, Joseph Henry Papers, 6493.

83. *Annual Report for 1856*, 234.

84. *Annual Report for 1852*, 87–88. Barton S. Alexander was at the time superintending the construction of a military and naval asylum for the District of Columbia and was assigned to the Smithsonian by Colonel Totten.

85. *Annual Report for 1854*, 70.

86. *Annual Report for 1853*, 68.

87. *Annual Report for 1854*, 70.

88. Joseph Henry, "On Acoustics Applied to Public Buildings," *Annual Report for 1856*, 221. This paper was read by Henry before the American Association for the Advancement of Science in August 1856.

89. *Annual Report for 1856*, 231.

90. *Annual Report for 1854*, 27–29.

91. Joseph Henry Desk Diary, 20 March 1858. The

painting of Washington, *Patriae Pater*, completed in 1824, depicted Washington as seen through an oval window. It was purchased for the U.S. Capitol by Congress in 1832 for $2,000 and now hangs in the Old Senate Chamber. *Glenn Brown's History of the United States Capitol*, with an introduction and annotations by William B. Bushong (Washington, D.C.: U.S. Government Printing Office, 1998), 248, 251.

92. Bernard Courlaender (ca. 1823–98) immigrated to Baltimore, Md., about 1853. He organized the piano department at the Peabody Conservatory in Baltimore and was connected with that institution until his death. *Washington Post*, 15 April 1898, 7.

93. Program for "Soiree Musicale," 1859, SICC, SI.2005.008.

94. *Annual Report for 1858*, 42–43.

95. *Annual Report for 1849*, 18. For further information on Robert Hare, consult Charles Coulston Gillespie, editor in chief, *The Dictionary of Scientific Biography*, vol. 6 (New York: Scribner, 1972) and Clark A. Elliott, comp., *Biographical Index to American Science: The Seventeenth Century to 1920* (Westport, Conn.: Greenwood Press, 1990).

96. *Annual Report for 1856*, p.45.

97. Rhees, *An Account of the Smithsonian*, 1857, 27.

98. U.S. Senate, "Report of the Special Committee of the Board of Regents Relative to the Fire," 38th Congress, 2d session, 21 February 1865, S. Rept. 129, 3. The King portraits were commissioned by the Bureau of Indian Affairs and had come to the Smithsonian as part of the National Institute collections.

99. *Annual Report for 1857*, 36.

100. *Annual Report for 1857*, 35. Also known as *The Dying Gaul,* the statue, as reported by Joseph Henry, was the work of the English sculptor Joseph Gott. However, the catalogue of a major exhibition of Gott's work in England in 1972 stated that the statue was most certainly by John Gott, a sculptor from Albany, N.Y. Terry Friedman, *Joseph Gott, 1786–1860, Sculptor, Leeds and Liverpool* (Leeds: Temple Newsam House, Stable Court Exhibition Galleries; Liverpool: Walker Art Gallery, 1972). Until 1854 John Gott's occupation was listed as "drain tile manufacturer" in the Albany city directory (*Munsell's Albany Directory*, 1852–54). He is first listed as a sculptor beginning in 1855, and in 1856 he secured a patent for a sculpture bust of John C. Frémont; as evidenced by the patent photograph, he was not an accomplished artist. It is thus not completely clear whether the sculptor of the *Dying Gladiator* that was exhibited in the Castle was John Gott or Joseph Gott. No doubt the work was sculpted well before its 1853 exhibition in New York—a time when John Gott was not known as a sculptor.

101. *Prof Baird's Proposed Circular,* January 1865, SIA, William J. Rhees Collection, 1878–1907, RU 7081, box 14. Page four of this draft document account of the fire by Baird stated that the sculpture had been shown at the Crystal Palace Exhibition in New York and that its original owner, Frederick W. Risque, an attorney, sold the sculpture before the fire to J. C. McGuire for $1,000.

102. *New York Times*, 13 November 1854, 6.

103. *Annual Report for 1857,* 35–36. The statue was on loan to the Smithsonian from its owner, F. W. Risque. It had arrived in Washington in November 1854 and was exhibited at Morrison's Building (4½ Street near Pennsylvania Avenue) by Risque for a charge of 25 cents. *The [Washington] Daily Globe* (27 November 1854, 7 December 1854, and 8 December 1854). The statue was

sent to the Smithsonian from the U.S. Capitol on 17 April 1857. Fiscal Records, Smithsonian Institution, June 1856–December 1859, vol. 2, p. 121, no. 175, SIA, RU 110, box 1, folder 1. The entry reads: "J. Cagliari—removing from Hall of Capitol Dying Gladiator to Smithsonian Institution—40.00." The statue was subsequently purchased from the estate of F. W. Risque by J. C. McGuire, a Washington auctioneer; Risque died 28 March 1862 and his estate was sold on 4 April 1863 by J. C. McGuire Auction Company. Joan M. Dixon, *National Intelligencer Newspaper Abstracts, Special Edition: The Civil War Years* (Westminster, Md,: Heritage Books, 2007), 269, 270, 279, 521, 523. As owner of the statue, McGuire was reimbursed $1,000 for his loss. Rothenberg, Dorman, Rumm, Theerman, *Joseph Henry Papers*, vol. 10, 475.

104. *Annual Report for 1864*, 56, 60.

105. Barton S. Alexander to Joseph Henry, 25 January 1865. Testimony related to U.S. Senate, "Report of the Special Committee of the Board of Regents Relative to the Fire," 38th Congress, 2d session, 21 February 1865, S. Rept. 129, 3.

106. Testimony of William J. Rhees, "Origin of the Fire at the Smithsonian Institution, February 21, 1865," 38th Congress, 2d session, S. Rept. 129, 24–25. SIA, RU 7081, box 14.

107. DeBeust does not mention the ice on the alarm box in his testimony to the Senate. *The Washington Post* reported this fact on the day of the fire. *Washington Post*, 24 January 1865, 2d ed.

108. Testimony of William DeBeust, "Origin of the Fire at the Smithsonian Institution, February 21, 1865."

109. *Evening Star*, 25 January 1865, 2d ed.

110. Testimony of Henry W. Elliott, "Origin of the Fire at the Smithsonian Institution, February 21, 1865."

111. Joseph Henry to Louis Agassiz, 30 January 1865, William Jones Rhees Collection, Huntington Library, San Marino, Calif.

112. Testimony of Henry Horan, "Origin of the Fire at the Smithsonian Institution, 21 February 1865."

113. Mary Henry Diary, 25 January 1865, SIA, RU 7001, box 51.

114. Mary Henry Diary, 25 and 26 January 1865.

115. Ibid.

116. Mary Henry Diary, 26 January 1865.

117. C. B. Young to Spencer F. Baird, 3 September 1870, SIA, RU 7002, box 36, folder 14.

118. Rothenberg, Dorman, Rumm, Theerman, *Joseph Henry Papers*, vol. 10, 478. It was erroneously reported in the 11 February 1865 *National Intelligencer* that Varden died because of an illness contracted while trying to "preserve the property under his charge" on the day of the fire.

119. Joseph Henry Desk Diary, 28 January 1865. The roof was erected with the help of the secretary of war.

120. Joseph Henry Desk Diary, 31 May 1867.

121. *Annual Report for 1865,* 19.

122. Joseph Henry to N. B. Chamberlain, 15 January 1869, SIA, Joseph Henry Papers, 49624. The Civil War had brought many problems for the Secretary concerning the lecture hall, as more people petitioned to use the space to promote their own political interests.

123. *Annual Report for 1869,* 26.

124. Joseph Henry to Felix Flugel of Leipsic, Saxony, 17 August 1868, SIA, Joseph Henry Papers, 48944.

125. *Annual Report for 1870,* 13. $10,000 was appropriated "for the preservation and exhibition of the national collection" and $10,000 "toward the preparation of the

second story of the building for the better care and display of the specimens."

126. *Annual Report for 1870,* 35. "The upper room . . . is entirely free from all hindrance to an arrangement with a view to the best exhibition of the collections."

127. *Annual Report for 1871,* 39–40.

128. Joseph Henry was likely introduced to Hawkins through Robert Barclay, director of the Montrose Natural History and Antiquarian Society in England. Barclay wrote to Henry, praising Hawkins as "the eminent Fossil constructive anatomist of London" and alerting Henry to Hawkins's upcoming lecture tour in America. Robert Barclay to Joseph Henry, 14 April 1867, SIA, Joseph Henry Papers, RU 26, box 1. Within a year Henry had become a solid advocate for Hawkins, writing to Nathaniel Morrison of the Peabody Institute to describe the lecture Hawkins gave at the Smithsonian in June 1868. The audience was "comprised of some of the higher officials of the government and a number of the principal men of science of this city and that all were delighted with his subject and the manner in which he illustrated it, by means of extemporaneous sketches with colored crayons on a large surface of blackened canvas." Joseph Henry to Nathaniel Morrison, 12 June 1868, SIA, Joseph Henry Papers, vol. 10, RU 33, box 3B.

129. Benjamin Waterhouse Hawkins to Joseph Henry, 10 April 1871, SIA, Joseph Henry Papers, vol. 113, p. 3, RU 26, box 38.

130. Joseph Henry to John Torrey, 3 May 1871, SIA, Joseph Henry Papers, RU 7001, box 4.

131. Joseph Henry to Benjamin Waterhouse Hawkins, 8 May 1871, SIA, Joseph Henry Papers, vol. 113, RU 26, box 38. Henry wrote that "the appropriation thus far made by Congress for the completion of the building is twenty thousand dollars and at least sixteen thousand dollars of this amount will be required to meet the contracts already made leaving but four thousand dollars with which to commence putting up the cases. We hope however to obtain another appropriation next winter, and, as rapidly as our means will permit, we intend to carry out in a general way the plans you have prepared."

132. Joseph Henry Desk Diary, 2 February 1872.

133. *Annual Report for 1871,* 39–41. For the number of paintings on exhibit, see Joseph Henry Desk Diary, 27 February 1872.

134. *Annual Report for 1879,* 40–41.

135. Joseph Henry Desk Diary, 8 May 1872. "Mr. Palmer the workman from Mr. Hawkins commenced to put up the restored Irish Elk." The elk was a gift from Hawkins. *Annual Report for 1872,* 48. It is unclear if this was the skeleton or the mounted skin, which were exhibited side-by-side in the hall. Stereograph, SI.2003.013.

136. *Annual Report for 1873,* 50.

137. *Annual Report for 1873,* 35.

138. Joseph Henry to Professor H. A. Ward, Rochester, N.Y., 29 July 1873, SIA, Joseph Henry Papers, 5525.

139. The whole room was devoted to ethnology, "this being a branch of science attracting perhaps at the present time more attention than almost any other." *Annual Report for 1873,* 35. The casts of prehistoric animals were moved to the Lower Main Hall as part of a natural history exhibit. *Annual Report for 1874,* 121.

140. Joseph Henry Desk Diary, 10 January 1875.

141. *Annual Report for 1874,* "Report of Special Committee on the Museum," 126.

142. Rhees, *Visitor's Guide*, 1880, 63–93.

143. *Annual Report for 1876,* 10. The Tsimshian house

front, catalogue no. 410732, was donated by James G. Swan, an employee of the Interior Department's Indian Bureau.

144. *Annual Report for 1885,* "Report on National Museum," 163, 175.

145. *Annual Report for 1886,* part 2, 111. See also *Handbook to the National Museum* (Washington, D.C.: 1886), 50–57.

146. "Report on the Operations in the Department of Antiquities, U.S. National Museum, During the Year 1884," Report of Curator Charles Rau, SIA, RU 158, box 4. Spears were taken off the walls on 10 July 1885. Henry Horan to George Brown Goode, *Semi Annual Report for July to December 1885,* SIA, RU 158, box 22.

147. *Annual Report for 1885,* part 1, 22–33. The museum received a cast of a Mexican calendar stone from the National Museum of Mexico in 1879 *(Annual Report, 1879, 11),* which is listed on page 70 of the 1880 guidebook. As it was inside case 55, it appears that it was not a large calendar stone (12 feet in diameter) acquired in 1885 and seen hanging on the wall.

148. *Annual Report for 1888,* 57. Rau died on 26 June 1887, and Wilson was appointed honorary curator on 1 December 1887; by 1890 he was listed as curator. *Annual Report for 1890,* 27.

149. *Report of the National Museum for 1891,* 188.

150. Ibid.

151. Curator Thomas Wilson's report for FY 1894, SIA, RU 158, box 4.

152. Victor Mindeleff, *A Study of Pueblo Architecture in Tusayan and Cibola,* introduction by Peter Nabokov (Washington, D.C.: Smithsonian Institution Press, 1989), ix.

153. Nabokov, introduction, *A Study of Pueblo Architecture,* x.

154. *Annual Report for 1909,* 25. Receipt by the Smithsonian of significant collections of art from Harriet Lane Johnson, Charles Freer, and William T. Evans, combined with the Institution's relatively minor collection of prints and sculpture already on hand, prompted the proposal to create a National Gallery of Art.

155. *Report of the National Museum for 1903,* 299.

156. *Report of the National Museum for 1911,* 43–44.

157. Bess Furman, "Grass Is Her Liferoot," *New York Times,* 12 June 1958, 37.

158. *New York Times,* 26 September 1963, 35.

159. "A Custodian of Grass," *Christian Science Monitor,* 20 September 1940, 9.

160. "Agnes B. Chase, U.S. Botanist," *Washington Post,* 26 September 1963, B11.

161. *Index to Grass Species,* Agnes Chase and Cornelia D. Niles, comps. (Boston: G. K. Hall, 1962), 3 vols. Her death was reported in *Annual Report for 1964,* 68.

162. *Annual Report for 1928,* 29, and *Annual Report for 1954,* 27.

163. Ellis L. Yochelson, *The National Museum of Natural History: 75 Years in the Natural History Building* (Washington, D.C.: Smithsonian Institution Press, 1985), 108.

164. The plaster had been removed from the ceiling and replaced with metal sheeting between 18 September and 29 December 1924 because it had deteriorated and large sections of it had fallen. *Annual Report for 1925,* 18–19.

165. *Annual Report for 1969,* 483–84. The recommended site was the proposed Market Square development on Pennsylvania Avenue, N.W., across from the National Archives.

166. *Annual Report for 1972,* 138.

167. *Washington Post,* 19 October 1970.

168. Richard H. Howland to Phillip Ritterbush, 15 July 1966, SIA, RU 99, box 46.

169. The move occurred during the week of 10 August 1998.

170. Proverbs 31:31. A shortened version, inscribed above the door to the Women's Pavilion at the 1876 Centennial Exhibition in Philadelphia, read: "Let Her Works Praise Her in the Gates."

171. *Annual Report of the National Museum for 1891,* insert, 186.

172. The tapestry, on loan to the SICC from the Smithsonian American Art Museum, a gift of Mrs. Philip Coffin, is still on view in the former Wilson Center library.

173. Michael Dunn, "The Fall of Troy Superseded in Horror," *The Woodrow Wilson Center Report* 5, no. 2 (1993): 5. The conference participant was the psychiatrist Bennett Simon of Harvard Medical School.

174. Margaret R. Scherer, *The Legends of Troy in Art and Literature* (New York: Phaidon, 1963), 124.

The West Wing and the West Range

1. Joseph Henry Desk Diary, 5 February 1850, SIA, Henry Collection, RU 7001, box 14. "Prof Jewett commenced moving today into the library west wing." For reference to the main library, see *Annual Report for 1853,* 30.

2. *Annual Report for 1850,* 30.

3. *Annual Report for 1852,* 27. Stanley's paintings were installed by February 1852. Joseph Henry Desk Diary, 9 February 1852.

4. Rhees, *Journals,* 119, 133, 138.

5. *Annual Report for 1853,* 30.

6. *Annual Report for 1857,* 31.

7. *Annual Report for 1853,* 30.

8. Diary of Francis Ormand French, 31 December 1851, Library of Congress, Manuscript Division, Benjamin Brown French Family Papers. During the first months of the Institution's history, Benjamin Brown French served as Assistant Secretary under William Jervis Hough and extended to Joseph Henry the invitation to serve as Secretary. He was later named the commissioner of public buildings and grounds, a position that included supervising the maintenance and design of the Smithsonian grounds.

9. John Varden Papers, 1829–63, SIA, RU 7063, box 1, Diary, 1857–63. Varden, the caretaker of the museum, was responsible for installing the collections. The last entry regarding the art gallery was on 22 January 1863, when he was instructed to hang the portrait of George Washington.

10. Notable busts and sculpture groups on the north side of the hall were President Martin Van Buren; *Sleeping Child,* a subject popular in the Renaissance (fifth pedestal); Joel R. Poinsett, founder of the National Institute and namesake of the poinsettia plant (sixth pedestal); Diana and Apollo (far end); and a sculpture group designed to ornament the U.S. Capitol (in the blind arch).

11. Rhees, *Visitor's Guide,* 1863, 61.

12. *Annual Report for 1866,* 14, and *Annual Report for 1874,* 65.

13. *Annual Report for 1868,* 34, and Joseph Henry Desk Diary, 11 April 1871. "The large room formerly occupied by the library having had the old and decayed floor replaced with iron girders and brick arches will be ready for the meeting of the National Academy on Tuesday one week from today. The outer range will be used as the meeting room for the committee of the academy."

14. *Annual Report for 1863,* 55–56. This object is also visible in the top photograph on p. 71 of this book.

15. The hall's first use was for the meeting of the National Academy on 18 April 1871, before the exhibits were installed. Joseph Henry Desk Diary, 11 April 1871, box 15. Henry noted after the meeting that the hall's empty condition produced a reverberation. Joseph Henry Desk Diary, 20 April 1871.

16. Rothenberg, Dorman, Rumm, and Theerman, *The Papers of Joseph Henry,* vol. 10 (Washington, D.C.: Smithsonian Institution Press, 2004), xxxv.

17. Rexmond C. Cochrane, *The National Academy of Sciences: Its First Hundred Years, 1863–1963* (Washington, D.C.: National Academy of Sciences, 1978), 17. Annual meetings of the academy were held in the Castle until 1879, when the space proved inadequate. Meetings that year and the next were held in the vestry of All Souls Church and beginning in 1881 in the newly completed National Museum (Arts and Industries Building). *Annual Report for 1879,* 64–65, and *Annual Report for 1881,* xii. The academy continued to occupy office space in the Castle.

18. *Annual Report for 1871,* 38. The floor was raised 18 inches. Joseph Henry Desk Diary, 23 February 1871.

19. Joseph Henry Desk Diary, 26 February 1872.

20. Mary Henry Diary, 29 October 1867, SIA, RU 7001, box 51. Henry Wood Elliot (1846–1930), an artist and a naturalist, sometimes served as Joseph Henry's private secretary, taking dictation and performing other related duties. Rothenberg, Dorman, Rumm, Theerman, *The Papers of Joseph Henry,* 2007, vol. 11, 397, n2.

21. Mary Henry Diary, 25 December 1866.

22. *Washington Post,* 26 April 1903, 2.

23. Joseph Henry and Salmon P. Chase to Congress, 1 May 1868, SIA, William J. Rhees Collection, RU 7081, box 10.

24. *Report of the National Museum for 1885,* part II, 803. Joseph Henry wrote to Shindler that "you can have wall-room at the Institution for your Indian portraits though if placed here they will be at your own risk." Henry to A. Z. Shindler, 18 May 1870, Records of the Secretary, Outgoing Correspondence for December 1869–May 1870, RU 33, box 6. Paula Fleming, formerly of the National Anthropological Archives, has conducted much research on Shindler and provided this reference.

25. Richard Rathbun, *The National Gallery of Art,* 1909, originally published in *U.S. National Museum Bulletin* 70 (1909): 32. The portrait of Guizot was painted in 1841 by the American artist George Peter Alexander Healy (1813–94).

26. John Varden Diary, 21 February 1862. "Solomon & Jim helping me hang Constantinople."

27. John Varden Diary, 28 February 1861. "Woltz at work making 1 doz spit boxes ordered by S F Baird."

28. Joseph Henry Desk Diary, 4 January 1858. Glass doors, given by the secretary of the interior, were used to enclose the cloisters.

29. Rathbun, *The National Gallery of Art,* 70–71. These sculptures and several portrait busts from the art collection were loaned to the Corcoran Gallery of Art in 1874 for safekeeping.

30. *Report of the National Museum for 1917,* 95. Smillie had done photographic work for the Institution in 1869–70 and was hired in June 1871. Thomas W. Smillie, "History of the Department of Photography," July 1906. Records of the Assistant Secretary in charge of the U.S. National Museum (Richard Rathbun), 1897–1918, SIA, RU 55, box 20. Joseph Henry Desk Diary, 24 March 1870, states that the Regents' Room was used for photography before this studio was created. The photograph of the sculpture in the cloister was inscribed by William H. Holmes, "In 1871–1872, I studied photography with Mr. Smillie in the room next this in the Smithsonian Building."

31. For the type of armor: Paul Taylor to Heather Ewing, memorandum, 31 July 1992, office of the curator of the SICC. For all other data, see http://www.wakagashira.com/history.

32. Joanna C. Scherer and Vicki Simon, "Red Cloud's and His Uncle's Shirt: Historical Representation in the Museum as Seen through Photo Analysis." For more information, see http://anthropology.si.edu/redcloud/index.htm.

33. Richard Stamm and Paula Fleming, "The Castle Stereos: Views of Exhibits in the Smithsonian Institution," *Stereo World* (March–April 2010): 18. Extensive research on the mannequins and costumes was performed by Paula Fleming, photo historian and photo archivist (retired), Smithsonian National Anthropological Archives.

34. Rhees, *Visitor's Guide*, 1863, 68. The description of Kane's outfit was reprinted in the Smithsonian guide from Kane's account of his expedition.

35. *Annual Report for 1881*, 105. "The fitting up of the west range of the Smithsonian building for the reception of alcoholic vertebrates—a work now nearly completed—will enable the curator of this department to revolutionize its arrangement during the coming year." *Annual Report for 1882*, 143–44: the assignment of the West Wing and the occupation of the West Range by marine invertebrates.

36. Henry Horan to George Brown Goode, Semi-Annual Report, 31 May 1882, SIA, RU 158, box 22.

37. *Annual Report for 1888*, 17–18.

38. *Annual Report for 1878*, 40–41.

39. The Albert Memorial was unveiled and dedicated by Queen Victoria in 1876. The four corner pieces depict the four continents, each symbolized by an indigenous animal surrounded by allegorical figures: Africa, a camel; Asia, an elephant; Europe, a bull; and America, a bison.

40. Rhees, *Visitor's Guide*, 1880, 59.

41. *Report of the National Museum for 1885*, 27, 49. Only the wall cases were used for marine invertebrates. Rhees, *Visitor's Guide*, 1886, v–vi. "Keramics" were shown located in the West Main Hall and the West Court of the Arts and Industries Building, while Doulton's group, *America*, was still located in the West Wing of the Castle.

42. Report of the Building's Supervisor, 1889–97, SIA, RU 158, box 23, folder 4: "1 July 1891. The terra-cotta group 'Guiding the Course of America' was removed from the Chapel [West Wing], Smithsonian building and packed in crates ready for the disposition of the owners Mssrs Dalton [Doulton] and Company of England. To successfully remove the same, it became necessary to cut a hole in the roof of the Chapel. The heavy work was done by Knox's Express, and the material taken out through the hole opening in the roof." Report of the Building's Supervisor, 24 April 1892, 49, states that the *Americas* group was shipped to Chicago for the World's Columbian Exposition.

43. Ibid. The work carried out by Cluss & Schulze, which provided a wood floor, was nonetheless considered fireproof because the supporting members consisted of iron beams and brick vaulting.

44. Adolf Cluss and Paul Schulze to Samuel P. Langley, 10 April 1888, Records of the Office of the Secretary, 1882–90, SIA, Incoming Correspondence, RU 30, box 3. This letter is inscribed on top, "Do Nothing."

45. *Report of the National Museum for 1893*, 165–66. The marine invertebrates had actually been put on display in 1887. However, because of the closing of the West Range for fireproofing, the West Wing was inaccessible. The exhibit of marine invertebrates was then open to the public for a brief time in 1889–90. *Report of the National Museum for 1887*, 128–29; *Report of the National Museum for 1888*, 175; and *Report of the National Museum for 1889*, 381.

46. *Report of the National Museum for 1897*, 53, and *Report of the United States Government Exhibit at the Tennessee Centennial Exposition Nashville* (Washington, D.C.: U.S. Government Printing Office, 1901), plates 30–31.

47. *Report of the National Museum for 1901*, 65, 187–88.

48. *Report of the National Museum for 1903*, floor plan of the Arts and Industries Building, plate 25 and p. 300: reptiles and fishes in the southeast range of Arts and Industries; floor plan of the Smithsonian Building, plate 28 and p. 303: insect exhibition hall in the Castle.

49. *Report of the National Museum for 1901*, 66.

50. *Report of the National Museum for 1902*, 59–60.

51. *Report of the National Museum for 1897*, part II, "Memoir of George Brown Goode," 55. George Brown Goode (1851–96) is known as a museum administrator, a historian of science, and an ichthyologist.

52. *Report of the National Museum for 1913*, 46.

53. See http://americanhistory.si.edu/starspangledbanner/family-keepsake.aspx.

54. "Real Star-Spangled Banner," *Washington Post*, 21 July 1907, MS 4.

55. Charles Walcott to Elliott Woods, 10 October 1908, SIA, Records of the Office of the Secretary, 1907–24, RU 45, box 79. Congress transferred the statue to the Smithsonian because of concern over the work's deterioration resulting from exposure.

56. "Dealer Gets Letter of Sculptor of Washington's Statue," *Washington Post*, 17 May 1914, 30.

57. *Annual Report for 1908*, 28.

58. Draft of the minutes of the first meeting of the Advisory Committee on Painting and Sculpture for the National Gallery of Art, 16 April 1908, SIA, RU 45, box 78.

59. *Report of the National Museum for 1963*, 21.

60. A series of photographs shows the preparations for the removal of the statue. SIA, RU 562, "Buildings Pictures" folder.

61. *Report of the National Museum for 1914*, 91–92.

62. "Restoring the Flag, Woman Is Engaged in Repairing Star-Spangled Banner," *Washington Post*, 19 May 1914, 4.

63. "Display of Graphic Arts," *Washington Post*, 21 July 1912, 4.

64. *Report of the National Museum for 1893*, 25.

65. *Report of the National Museum for 1917*, 25, and *Report of the National Museum for 1919*, 58. The first figure was installed in 1917, the second in 1919. By at least 1930 and possibly 1927, the mannequins and the case were located at the west end of the Lower Main Hall. *Brief Guide to the Smithsonian Institution*, 1930, 63.

66. *Report of the National Museum for 1921*, 123.

67. The photograph can be dated to between 1931 and 1934. Twenty-one-year-old Robert Mooney was listed as "clerk, govt." in the 1930 U.S. Census. He resigned his position in the Division of Graphic Arts, accepting a position at the Internal Revenue Service in 1934. "The Federal Diary," *Washington Post*, 5 November 1934, 20.

68. *G. A. 100: The Centenary of the Division of Graphic Arts*, SIA, catalogue for an exhibition at the National Museum of American History, May 1986, 30.

69. Ibid., 35–41.

70. *Report of the National Museum for 1938*, 68.

71. *Report of the National Museum for 1942*, 73. The Department of Engineering and Industries, under which the Division of Graphic Arts fell, changed electric service from direct current to alternating current, which made it possible to "properly illuminate . . . a number of important exhibits in several sections of the Department."

72. *Annual Report for 1954*, 2, 25.

73. "How Prints Are Made," *Washington Post*, 24 October 1926, SM7.

74. *Annual Report for 1956*, 4, 38, and *Annual Report for 1858*, 40.

75. Frank A. Taylor to Leonard Carmichael, memorandum, 30 January 1956, SIA, RU 276, box 39.

76. Invitation from the Regents and the Secretary of the Smithsonian Institution, SIA, RU 276, box 39.

77. *Report of the National Museum for 1959*, 30.

78. *Annual Report for 1971*, 84.

79. A. F. Michael to Richard H. Howland, 17 June 1970, SIA, RU 99, box 384. In a telephone conversation with Cynthia Field on 1 December 1992, Howland stated that the choice of ceiling treatment was made because Sainte Chapelle was deemed to be an appropriate source for the period of restoration and its proportions were approximately the same as those of the West Wing.

80. James M. Goode, correspondence and memoranda relating to the escutcheons, 1971, Smithsonian Building Collection, AHHP.

81. Nan Robertson, "Group of Ten Will Confer in Castle on Mall," *New York Times*, 15 December 1971, 91.

82. Edwin L. Dale Jr., "The Dollar: Why It Feels So Good to Devalue," *New York Times*, 26 December 1971, E1.

83. *Annual Report for 1972*, 21.

84. Ibid., 115.

85. *Annual Report for 1974*, 6.

86. Mary Grace Potter to Robert Mason, 19 December 1974, attached to a letter from Potter to James M. Goode, 24 February 1975, SIA, Records of the Office of the Secretary, 1975, box 8.

87. The essay "Painting as a Pastime" was originally published in Churchill's book *Amid These Storms* (New York: Scribner, 1932).

88. Winston Churchill, *Painting as a Pastime*, 1950 (Reprint, New York: Cornerstone Library, 1965), 13. This reprint was a complete, unabridged copy of the 1950 McGraw-Hill hardcover edition.

89. Marilyn Hoffman, "Chartwell: A Look into the Home of Winston Churchill and His Family," *Christian Science Monitor*, 25 August 1983, 11.

90. Leslie Judd Portner, "Churchill to Open Own Show Here," *Washington Post*, 2 March 1958, E8.

91. "Churchill's Art Seen by 223,000," *Washington Post*, 21 May 1958, B1.

92. "A New Smithsonian Exhibition Takes Visitors into Secretary Madeleine Albright's Jewelry Box," press release, 15 April 2010.

The Towers

1. Joseph Henry Desk Diary, 23 April 1850, SIA, Henry Collection, RU 7001, box 14. Henry believed that "the building would be improved by so doing."

2. *Annual Report for 1864*, 38.

3. Horatio Greenough, *The Travels, Observations, and Experience of a Yankee Stonecutter* (New York: 1852). A facsimile reproduction with an introduction by Nathalia Wright (Gainesville, Fla.: Scholars' Facsimiles and Reprints, 1958), 44–47.

4. Owen, *Hints on Public Architecture*, 14. "There are nine

towers in all, including a small one at each wing." The two small towers to which Owen refers are the north tower attached to the West Wing and the bell tower on the east front of the East Wing, which was demolished during the 1883–84 renovation of the wing by Adolf Cluss. Although Owen referred to the small tower attached to the western face of the South Tower as a "turret," today it is considered the ninth tower, as the terms are synonymous.

5. Joseph Henry to Asa Gray, 6 November 1852, Harvard University, Peabody Museum of Archeology, Gray Herbarium. Henry was in the South Tower office from 1852 to about 1861, when he moved to the North Towers. His office suite included three rooms, one in each tower and the third in the connecting room between them.

6. Owen, *Hints on Public Architecture*, 107.

7. Rhees, *Journals*, 657.

8. Joseph Henry Desk Diary, 8 March 1865. "Wrote to Secretary of War thanks for assistance in protecting the Inst. by roof."

9. Joseph Henry to Spencer F. Baird, 4 September 1866, SIA, Joseph Henry Papers, 23607.

10. Joseph Henry Desk Diary, 16 November 1860. "The round windows proposed by Mr. Cluss to give light to one of the rooms in the large rear tower have been cut[. Make] a striking difference in the appearance. I cannot say for better or worse."

11. *Annual Report for 1867*, 103.

12. Rhees, *Visitor's Guide*, 1865, 18.

13. *Annual Report for 1867*, 102. Also: Thos. Evans, Contract for Plumbing Expenditures on Building, 4 April 1867, RU 7081, box 5, folder 4. "Specification of Plumbers Work, required on Reconstruction of Smithsonian Building. South Tower and adjoining spaces: One water closet and wash basin in cellar. One water closet, large size china urinal and wash basin on 1st floor. One water closet, bathing tub with copper-tinned and planished shower and wash basin with attached swing urinal on half story above vestibule. One wash basin with swing urinal on second story. One wash basin with attached urinal on third story."

14. Rhees, *Visitor's Guide*, 1887, 24. Commodore Jesse Duncan Elliott, who brought the sarcophagus to the United States in 1839, wrote to the president and the directors of the National Institute, 8 April 1845, explaining why Andrew Jackson had refused the honor.

15. Rhees, *Visitor's Guide*, 1887, 23.

16. John Varden Diary, 28 November 1860: ". . . removed the Sarcophagus inside of the South door."

17. Rhees, *Visitor's Guide*, 1869, 15–16.

18. Joseph Henry Desk Diary, 29 June 1871. "During my absence a brick pier has been built under the arch of the south entrance of the main building. This arch was giving way under the pressure of the heavy sarcophagus."

19. Solomon G. Brown to Spencer F. Baird, 15 July 1864, SIA, RU 7002, box 16. *Annual Report for 1895*, 5.

20. *Annual Report for 1899*, 8.

21. *Annual Report for 1901*, 555.

22. Samuel P. Langley to Richard Rathbun, 10 October 1899, SIA, RU 55, box 17. At the turn of the century, Hornblower & Marshall was also involved in alterations to the Arts and Industries Building and Holt House at the National Zoological Park. By 1904 the firm was preparing designs for Smithson's crypt in the Smithsonian Building, as well being in the midst of two major Smithsonian construction projects: the National Museum of Natural History on the Mall and the first Small Mammal House at the National Zoo.

23. J. S. Goldsmith to J. E. Watkins, 26 April 1900, SIA,

RU 55, box 17. On the role of the architects, see Hornblower & Marshall to Richard Rathbun, 19 October and 28 October 1899, Records of the Office of the Secretary, 1891–1906, SIA, RU 55, box 17.

24. Hugo Mullerett to Frederick W. True, 26 January 1901, SIA, RU 55, box 17. Mullerett designed the aquarium for the Smithsonian.

25. Samuel P. Langley to Richard Rathbun, 30 November 1898, Records of the Assistant Secretary in Charge of the U.S. National Museum, 1897–1918, SIA, RU 55, box 17.

26. A Boston native and a former art instructor at the Cleveland Art School, she arrived in Washington in 1894 to set up a decorating firm with her former classmate and friend, Elizabeth B. Sheldon. The partnership, which lasted only about a year, was named Sheldon and Temple. One of its first commissions was to design the interiors of the Women's Building at the Atlanta Cotton States and International Exposition in 1895. Temple was also selected to design the Government Building for the Louisiana Purchase Exposition, held in St. Louis in 1904. For more biographical information on her, see Linda NeCastro, "Grace Lincoln Temple and the Smithsonian's Children's Room of 1901," M.A. thesis, Bryn Mawr College, 1988; Jessie Fant Evans, "Pioneer Career Woman Here Is Authority in Art World," *Washington Star*, 29 December 1940; "Miss Grace Temple D.C. Decorator Dies," *Washington Post*, 24 February 1953, 16.

27. *Annual Report for 1901*, 555. Albert Bigelow Paine's four-volume biography of Mark Twain was published in 1912; his other works on Twain were *The Boy's Life of Mark Twain* (1916), ed., *Mark Twain's Letters*, 2 vols. (1917), *A Short Life of Mark Twain* (1920), and ed., *Mark Twain's Speeches* (1923).

28. *Annual Report for 1901*, 554–55. For a more complete history of the Children's Room, see Mary McCutcheon, "The Children's Room at the Smithsonian: 1901 to 1939," *Curator* 35, no. 1 (March 1992): 12.

29. *Annual Report for 1901*, 560.

30. *Annual Report for 1941*, 13.

31. *Annual Report for 1943*, 3.

32. *Annual Report for 1938*, 55.

33. *Annual Report for 1943*, 3.

34. *Annual Report for 1966*, 38. For the location of the shop: Robert Mason to S. Dillon Ripley, "Response to Space Reorganization Questions," memorandum, 25 March 1966, SIA, RU 99, box 46. Mason suggested eliminating the South Tower salesroom.

35. *Annual Report for 1972*, 115.

36. *Annual Report for 1974*, 244–47.

37. *Annual Report for 1990*, 161.

38. *Annual Report for 1901*, 555.

39. *Annual Report for 1899*, 8. At the time, it was thought that Henry was born in 1799, which he himself believed; his baptismal record, however, shows that he was born 17 December 1797. Nathan Reingold, Stuart Pierson, Arthur P. Molella, eds., *The Papers of Joseph Henry*, vol. 1 (Washington, D.C.: Smithsonian Institution Press, 1972), 3.

40. *Annual Report for 1856*, 227–29.

41. George C. Bartlett, *The Salem Seer: Reminiscences of Charles H. Foster* (New York: 1891), preface, and "Spiritual Swindling," *Boston Daily Globe*, 30 July 1873, 4. Emanuel Swedenborg (1688–1772) was a Swedish scientist, philosopher, and mystic. His religious doctrines formed the basis for the New Jerusalem Church. *Random House Webster's College Dictionary* (New York: Random House, 1991).

42. Mary Henry Diary, 17 March 1868.

43. Ann Braude, *Radical Spirits* (Boston: Beacon Press, 1989), 5.

44. Joseph Henry Desk Diary, 17 March 1868.

45. Mary Henry Diary, 17 March 1868.

46. Joseph Henry Desk Diary, 11 December 1852. "Took possession of the Regents' Room in the South Tower."

47. Rhees, *Journals*, 660. In a letter to his wife, Harriett, dated 6 July 1848, Henry made note of the "large table of the Smithsonian and chairs belonging to the table" being put together in one of the rooms. Henry was living in rented quarters while the building was under construction. Joseph Henry Papers, SIA, 7587.

48. Rhees, *Journals*, 695. The Regents voted on the choice of maroon leather at their 26 November 1847 meeting.

49. William J. Rhees, *James Smithson and His Bequest*, Smithsonian Miscellaneous Collections, 1880, no. 330, 15.

50. Smithsonian Fiscal Records, June 1856—December 1859, 31 March 1857, vol. 2, 161, p. 112, SIA, RU 110, box 1, folder 1. For Smithson's effects exhibited in the Regents' Room, see *Annual Report for 1857*, 34. See also Rhees, *Journals*, 78.

51. Rhees, *James Smithson and His Bequest*, 13–17.

52. The bronze medallion portrait of James Smithson was among his personal possessions brought back from England by Richard Rush after successfully prosecuting the Smithson bequest through the Court of Chancery. Smithson had scratched his name on the reverse side and attached a small tag to it that read "my likeness." Long thought to be by the Italian sculptor Antonio Canova, the medal was commissioned by Smithson at an unknown date from Pierre Joseph Tiolier (1763–1819), engraver general of France, and marked with his distinctive letter *T* on the obverse side. The medal has also been attributed to Tiolier's son, Pierre Nicolas Tiolier (1784–1853), who succeeded his father as engraver general. However, the younger Tiolier signed his work "N Tiolier." The Smithson medallion is now in the National Numismatic Collection, National Museum of American History, Behring Center.

53. The portraits are mentioned in Rhees, *An Account of the Smithsonian*, 1857, 18. Smithson's library was placed in the library at the direction of Joseph Henry. Joseph Henry Desk Diary, 4 March 1858. The Berghem painting is mentioned in Rhees, *Smithson and His Bequest*, 16. There is no information that the painting was rescued from the room during the fire, indicating that it may have been moved sometime before 24 January 1865.

54. *Annual Report for 1877*, 9.

55. Rhees, *Smithson and His Bequest*, 16. The price paid was $100 for two portraits, one of Smithson and one of Henry Dickinson, Smithson's half-brother. *Annual Report for 1877*, 9. The reference for John's biography is E. Benezit, *Dictionnaire critique et documentaire des Peintres, Sculpteurs, Dessinateurs et Graveurs, Librairie Grund* (Paris: 1976), 84.

56. A list of the objects is found in *Annual Report for 1880*, 3–4.

57. Joseph C. Hornblower to Richard Rathbun, 23 April 1900, SIA, RU 31, box 35. The brick was similar to the exterior of the W. J. Boardman house of 1893, located at 1818 P Street, N.W., which was one of Hornblower & Marshall's most important commissions. See also Anne E. Peterson, *Hornblower and Marshall, Architects* (Washington, D.C.: Preservation Press, 1978), 18.

58. Roger W. Moss, *Lighting for Historic Buildings* (Washington, D.C.: Preservation Press, 1988), 184. The Welsbach burner was patented in 1885 and used in this country from 1890 until its replacement by electricity. See also Denys Peter Myers, *Gaslighting in America* (Washington, D.C.: U.S. Department of the Interior, 1978), 207. Early electric lighting devices had undesirable drawbacks, such as the need to string wiring and frequent power failures.

59. *Annual Report for 1901,* xix.

60. *Annual Report for 1902,* xiv.

61. Alexander Graham Bell to Samuel P. Langley, with attached notes by William Henry Bishop, 15 March 1904, Secretary's files, 1904, SIA, RU 7000, box 4, folder 10. U.S. consul in Genoa, Italy, describing the exhumation of Smithson's remains in Italy. The glass negatives taken by Mrs. Bell are in the Prints and Photographs Division, Library of Congress, Gilbert H. Grosvenor Collection.

62. *Annual Report for 1904,* xx–xxiii.

63. Ibid., xxiv.

64. *Annual Report for 1912,* 130.

65. *Report of the National Museum for 1911,* 44.

66. For a history of the CWA, see Bonnie Fox Schwartz, *The Civil Works Administration, 1933–1934: The Business of Emergency Employment in the New Deal* (Princeton, N. J.: Princeton University Press, 1984).

67. *Report of the National Museum for 1934,* 35.

68. "100 Mechanics and Scientists Given Work of Refurbishing Smithsonian Institution," *Washington Post,* 6 December 1933, 15.

69. Richard H. Howland to Philip Ritterbush, 15 July 1966, SIA, Records of the Office of the Secretary, 1964–71, RU 99, box 46. See also accession card SI.65.88, AHHP, SICC.

70. *Paul and Virginia* was a popular French novel by Jacques-Henri Bernardin de Saint-Pierre, first published in 1788. It told the tragic story of a pair of French children raised on a tropical island who grow to love each other but are separated and ultimately die young. The novel was reprinted countless times in Europe and the United States and inspired songs, poems, plays, and objects such as the girandole.

71. The painting depicts William Jervis Hough, his wife, two daughters, and son; painted by J. Brayton Wilcox, ca. 1847–49, it measures more than five-feet square. It was a gift to the Smithsonian's National Portrait Gallery in 1969 from Violet Shepherd, Hough's great-granddaughter.

72. Rhees, *The Smithsonian Institution*, vol. 1, 423–27. The use of the word *Regent* for the members of the governing board was introduced in this piece of legislation by William Jervis Hough, a congressman from the state of New York, where the term *Regents* has been in continuous use for the governors of the state university.

73. Rhees, *Journals,* 2.

74. James M. Hobbins to Richard Stamm, 10 May 2001, Office of the Curator, SICC.

75. "Doors & Keys, April 1879," SIA, RU 7081, box 21. Ridgway had sleeping quarters in the room directly above this office on the sixth floor in 1875. Alexander Wetmore, *Biographical Memoir of Robert Ridgway, 1850–1929* (Washington, D.C.: National Academy of Sciences, 1932), 62. See also Robert Ridgway to Spencer F. Baird, 6 December 1875, RU 7002, box 32, "Should you need me I will be in the South Tower."

76. Harry Harris, "Robert Ridgway, with a Biography of His Published Writings," reprinted from *The Condor* 30 (January 1938): 15–20.

77. Robert Ridgway, "Spencer Fullerton Baird," *The Auk* 5, no. 1 (January 1888).

78. Harris, "Robert Ridgway," 32.

79. Ridgway was in the South Tower office between 1875 and 1895. *Report of the National Museum for 1895,* 55–56, states that he was writing primarily out of his home. See also *Annual Report for 1929,* 20–21.

80. For biographical information, see Alexander Wetmore, *Biographical Memoir of Robert Ridgway,* 57–101. For a bibliographic reference, see Charles C. Gillespie, ed., *Dictionary of Scientific Biography,* vol. 11 (New York: Scribner, 1981), 443.

81. "Curious Experiences . . . ," *Washington Post,* 2 September 1886, 2.

82. Wilton Dillon to Richard E. Stamm, interview, 7 October 1992.

83. Wilton Dillon, "Elizabeth Taylor and Mr. Smithson's Ghost," unpub. essay, Office of the Curator, SICC.

84. The portrait (ca. 1928) is of a young socialite, Kate Hyde Scully, who met the artist Howard Chandler Christy while on a trans-Atlantic cruise. Christy expressed a great desire to paint a portrait of Kate, then fourteen years old, as she was "such a beautiful young lady." In 1945 Kate Scully married Lieutenant Commander A. Smith Bowman Jr., USNR, owner and namesake of the A. Smith Bowman Distillery in Virginia. She died in 1960 at the age of forty-six.

85. Dillon, "Elizabeth Taylor and Mr. Smithson's Ghost."

86. "Reliable Source: A Castle Roost," *The Smithsonian Torch* (August 1980): 4.

87. Alexander Wetmore to S. Dillon Ripley, memorandum, 15 November 1971, SIA, RU 99, box 509.

88. "Owls Protect Smithsonian from Starlings," *Washington Post,* 24 December 1933, SM5.

89. Alexander Wetmore to S. Dillon Ripley, 15 November 1971, memorandum, Office of the Curator, SICC, Owls file.

90. Ibid.

91. Bart Barnes, "Louis Halle Jr., Naturalist and Author, Dies at 87," *Washington Post,* 22 August 1998.

92. *Annual Report for 1886,* 45. The quotation is from "Autobiographical Memoir of Mary Jane Rathbun," unpub. ms., Mary Jane Rathbun Papers, SIA, RU 7256, box 8.

93. "S.I. Barn Owl Re-Establishment Research Project," Guy A. Greenwell to John D. Blackwell, 10 September 1973, SIA, RU 157, box 48.

94. "Where's Athena?," *Smithsonian Torch* (January 1976): 7.

95. Kathryn Lindeman, "Increase and Diffusion Reinstate Barn Owl Tradition in SI Tower," *Smithsonian Torch* (June 1977): 2.

96. James Dodd, 9 September 1977, Owl Record, Smithsonian Building Collection, AHHP.

97. Mary Henry Diary, 10 July 1864.

98. Henry had established a nationwide network of observers in 1849, the forerunner of the present-day National Weather Service. For a detailed discussion of the Smithsonian's meteorological project, see *Joseph Henry: Father of Weather Service,* by Frank Rives Millikan, historian, Joseph Henry Papers Project, http://siarchives.si.edu/history/jhp/joseph03.htm.

99. U.S. Congress, Senate, "Report of the Special Committee of the Board of Regents Relative to the Fire," 38th Congress, 2d session, 21 February 1865, S. Rept. 129, 25. Force helped remove these records during the 2fire of 1865, ensuring their survival; as he testified

afterwards, "I remained in the rooms, directing what was most important to be removed, until driven out by the smoke, and then left by way of a ladder from the north portico, on which stones were then falling from the walls of the building."

100. William B. Taylor, "A Memoir of Joseph Henry, A Sketch of His Scientific Work," *Bulletin of the Philosophical Society* (1879): 324–25.

101. Carl Sandburg, *Abraham Lincoln: The Prairie Years and The War Years* (New York: Harcourt, Brace and World, 1954), 260–61.

102. Mary Henry Diary, 26 January 1865, SIA, RU 7001, box 51.

103. *Annual Report for 1884,* 9.

104. W. T. True to L. L. Oliver, 20 February 1948, SIA, RU 157, series 3, box 69. Webster Prentiss True was chief of the Editorial Division, the precursor of the Smithsonian Institution Press.

105. The flagpole is mounted inside the tower's twelfth-floor room and rises through a hole in the roof, projecting thirty-two feet above the roof level. The weathervane at the top of the pole is 177 feet above ground.

106. Joseph Henry to Spencer F. Baird, 24 August 1863, SIA, RU 7002, box 25.

107. "Origin of the Fire at the Smithsonian Institution," 21 February 1865, SIA, RU 7081, box 14.

108. Records of the North Pacific Exploring Expedition Collection, 1852–61 and n.d., SIA, RU 7253, box 1.

109. Joseph Henry Desk Diary, 24 January 1865.

110. "Smithsonian Rules and Regulations," January 1872, SIA, RU 7081, box 5, 19–41. "Doors & Keys, April 1879."

111. Joseph Henry Desk Diary, 26 September 1872, box 15. The Catlin sketches were first installed in February. Joseph Henry Desk Diary, 27 February 1872.

112. *Annual Report for 1872,* 41.

113. Thomas R. Henry, "Smithsonian Tower Romance Revealed by Visiting Mayor Iowa Official as Boy Carried Meals to Struggling Painter of Indian Subjects in Loft of Institution." From a longer (ca. 1922) newspaper article with no citation, found in SIA, RU 7081, box 42, Catlin folder.

114. *Annual Report for 1877,* 10.

115. "Report of the Special Committee of the Board of Regents Relative to the Fire," 31.

116. "Smithsonian Rules and Regulations," January 1872, SIA, RU 7081, box 5, 19–41. "Doors & Keys, April 1879."

117. *Annual Report for 1877,* 10.

118. Ibid., 9–11.

119. *Annual Report for 1929,* 102–4.

120. Charles G. Abbot to S. Dillon Ripley, 6 August 1968, SIA, RU 99, box 213.

121. Hugh McDiarmid, "Dr. Abbot Looks Back From Atop His Tower," *Washington Post,* 24 November 1966, G14.

122. *Annual Report for 1929,* 9.

123. McDiarmid, "Dr. Abbot Looks Back From Atop His Tower."

124. S. Dillon Ripley to James Bradley, "Renovation and Restoration of the Smithsonian Building," memorandum, n.d., SIA, RU 532, box 106, SI Project file.

125. *Smithsonian Torch* (May 1970): 1.

126. R. P. Wunder to S. Dillon Ripley, 18 May 1965, SIA, RU 99, box 46.

127. Two letters from Forrest E. Verdin to James M. Murphy, one dated 7 July 1966, stating the intended date of 17 July for installation of the clocks, and one dated

25 July 1966, reporting on the completion of the job, SIA, RU 532, box 103.

128. Joseph Gwilt, *The Encyclopedia of Architecture, Historical, Theoretical, and Practical,* ed. Wyatt Papworth (New York: Bonanza Books, 1982), 227–28. The earliest adaptation of a portico large enough to accommodate a carriage was thought to be at Longford Hall, Shropshire, England, designed about 1785 by the architect Joseph Bonami (1739–1808).

129. U.S. Patent Office, patent no. 360760, 5 April 1887.

130. Smith Hempstone Oliver and Donald H. Berkebile, "Wheels and Wheeling: The Smithsonian Cycle Collection" (Washington, D.C.: Smithsonian Institution, 1973), frontispiece. The other men in the photograph are identified as B. C. Poole, a patent attorney, with an associate (far left), and Edwin H. Hawley and W. H. Travis (left to right, right side of the tricycle). In the *Guide to the Smithsonian Institution Archives,* page 144, Hawley is identified as "preparator, Department of Arts and Industries." No listing of W. H. Travis as an employee of the Smithsonian or the National Museum could be found.

131. "A Steam Tricycle: A Novel Device that Suits Lazy Athletes," *Boston Daily Globe,* 2 February 1888, 5.

132. "Granddaddy of the Motorcycle, Steam Machine Invented in 1884 Was a Weird Contrivance," *Washington Post,* 13 July 1913, M1.

133. Owen, *Hints,* plate facing 105.

134. *Annual Report for 1904,* 5.

135. Gutzon Borglum to Alexander Graham Bell, 8 October 1904, Library of Congress, Gilbert H. Grosvenor Collection, J. Smithson file, container 272. Borglum's portrait of Smithson is similar to his portrait of Ruskin, ca. 1901, now in the Metropolitan Museum of Art, New York City.

136. James M. Goode to S. Dillon Ripley, memorandum, 17 May 1973, AHHP, Crypt Records.

137. "Exhumation and Re-internment of the Remains of James Smithson," memorandum, 5 October 1973, Office of the Curator, SICC. A copy of this document and the pathologist's report were also sealed inside the coffin.

138. John Sherwood, "Smithson Skeleton Unearthed," *Washington Star-News,* 5 October 1973, A3.

The Grounds

1. Section 4, "An Act to establish the Smithsonian Institution, for the Increase and Diffusion of Knowledge among Men," approved 10 August 1846. 9 Stat. 102, 29th Congress, sess. I, ch. 178, 1846.

2. Rhees, *Journals,* 6.

3. Rhees, *Journals,* 17.

4. *National Intelligencer,* 3 May 1847, 1.

5. *Annual Report for 1847,* 137. The report listed the articles: "The gold and silver coins of the United States; report of the Committee on Organization; Constitution of the United States; the New Testament; Declaration of Independence; Congressional Directory for 1847; Bulletins of the National Institute; report of the first National Fair at Washington; report of the United States agent appointed to receive the legacy of James Smithson; medal portrait of James Smithson; reports of the Commissioner of Patents; journal of the proceedings of the Board of Regents, 1846; with the previously described engraved plate.

"The address of the Chancellor of the Institution on laying the corner-stone; astronomical observations made at the National Observatory; a copy of the Directory of the city newspapers of the day.

"There was also deposited in the same cavity, by the Free Masons, a leaden casket containing the following articles, viz: An elegant copy of the Holy Bible, presented by the Rev. Charles A. Davis, on behalf of the Bible Society of Washington; a stereotype page of Bancroft's History of the United States; Constitution of the Grand Lodge of the District of Columbia; an impression of its seal in metal; a copy of its proceedings for 1846; a silver plate, inscribed with the names of the Grand and Subordinate Lodges of the District."

For reference to the engraved metal plate, see William J. Rhees, Smithsonian Miscellaneous Collections 329, 1879, 676–77.

6. *Annual Report for 1847,* 139.

7. *National Intelligencer,* 3 May 1847.

8. *Glenn Brown's History of the United States Capitol,* 2 vols., 1900 and 1903. Ann. ed., with introduction and annotations by William B. Bushong (Washington, D.C.: U.S. Government Printing Office, 1998), 68–77.

9. Hugh McDiarmid, "Smithsonian Forgets Site of Its Cornerstone Laid in 1847," *Washington Post,* 8 December 1966, F8.

10. Records of the Commissioner of Public Buildings and Grounds, National Archives and Records Administration, Letters Received, 3 March 1851, vol. 32.

11. The name "Smithsonian Pleasure Grounds" appears on Downing's 1851 "Plan Showing Proposed Method of Laying Out the Public Grounds at Washington," copy by N. Michler, 1867, in the National Archives.

12. Joseph Henry to George Perkins Marsh, 18 November 1851, SIA, Joseph Henry Papers, 29595.

13. *Annual Report for 1851,* 69.

14. *Annual Report for 1868,* 51–52.

15. Ibid.

16. Joseph Henry Desk Diary, 10 April 1872, SIA, Henry Collection, RU 7001, Box 14.

17. *New York Daily Times,* 30 July 1852, 2.

18. Rhees, *An Account of the Smithsonian Institution,* 1857, 37–40.

19. *Annual Report for 1883,* 2.

20. Smithsonian Institution news release, 25 May 1965, SIA, Joseph Henry folder, RU 99, box 93.

21. Joseph Henry to J. P. Lesley, esq., 8 March 1866, SIA, Joseph Henry Papers, 00092.

22. *Annual Report for 1978,* 24–25.

23. The statue was crated and put in storage in 1982 before the excavation of the South Yard for the Quadrangle museums and the Ripley Center.

24. S. Dillon Ripley to Richard H. Howland, memorandum, 5 December 1977, SIA, accession 09–007, AHHP files, box 31-S.

25. Edwards Park, "Around the Mall and Beyond," *Smithsonian Magazine* (February 1981): 27.

26. *Annual Report for 1853,* 20.

27. *Annual Report for 1859,* 38–39, 385–95.

28. Joseph Henry Desk Diary, 12 March 1875. "The mother of the Janitor of the Museum Mrs. Horan died in the little cottage on the grounds aged 75 years body taken to Ohio."

29. *Report of the National Museum for 1921,* 35–36. Although glowing in every respect, the report's description of Nelson Wood has this puzzling assessment: "Deficient in natural mechanical ability, it was only after the most persistent effort that he finally reached the point where he could make the bird skin take the form which he had mentally determined to be the natural and best position."

29. *Report of the National Museum for 1915,* 40.

31. *Report of the National Museum for 1903,* 260–61.

30. *Annual Report for 1885,* part 1, 6.

31. *Report of the National Museum for 1903,* 261.

32. "Amid Canon and Cliff," *Washington Post,* 22 June 1885, 1.

33. "A Clever Artist Dead," *Washington Post,* 4 July 1899, 7. Hendley worked at the Smithsonian from 1870 until leaving in 1892 to work for the Department of Agriculture, where he continued to craft lifelike fruits and animals.

34. "In the Wizard's Workshop," *Evening Star,* 10 April 1886, 2.

35. "Early Home of the Zoo," *Washington Post,* 23 August 1897, 2.

36. *Report of the National Museum for 1889,* 417.

37. *Report of the National Museum for 1888,* 44. The bison were a gift from Eugene G. Blackford, commissioner of fisheries for the State of New York.

38. *Report of the National Museum for 1889,* 417–18.

39. *Report of the National Museum for 1903,* 261.

40. *Guide to the Smithsonian Archives* (Washington, D.C.: Smithsonian Institution Press, 1996), 245.

41. *Annual Report for 1890,* 7.

42. *Annual Report for 1891,* 7.

43. *Annual Report for 1911,* 62, and *Annual Report for 1914,* 89.

44. *Annual Report for 1956,* 65.

45. *Annual Report for 1970,* 55. The Radiation Biology Laboratories were relocated from the Castle and "a number of small buildings in the old Astrophysical Observatory south of the Smithsonian Building."

46. *Annual Report for 1975,* 351.

47. *Annual Report for 1898,* 7.

48. *Annual Report for 1901,* 11.

49. Charles G. Abbot, "The Relations between the Smithsonian Institution and the Wright Brothers," *Smithsonian Miscellaneous Collections* 81, no. 5 (Washington, D.C.: 1928).

50. William E. Baxter, "Samuel P. Langley: Aviation Pioneer," part 2. http://www.sil.si.edu/ondisplay/langley/intro.htm.

51. *Annual Report for 1921,* 16.

52. *Report of the National Museum for 1927,* 185. The artillery was transferred from the War Department's Office of the Chief of Ordnance.

53. Scot Hart, "Smithsonian Gives Its Famed World War I Guns to Scrap Pile," *Washington Post,* 5 September 1942, 12.

54. *Annual Report for 1961,* 124.

55. *Annual Report for 1960,* 120, and *Annual Report for 1966,* 259–60.

56. *Annual Report for 1976,* 231.

57. Edwards Park and Jean-Paul Carlhian, *A New View From the Castle* (Washington, D.C.: Smithsonian Institution Press, 1987), 53.

58. *Annual Report for 1982,* 5.

59. Park and Carlhian, *A New View From the Castle,* 35.

60. Ibid., 154.

61. Ibid., 125.

62. Ibid., 135.

63. Ibid., 135–37.

64. Robert Dale Owen, *Hints on Public Architecture,* 1849, 108. "Designs submitted by the architect for cast-iron gateways, necessary to connect the Institution grounds with the adjoining streets, have been adopted."

65. *Annual Report for 1987,* 10.

BIBLIOGRAPHY

A Note on the Sources

Most of the information used in the preparation of this book came from primary sources located at the Smithsonian Institution. Numerous collections of papers housed in the Smithsonian Institution Archives have been researched, notably the Records of the Office of the Secretary. Other sources of manuscript material included the Manuscripts Division and the Division of Music of the Library of Congress.

The published edition of the Joseph Henry Papers, entitled *The Papers of Joseph Henry*—edited by Stuart Pierson (vol. 1), Arthur Molella (vols. 1–4), Nathan Reingold (vols. 1–5), Michele L. Aldrich (vol. 2), Marc Rothenberg (vols. 4–11), Paul H. Theerman (vols. 5–7), Kathleen W. Dorman (vols. 5–11), John C. Rumm (vols. 6–7), and Frank R. Milikan (vols. 9–11)—(Washington D.C.: Smithsonian Institution Press, 1972–2007)—was valuable for the additional information provided in the annotations to the documents. Many of the original documents reproduced and cross-referenced in the Joseph Henry Papers are available in the Smithsonian Institution Archives; a few were located in the archives of Brown University, Yale University, Harvard University, the Huntington Library, and the Workingmen's Institute of New Harmony, Indiana.

Also consulted was *The Papers of Robert Mills*, edited by Robert Alexander, with John Bryan and Pamela Scott (Wilmington, Del.: Scholarly Resources, 1990). The files of the Smithsonian Institution's Office of Architectural History and Historic Preservation contain many items collected over some fifteen years from Smithsonian sources and others by Richard H. Howland, James M. Goode, Cynthia R. Field, and the author.

Primary Sources

Annual Report of the Board of Regents of the Smithsonian Institution, abbreviated as *Annual Report for (year)*. Washington, D.C.: Smithsonian Institution, 1850–1991.

Henry, Joseph. Letters and diaries, unpublished, Smithsonian Institution Archives, RU 7001, box 15.

Henry, Mary. Letters and diaries, unpublished, Smithsonian Institution Archives, RU 7001, box 51.

Report of the United States National Museum, abbreviated as *Report of the National Museum for (year)*. Washington, D.C.: Smithsonian Institution, 1885–1964.

Rhees, William J., editor. *The Smithsonian Institution: Journals of the Board of Regents, Reports of Committees, Statistics, Etc.*, abbreviated as *Journals*. Washington, D.C.: Smithsonian Institution, 1879.

———. *The Smithsonian Institution: Documents Relative to Its Origin and History, 1835–1899*, abbreviated as *The Smithsonian Institution*. 2 vols. Washington, D.C.: U.S. Government Printing Office, 1901.

Additional Sources

Alexander, Edward P. *Museum Masters: Their Museums and Their Influence*. Nashville: American Association for State and Local History, 1983.

Arnot, David. *Animadversions on the Proceedings of the Regents of the Smithsonian Institution in their Choice of An Architect*. New York, 1847.

Baird, Donald. "Cloning a Dinosaur: Waterhouse Hawkins and the Skeleton of Hadrosaurus." Unpub. ms. n.d.

Beauchamp, Tanya Edwards. "Adolf Cluss: An Architect in Washington During the Civil War and Reconstruction." *Records of the Columbia Historical Society of Washington, D.C., 1971–72*. Washington D.C.: Columbia Historical Society, 1972.

Bell, Whitfield J. *A Cabinet of Curiosities: Five Episodes in the Evolution of American Museums*. Charlottesville: University Press of Virginia, 1967.

Bryan, John, editor. *Robert Mills, Architect*. Washington, D.C.: American Institute of Architects Press, 1989.

Carmichael, Leonard, and J. C. Long. *James Smithson and the Smithsonian Story*. New York: Putnam, 1965.

Cochrane, Rexmond C. *The National Academy of Sciences: Its First Hundred Years, 1863–1963*. Washington, D.C.: National Academy Press, 1978.

Cole, Donald B., and John J. McDonough, editors. *Benjamin Brown French: Witness to the Young Republic. A Yankee's Journal, 1828–1870*. Hanover, N.H.: University Press of New England, 1989.

Collins, Kathleen. *Washingtoniana Photographs: Collections in the Prints and Photographs Division of the Library of Congress*. Washington, D.C.: Superintendent of Documents, 1989.

Dall, William Healey. *Spencer Fullerton Baird: A Biography*. Philadelphia: Lippincott, 1915.

Downing, Andrew Jackson. *The Architecture of Country Houses*. 1850. Reprint, New York: Dover, 1969.

Elliot, Clark A., compiler. *The Biographical Index to American Science: The Seventeenth Century to 1920*. Westport, Conn.: Greenwood Press, 1990.

Ewing, Heather. *The Lost World of James Smithson: Science, Revolution, and the Birth of the Smithsonian*. New York: Bloomsbury, 2007.

Ewing, Heather, and Amy Ballard. *A Guide to Smithsonian Architecture*. Washington D.C.: Smithsonian Books, 2009.

Field, Cynthia R., Richard E. Stamm, and Heather P. Ewing. *The Castle: An Illustrated History of the Smithsonian Building*. Washington, D.C.: Smithsonian Institution Press, 1993.

Fleming, James Rodger. *Meteorology in America, 1800–1870*. Baltimore: Johns Hopkins University Press, 1990.

Gillespie, Charles Coulston, editor. *The Dictionary of Scientific Biography*, vol. 6. New York: Scribner, 1972.

Goode, George Brown. *The Smithsonian Institution, 1846–1896: The History of Its First Half-Century*. Washington, D.C.: De Vinne Press, 1897.

Goode, James M. *Capital Losses: A Cultural History of Washington's Destroyed Buildings*. 1979. 2d ed. Washington, D.C.: Smithsonian Institution Press, 2003.

———. *Outdoor Sculpture of Washington, D.C.* Washington, D.C.: Smithsonian Institution Press, 1974.

Greiff, Constance M. *John Notman, Architect*. Philadelphia: The Atheneum, 1979.

Gutheim, Frederick. *The Federal City: Plans and Realities*. Washington, D.C.: Smithsonian Institution Press, 1976.

Hafertepe, Kenneth. *America's Castle: The Evolution of the Smithsonian Building and Its Institution, 1840–1878*. Washington, D.C.: Smithsonian Institution Press, 1984.

Hendrickson, Walter Brookfield. *David Dale Owen: Pioneer Geologist of the Middle West*. Indianapolis: Indiana Historical Bureau, 1943.

Hinsley, Curtis, Jr. *Savages and Scientists: The Smithsonian Institution and the Development of American Anthropology, 1846–1910*. Washington, D.C.: Smithsonian Institution Press, 1981.

Holmes, William H. *Smithsonian Institution National Gallery of Art: Catalogue of Collections II*. Washington, D.C.: U.S. Government Printing Office, 1926.

Jones, Owen. *The Grammar of Ornament*. 1856. Reprint, New York: Portland House, 1986.

Kohlstedt, Sally G. "History in a Natural History Museum: George Brown Goode and the Smithsonian Institution." *The Public Historian* 10, no. 2 (spring 1988).

Leopold, Richard. *Robert Dale Owen*. 1940. Reprint, New York: Octagon Books, 1969.

Lessoff, Alan, and Cristoff Mauch. *Adolf Cluss, Architect: From Germany to America*. Washington, D.C.: Historical Society of Washington, D.C., 2005.

Longstreth, Richard, editor. *The Mall in Washington, 1791–1991*. Studies in the History of Art. CASVA Symposium Papers 14. National Gallery of Art Press. Hanover, N.H.: University Press of New England, 1991.

Lowe, David. *Lost Chicago*. Boston: Houghton Mifflin, 1975.

Maury, William. *Alexander "Boss" Shepherd and the Board of Public Works*. Washington Studies, no. 3. Washington, D.C.: George Washington University, 1975.

McCutcheon, Mary. "The Children's Room at the Smithsonian: 1901 to 1939." *Curator* 35, no. 1 (March 1992).

Mitchell, Vance & Company. *Picture Book of Authentic Mid-Victorian Gas Lighting Fixtures: A Reprint of the Historic Mitchell, Vance & Co. Catalog, ca. 1876*. New introduction by Denys Peter Myers. Reprint, New York: Dover, 1984.

Montgomery, Florence M. *Textiles in America, 1650–1870*. New York: W. W. Norton, 1984.

Moyer, Albert E. *Joseph Henry: The Rise of an American Scientist*. Washington, D.C.: Smithsonian Institution Press, 1997.

Nabokov, Peter, and Robert Easton. *Native American Architecture*. New York: Oxford University Press, 1989.

Newton, Roger Hale. *Town & Davis Architects: Pioneers in American Revivalist Architecture, 1812–1870*. New York: Columbia University Press, 1942.

Owen, Robert Dale. *Hints on Public Architecture*. 1849. New introduction by Cynthia R. Field. Reprint, New York: DaCapo, 1978.

———. *Threading My Way: An Autobiography*. 1874. Reprint, New York: Augustus M. Kelley, 1967.

Park, Edwards, and Jean-Paul Carlhian. *A New View From the Castle*. Washington, D.C.: Smithsonian Institution Press, 1987.

Parker, John Henry. *A Concise Glossary of Architectural Terms*. 1896. Reprint, New York: Bracken Books, 1989.

———. *A Glossary of Terms Used in Grecian, Roman, Italian and Gothic Architecture*. 2d ed. London: Charles Tilt, 1838.

———. *A Handbook for Visitors to Oxford*. Oxford: John Henry Parker, 1847.

Peterson, Anne E. *Hornblower and Marshall, Architects*. Washington, D.C.: Preservation Press, 1978.

Post, Robert. *The Centennial Exhibition: A Treatise upon Selected Aspects of the Great International Exhibition Held in Philadelphia on the Occasion of our Nation's One Hundredth Birthday. . . .* 1876. Reprint, Washington, D.C.: Smithsonian Institution Press, 1976.

Rathbun, Richard. *The National Gallery of Art, Department of Fine Arts of the National Museum*. 2 vols. Washington D.C.: U.S. Government Printing Office, 1909, 1916.

Rhees, William J. *An Account of the Smithsonian Institution, Its Founder, Building, Operations, etc., Prepared from the Reports of Prof. Henry to the Regents, and Other Authentic Sources*. Washington, D.C.: Thomas McGill, 1857, 1859, 1863, 1865, 1869, 1880.

———. *Visitor's Guide to the Smithsonian Institution and the United States National Museum*. Washington, D.C.: Judd & Detweiler, 1880, 1881, 1883, 1884, 1885, 1886, 1889, 1891, 1892.

Rivinus, E. F., and E. M. Youssef. *Spencer Baird of the Smithsonian*. Washington, D.C.: Smithsonian Institution Press, 1992.

Russell, Loris S. "Early Nineteenth-Century Lighting." in *Building Early America: Contributions Toward the History of a Great Industry*. Edited by Charles E. Peterson. Carpenters Company of the City and County of Philadelphia. 1976. Reprint, Lakeville, Minn.. Astragal Press, 1992.

Ryder, Richard C. "Dinosaurs Through the Stereoscope." *Stereo World* (March–April 1985): 4–17, 39.

———. "Hawkins' Hadrosaurus: The Stereographic Record." *The Mosasaur* (1986): 169–80.

———. "Megatherium: Stereo's Most Photographed Fossil." *Stereo World* (May–June 1984): 20–25, 33.

Sandburg, Carl. *Abraham Lincoln: The Prairie Years and the War Years*. New York: Harcourt, Brace, and World, 1939.

Sloan, Samuel. *Homestead Architecture*. Philadelphia: J. B. Lippincott, 1867.

Sturtevant, William C., general editor, and Wayne Suttles, volume editor. *Handbook of North American Indians: Northwest Coast*, vol. 7. Washington, D.C.: Smithsonian Institution Press, 1990.

U.S. Congress, Senate, "Report of the Special Committee of the Board of Regents Relative to the Fire," 38th Congress, 2d session, 21 February 1865, S. Rept. 129.

Viola, Herman, and Carolyn Margolis, editors. *Magnificent Voyagers: The Exploring Expedition, 1838–1842*. Washington, D.C.: Smithsonian Institution Press, 1985.

Von Rosenstiel, Helene, and Gail Caskey Winkler. *Floor Coverings for Historic Buildings*. Washington, D.C.: Preservation Press, 1988.

Wilk, Christopher. *Thonet: 150 Years of Furniture*. New York: Barron's, 1980.

———. "Thonet and Bentwood," in *Nineteenth Century Furniture: Innovation, Revival and Reform*. Introduction by Mary Jean Madigan. *Art and Antiques*. New York: Billboard, 1982.

Wilson, Richard Guy. *McKim, Mead & White, Architects*. New York: Rizzoli, 1983.

Withey, Henry F., and Elsie Rathburn Withey. *Biographical Dictionary of American Architects (Deceased)*. Los Angeles: New Age, 1956.

Yochelson, Ellis. *National Museum of Natural History: 75 Years in the Natural History Building*. Washington, D.C.: Smithsonian Institution Press, 1985.

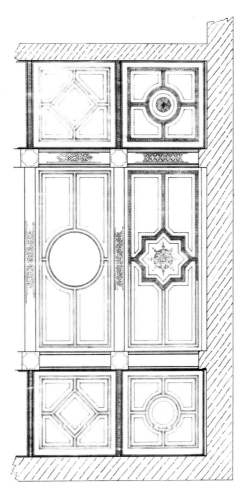

Gable end of the ceiling in the hall of the West Range showing the proposed decoration scheme. Drawing by Cluss & Schulze, May 1888.

ACKNOWLEDGMENTS

For the first edition of this book, I was privileged to serve as coauthor with my former colleagues Cynthia R. Field and Heather P. Ewing. The extremely high standards that Cynthia set as lead author on that volume have served as a guide not only for this book but for all aspects of my subsequent work at the Smithsonian. For her influence and guidance, I am truly grateful. The research that Heather and I conducted for the first edition, touching on the stories of the people who lived and worked in the Castle, provided inspiration for this revised and updated version. Heather's biography of James Smithson is now the definitive reference on the life of the Institution's benefactor.

I am also grateful to many colleagues past and present who supported me in this work, for without their help this book would not have been possible. Thanks are due current Smithsonian colleagues Pam Henson, Helena Wright, and Joan Boudreau, as well as former staff members Paula Fleming, Susan Myers, Kathleen Darmon, and Alan Bain for their institutional memory and specialized knowledge, of which they freely shared. The Smithsonian is indeed extremely fortunate to have many such "treasures." Special thanks go as well to Paula Fleming for generously sharing her research and for collecting the treasure trove of stereograph images of the Castle.

Two former colleagues, Rodris Roth and David Shayt, both now deceased, contributed in different ways: Rodris through her unbridled enthusiasm for and deep knowledge of nineteenth-century American furnishings and David for fulfilling a long-planned proposal to install a bell in the Castle's tower.

Smithsonian Institution Archives staff Ellen Alers and Tammy Peters cheerfully provided access to the Institution's historic records and images. I am especially indebted to the extra effort and attention afforded me by Marguerite Roby in tracking down the many obscure historic photographs that I requested and to Michael Barnes for digitizing them with great speed and efficiency.

The Smithsonian has recognized the importance of photographically documenting its collections and events from the early 1870s, beginning with the Smithsonian's first photographer, Thomas W. Smillie. In addition to Smillie's wonderful, rare images, the work of recent photographers from the former Office of Photographic Services is featured in either this or the first edition. Among them are Harold Dorwin, Richard Farrar, Alfred F. Harrell, Richard Hofmeister, Dane Penland, Jeff Ploskonka, Ken Rahaim, Albert Robinson, Richard Strauss, Hugh Talman, Jeff Tinsley, and Rick Vargas. I am extremely fortunate that among these fine photographers is Eric Long; the spectacular photographs that he artfully composed to document the Castle's offices and meeting rooms enhance this volume in ways that only a seasoned professional can achieve. He is truly a master of the photographic art.

For their patience and perseverance with the sometimes mysterious (for me) and always arduous editing and review process, Smithsonian Books Director Carolyn Gleason and the project editor Christina Wiginton have earned my gratitude. Thanks are also due the text editor and indexer extraordinaire Diane Maddex. Initial review of the footnotes and the bibliography was deftly conducted by the Smithsonian volunteer Alexandra Penland, who whipped both into shape in record time. Thanks go to Amy Lemon, program coordinator of the Smithsonian's Behind-the-Scenes Volunteer Program, for directing Alex to this project.

The book's elegant design is the result of Robert Wiser's keen artistic vision and expertise.

For insight gained on related topics outside the Smithsonian, my appreciation goes to William C. Allen, historian emeritus of the U.S. Capitol, and Laura Lyn Sears and Diane Michalski of The Grove, Robert Kennicott's home their enthusiasm for all things Kennicott was infectious.

Office of the Secretary staff members Catherine Beliveau and Kemble Dycus were always accommodating in providing access to the Secretary's offices and parlor for photography, as were LeShawn Burrell-Jones, special assistant to the Under Secretary for History, Art, and Culture, for access to his meeting room (the Art Room) and Debra Woods for access to the Regents' Room and library. I am honored that the Secretary contributed the foreword to this book.

Recognition is also due my office colleagues for their encouragement and support. Thank you Walt Ennaco, Sharon C. Park, and Amy Ballard—whose "fifteen minutes of fame" as feeder of the owls has now lasted well over three decades. Peter Muldoon and Paul Westerberg dutifully attended to Castle Collection needs while my nose was buried in this manuscript.

Finally I express my gratitude to Wilton Dillon for sharing his Ripley-era South Tower memories with such eloquence and poetry. It was my great privilege and good fortune to have begun my career at the Smithsonian during the height of a golden era in the Institution's history and to have worked directly for James M. Goode and Richard H. Howland, with the Castle Collection established as a result of S. Dillon Ripley's foresight, imagination, and whimsy.

Richard E. Stamm

Model for the Smithsonian Building from the north, by James Renwick, Jr., 1846.

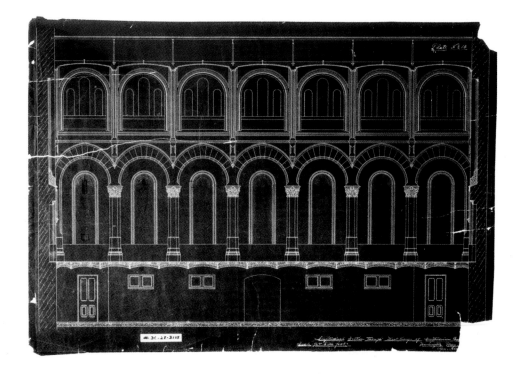

Fireproofing scheme for a section of the West Range. Blueprint by Cluss & Schulze, March 1887.